Colombia
Inside the Labyrinth

Jenny Pearce

To my parents, Joan and Neville Pearce

First published in Great Britain in 1990 by Latin America
Bureau (Research and Action) Limited, 1 Amwell Street,
London EC1R 1UL

British Library Cataloguing in Publication Data
Pearce, Jenny
    Colombia: inside the labyrinth
    1. Colombia,
    I. Title II. Latin America Bureau
    986.1

ISBN 0 906156 44 0 Pbk
ISBN 0 906156 45 9 Hbk

Written by Jenny Pearce
Edited by Selina Cohen and James Ferguson
Additional research by Beatriz Echeverría

Cover photograph by Julien Frydman/Sygma
Cover design by Andy Dark
Text design by Fiona MacIntosh

Photographs on pages 18, 19, 21, 34, 39 by courtesy of Museo
de Arte Moderno de Bogotá

Typeset, printed and bound by Russell Press, Nottingham
NG7 4ET
Distribution in USA by Monthly Review Press, 122 West 27th
Street, New York, NY 10001

Contents

Inserts

Tables/graphs

Maps of Colombia

Geographical note

Colombia is a country of very diverse regions. Three main geographical areas can be identified:

1. The mountainous region of the west, where three mountain ranges of the Andes, the Western, Eastern and Central Cordillera, cut the country and define its climatic variations. Deep valleys separate the ranges, notably those of the two great rivers, the Cauca and Magdalena. This region covers 26 per cent of the country's surface but 80 per cent of the population lives there. It is the centre of the country's economy.

2. To the east there is a low-lying flat region made up of huge savannahs or plains (*llanos*) to the north and extensive forests to the south. Less than 2 per cent of the population live in this territory.

3. A third region is shaped by the Pacific and Caribbean coasts. It consists of 19 per cent of all national territory and 19.4 per cent of the population live there.

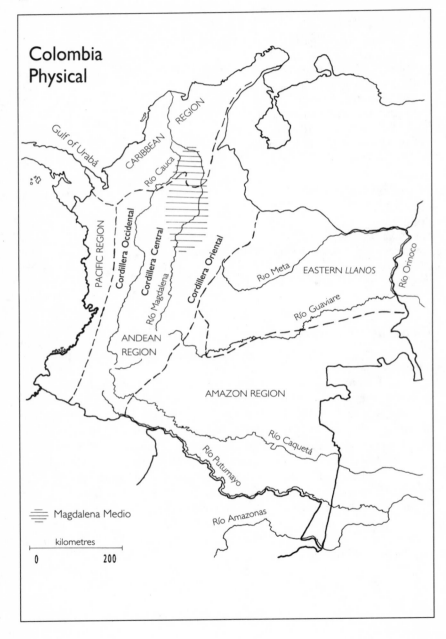

Colombia Physical

Gulf of Urabá

CARIBBEAN REGION

Río Cauca

PACIFIC REGION

Cordillera Occidental

Cordillera Central

Río Magdalena

Cordillera Oriental

Río Meta

EASTERN *LLANOS*

Río Orinoco

Río Guaviare

ANDEAN REGION

AMAZON REGION

Río Caquetá

Río Putumayo

Río Amazonas

Magdalena Medio

kilometres

0   200

Colombia
Political

CARIBBEAN SEA

San Andrés & Providencia

PANAMA

PACIFIC
OCEAN

VENEZUELA

Barranquilla
Atlántico

La Guajira

Magdalena

Cesar

Sucre

Córdoba

Bolívar

Norte
de
Santander

Bucaramanga

Barrancabermeja

Antioquia

Medellín

Santander

Arauca

Chocó

Caldas

Boyacá

Casanare

Risaralda

Cundinamarca

Quindío

Bogotá

Vichada

Valle

Cali

Tolima

Meta

Guainía

Huila

Cauca

Nariño

Vaupés

Caquetá

Putumayo

ECUADOR

Amazonas

BRAZIL

PERU

kilometres

0   200

Colombia in Brief

Country and People

Land area	1,141,748 sq km
Coastal region	1,300 km Pacific
	1,600 km Caribbean

Population (1988)	30.8m
Annual growth rate(1987)	1.7%
Urban (1987)	69.1%
Bogotá	3.98m
Medellín	1.47m
Cali	1.35m
Barranquilla	0.9m

The people:
(ethnic composition approx.)

Mestizos (mixed Spanish and Indian)	70%
European	22%
Amerindian	2%
African	6%

Language:	Spanish
Religion:	Roman Catholicism 96 per cent
Literacy:	64.3% (1964)
	82.1% (1985)

Secondary education:

% of age group in secondary education
56 per cent (1986)
17 per cent (1965)

Health:

Infant Mortality (per 1,000 live births)	99 (1965)
	46 (1987)
Life expectancy at birth	56 (1965)
	66 (1987)

Population per doctor   1,190 (1984)

Malnutrition: 20% of children under five suffer from malnutrition and a further 19.7% are at risk.

(regional differences in these figures are very great. Life expectancy in the Chocó is 47 years, and 144 children under one die in every 1,000 live births. Cauca and Nariño are not far off these, while the city of Cali has a life expectancy of 70 and infant morality for children under one of 36 per thousand live births, 1987 figures)

The Economy
Total Gross Domestic Product
(GDP) US$31,940 million
GDP per capita (1987) US$1,372
Real GDP growth rate (%):

1950-65	1967-74	1974-79	1980-83	1983-86	1987	1988
4.9	6.5	5.0	1.6	3.6	5.3	4.2

(1978-88 average: 3.6%)

Inflation: 28.1 % (1988) 23.3% (1987) annual average 1978-88 23.3%

Employment:
Economically active population (millions):   11.30 (1985)

Men	7.02
Women	4.28

by sector

	1951	1964	1974	1984
Agriculture	55.9	49.0	41.9	32.7
Mining	1.7	1.6	0.8	1.1
Manufacturing industry	12.7	13.2	14.3	16.4
Construction	3.7	4.5	4.7	5.0
Electricity, gas and water	0.3	0.3	0.5	0.3
Commerce	5.6	8.9	12.6	17.8
Transport and Communications	3.6	3.9	4.1	4.5
Other services:	16.5	18.6	21.0	22.2
Domestic		9.8	5.9	3.6
Non-Domestic		8.8	15.2	18.6

Unemployment %	1985	1986	1987	1988
	13.1	12.5	10.1	10.2

Distribution of land ownership (excludes Antioquia and Chocó)

Size of farms (hectares)	No. of farms	%	Area (hectares)	%	Average size (hectares)
less than 3	1,095,919	56.9	1,027,246.5	2.8	0.9
3 to 20	561,508	29.16	4,320,138.8	11.7	7.7
20 to 100	209,129	10.86	8,956,001.8	24.2	43.0
100 to 500	51,705	2.69	9,821,378.3	26.5	189.9
more than 500	7,110	0.37	12,881,780.6	34.8	1,811.8
Total	1,925,372	100.00	3,006,536.9	100.0	19.2

Catastro Nacional, 1984

The country has 114 million hectares distributed in the following way: 4 million under cultivation, 23 million in pasture and ranching, 20 million in non-cultivable pasture, 40 million in woods, and the rest in towns rivers and lakes.

Trade:	1987	1988
Exports in US$ millions	5,661	5,310
Imports in US$ millions	3,793	4,400

Principal Exports, % of total (1988):

Coffee 32.6
Petroleum and derivatives 19.6
Textiles, clothing, leather and footwear 6.6
Coal 6.1
Bananas 5.0
Chemical products 4.2
Flowers 3.8

Markets:

(May 1989) US (25.5%), West Germany (13%), Holland (8.6%), Japan (5.3%) Panama (4.6%), Venezuela(4.5%), French (3.2%), Spain (2.6%) United Kingdom (2.6%)

Principal Imports % of total (1988):
Intermediate goods (50%)
Capital goods (34.6%)
Main sources of imports US 34.9%, EC 21.1%
Foreign debt: US$114,000 million (1983)
US$167,000 million (1988)
as % of GNP 45.3 (Brazil 33.7, Argentina 65.5, Mexico 69.6 1987)
Debt service/export earnings ratio 46.4% (1988)

Sources: Banco de la República 1989, DANE 1987, Barco 1987, Economist Intelligence Unit, Inter-American Development Bank, World Bank 1989, *Financial Times*

Political Parties and Movements

Partido Liberal (Liberal Party) and ***Partido Social Conservador*** (Social Conservative Party)

The Liberal Party, like its counterpart, the Conservative Party (officially renamed the Social Conservative Party in 1987), emerged in the years after independence from Spanish rule. By the 1850s, both parties were formally established and could mobilise an electorate and command support in the battlefield. Neither party could be identified clearly in terms of distinct economic or social interests, although the Liberals were associated with anti-clericalism. Both were loose coalitions of large landowners and merchants, with strong regional roots and considerable autonomy. The Liberal Party wooed the urban vote as towns and cities grew in the first decades of the 20th century, reversing the inbuilt majority of the Conservatives which was based on their greater strength in the rural areas.

Following the inter-party violence of the 1940s and 1950s, the parties reached an agreement to alternate the presidency for sixteen years and to distribute all national and local legislative seats, posts in the cabinet, the judiciary and all levels of public administration between the two parties. Although competitive elections were resumed in 1974, in practice power-sharing arrangements continued. Colombia has been ruled by *de facto* coalition since 1986, when for the first time the Liberals did not govern with the Conservatives, who were expected to evolve towards a genuine party of opposition. Although President Virgilio Barco made an agreement with the Conservatives for its repeal, Article 120 of the constitution still requires the majority party to offer 'adequate and equitable' representation in the executive branch to the party with the second highest number of votes. The repeal will depend on the passage of the constitutional reform through Congress.

Colombia's two traditional parties remain archaic institutions rather than modern parties built around programmatic agreements and some form of internal democracy. Regional party bosses still dominate both parties, their influence resting on capacity to mobilise the electorate through time-honoured mechanisms of manipulation and vote-buying. The Liberal Party in government may face as much opposition from its own 'members' in Congress as from those of the Conservative Party. Nor has the Conservative Party yet evolved into a serious party of opposition, with a clear set of policies and objectives.

Unión Patriotica (Patriotic Union, UP)

The UP was set up in 1985 in the wake of President Belisario Betancur's peace initiative. It was organised by the Communist Party (founded in

1930) which intended it to involve a broad range of forces, beyond the party members. Initially it was also to be a vehicle for the reinsertion of the Fuerzas Armadas Revolucionarias de Colombia (FARC) guerrillas into political life, but assassinations of guerrillas who attempted this soon led members of the FARC to abandon such an option. The UP has been targeted by right-wing paramilitary groups, and has lost over 700 of its activists since it was founded. The assassinations include its leader, Jaime Pardo Leal, who was killed in 1987. During 1989, the UP moved to become an independent force from the Communist Party, under the leadership of Bernardo Jaramillo. Despite the assassinations, the UP has established itself as the main opposition party to the traditional parties, but its vote is still very small.

Frente Popular (Popular Front, the FP)

The FP was legally constituted in 1989 after five years of discussions by the *Partido Comunista-Marxista Leninista* (Communist Party Marxist-Leninist, PC-ML). The PC-ML, which began as a Maoist party, also has an armed wing, the *Ejército Popular de Liberación* (Popular Army of Liberation, EPL). The FP emerged out of the peace initiatives of the early 1980s, and was an attempt by the PC-ML to take advantage of the political spaces it hoped would open up. The FP was also intended to incorporate non-party members and has put forward candidates to elections. An estimated 50 FP activists have been killed since the movement was founded.

A Luchar (To Struggle)

A Luchar was set up in 1984, bringing together those who rejected the peace plan and electoral politics. For this reason, it has been associated with the politics of the *Ejército de Liberación Nacional* (Army of National Liberation, ELN), although it insists on its complete autonomy from the guerrilla organisation. It brought together a number of independent workers collectives, and Trotskyist groups. One of these, the *Partido Socialista Revolucionario* (Revolutionary Socialist Party, PSR) has remained inside the party. Another Trotskyist group, the *Partido Socialista de los Trabajadores* (Socialist Workers Party, PST) split, with a sector leaving *A Luchar* and remaining an independent party. *A Luchar's* emphasis has been on popular mobilisation and it has not participated in elections. At least 100 of its activists have been assassinated between 1984 and 1989.

Colombia Unida (Colombia United)

This movement was set up in September 1989 by 43 prominent intellectuals and politicians, including the former Attorney-General,

Carlos Jímenez Gómez, sociologist Orlando Fals Borda and politician and human rights campaigner, Alfredo Vásquez Carrizosa, to offer the country a new vision of 'authentic democratic and pluralist character, in opposition to the oligarchic monopoly on power, and autonomous *vis-a-vis* the traditional left and the insurgent movement'. (*Convocatoría a la convencíon democrática 'Colombia Unida'* 1-3 September 1989, Bogotá)

Movimiento de Restauración Nacional (Movement of National Restoration, MORENA)
This party of the extreme right was set up in July 1989. It was supported and promoted by ACDEGAM, the Association of Peasants and Ranchers of Magdalena Medio, which since 1983 has been engaged in a war against 'communist subversion' in this area of the middle Magdalena river. Considerable evidence exists of ACDEGAM's sponsorship of paramilitary groups who have assassinated hundreds of political activists and trade union and peasant organisers. Leading members of the Medellín cocaine cartel are reputed to be involved both with ACDEGAM and MORENA.

Introduction

Bolívar's Knot

On 18 August 1989, Luis Carlos Galán, the politician most likely to be the Liberal Party's candidate in the 1990 presidential election, was shot dead while addressing a crowd in Soacha on the outskirts of the Colombian capital, Bogotá. The assassination took place in front of the TV cameras and in spite of the presence of Galán's 22 bodyguards; it was ordered by some of the country's most powerful traffickers in cocaine, known collectively as the Medellín cartel.

The cartel's previous victims have included the Minister of Justice, Lara Bonilla; Guillermo Cano, the editor of the leading daily newspaper, *El Espectador*; Attorney-General Carlos Mauro Hoyos and Jaime Pardo Leal, the leader of the important opposition movement, the Patriotic Union (UP). It has also included dozens of judges, magistrates, policemen and soldiers and other members of the traditional establishment. They are mostly victims of what Colombian journalist, Antonio Caballero, called in an article in *El Espectador* (1 October 1989) the cocaine cartel's 'commercial war'; this is the war waged in order to protect its business interests and, in particular, to prevent the extradition of its members to the United States.

There is another war and another far more numerous set of victims, in this case mostly from the lower echelons of Colombian society: the 'political war', also known as the 'dirty war'. This time the cartel does not stand alone, but is allied with members of the traditional elite: businessmen, landowners and members of the armed forces. This war cost the lives of an estimated 8,000 peasants, workers, opposition politicians and left-wing activists between 1986 and the first four months of 1989. Some of these were victims of a new phenomenon, mass killings, often in areas which are heavily militarised and where the massacres could not have taken place without the connivance of members of the security forces.

Among the victims of the 'political war' was Daniel Espitia, the national treasurer of the peasant movement ANUC. Daniel was shot dead on 9 August 1989 by paid assassins. Two months previously I had met him when he visited Britain as part of a delegation organising a Latin American response to the 1992 anniversary of the 'discovery' of the sub-continent.

Daniel Espitia came from the town of Montería in Córdoba. In this town, there are seven miserable shanty towns of some 30,000 people, created by land invasions; 75 per cent of the shanty towns are peopled by refugees from the political killings and army bombings of peasant villages which had escalated during 1988 and 1989. The rest give shelter to the victims of floods which devastated the area in 1988. Daniel was helping to organise the local people. His brother had been killed in a massacre in El Tomate in 1988 along with 15 others including several children; his father was assassinated six weeks before his own death, and his wife had left him and their seven children because she could no longer stand the fear in which they lived.

The murder of Galán was part of both the 'commercial war' and the 'political war'. He was deeply alarmed at the drug barons' penetration of the country's political institutions and in favour of extradition of the major

Daniel Espitia in London, 1989.

Chris Stadtler

cocaine traffickers. But also, though a member of the traditional political establishment, he was, in Colombian terms, a reforming politician, whose political career had centred on the modernisation of the archaic institutions of the state and the corrupt political practices associated with them. He had won some sympathy among the substantial middle class of Colombia's large cities, and it is likely that as presidential candidate for a united Liberal Party (PL), he would have won the 1990 election.

His murder, rather than that of Daniel and thousands like him, finally made the government recognise that in just a decade, the cocaine barons had not only become some of the wealthiest men in the world, but they had also become a virtual 'state within a state', associated with an extreme right-wing political project. The Movement of National Restoration (MORENA) had been launched just over a week before Galán's killing, and was known to represent politically many of those forces which had been involved in the killings and assassinations of the 'dirty war'. These are the words of General Miguel Maza Márquez, head of the government's security police (DAS):

> We realised that the drug traffickers no longer operated like ordinary criminals, like the mafia. They were becoming a small state within the Colombian state . . . This small state has a very organised military infrastructure and a political arm in formation in the MORENA party in the Magdalena Medio region, a territory that the drug traffickers were on the point of controlling totally. (*La Prensa* 11 October 1989)

The rise of the cocaine barons is not, as some would have it, the cause of the present crisis of Colombia's political order. It is merely a thread of that crisis, a comparatively recent manifestation of a historically rooted crisis. For some the crisis has so many strands to it, that they see no clear explanation or pattern which could clarify it. Colombia is seen as a tangled knot with no discernible beginning or end. It is a country of so many extraordinary happenings identified in the minds of many with the Macondo of the García Márquez novel, *One Hundred Years of Solitude*, implying that it inhabits the realm of magical realism and defies explanation and analysis.

But García Márquez himself believes his novels have roots in reality. In a rare interview in March 1989, he spoke about his most recent book on the last journey of Bolívar, who led Colombia's struggle for independence from Spanish rule, *El General en su laberinto*:

> 'The General' has a greater importance than all the rest of my work. It shows that all my work corresponds to a geographic or historical reality. It is not magical realism and all these things

which are said. When you read Bolívar, you realise that all the
others have, in some way, a documented base, an historical
base, a geographic basis which is proved with 'The General'.
(*Semana* 14 March 1989)

This book is an attempt to find some threads in Colombia's labyrinthine
past and present which might explain its contemporary crisis to
non-Colombians. It traces the knot back to Bolívar, because some of the
fundamental dilemmas of building a nation were posed during the
struggle for independence and never subsequently resolved.

Bolívar's search for a formula which would create a strong, coherent
and effective state, bringing together the disparate parts of the former
Spanish Empire, was thwarted by the parochial vision of the local elites
of the region, who immersed themselves in their own power struggles
in the post-independence years. Those elites imported democratic
formulae from Europe, drew up impressive constitutions and established
parties which even took their names from similar parties in the old world.
But these formulae bore no resemblance to the political reality, which
had a profoundly elitist, undemocratic and unstable character.

This book is written from the perspective of those who have given
their lives to fight for a better society, the many activists of the popular
movement, such as Daniel Espitia, who have been targeted by the army
and right-wing paramilitary groups for extermination. The question of
who can unravel Bolívar's knot is of vital importance to the future of this
popular movement. And in the late 20th century, the aspirations of Daniel
Espitia and others, go beyond the construction of a strong and effective
state — the vision of Bolívar — to one based fundamentally on principles
of social and economic justice.

* * * * * *

The book begins from the premise that some threads can be untangled,
while accepting that the Colombian story is one of the most complex in
Latin America and that a book of this sort could not possibly do justice
to all of them. Just one region of this geographically and culturally diverse
country could have more than filled this book.

It is divided into three parts and each one will introduce the threads
which it hopes to unravel. **Part One** introduces the historical dimension.
It traces the 'birth of the political order' and establishes the historic roots
of a distinction which appears again and again among Colombian writers,
between the 'formal' Colombia and the 'real' Colombia.

There is a Colombia which is constitutional and legalistic, which
boasts all the trappings of a modern polity. This is the Colombia which
is often described in the world's press as the most democratic country in

Latin America. But there is also a 'real' Colombia of the people, where the rule of law barely holds, deprivation and poverty are the norm and democracy is just a word on a historic document.

Loyalty to two traditional political parties for many years was the link between the two worlds; the people fought out the bitter party conflicts on behalf of the ruling oligarchy and their own allegiances to the two parties which divided that oligarchy were sealed through generations of bloody vendettas. A tradition of party political violence was established which culminated in the late 1940s and 1950s in the last great civil war between the parties: *La Violencia*. The final phase of *La Violencia*, was one of social banditry and lasted until 1965.

During these years of *La Violencia*, forms of 'private justice' emerged which were to appear again and again in the 1980s. There was the figure of the hired assassin; the *pájaro* was linked to the political parties and local landowners in the 1950s but his professional equivalent, the *sicario* was a dominant figure of the killings a few decades later. The paramilitary groups and self-defence groups were also part of the landowners' arsenal of attack and revenge during *La Violencia*. And extortion, the *boleteo*, was associated with the police during the 1940s and 1950s and returned again in the 1980s when the Communist Party-affiliated FARC guerrillas, in particular, used kidnapping threats to raise money from landowners.

Part Two traces the crisis of the political order which emerged from *La Violencia*, between 1966 and 1986. This period begins with one frustrated attempt at reform, by President Lleras Restrepo and ends with the failure of another, by Belisario Betancur. The thread running through this part, is the political order's inability to deal with the dramatic social and economic change which accompanied economic modernisation, in particular the shift in just a few decades from a predominantly rural to an urban society.

The state became a mediator through which members of the ruling elite distributed power and privileges among themselves. Social order was maintained by clientelist loyalties based on political manipulation and administrative corruption and by repression, according to a Colombian lawyer and politician:

> In Colombia the State of Law disappeared a long time ago; I maintain that the State of Law was slaughtered on 9 April[1] and authority was reestablished on the basis of the second constitution which is the 'state of siege' and on the

1. 9 April 1948 was the date of the murder of Jorge Eliécer Gaitán, Colombia's populist leader, it marked the beginning of *La Violencia* and Colombia has lived under a State of Siege almost continuously since then.

> understanding that the armed forces play a role in sustaining
> political power, by controlling the defence portfolio. (Vázquez
> Carrizosa quoted in Rodríguez 1988:43)

The uneven and unrestricted expansion of capitalism brought poverty at
the same time as it created wealth. Two economies emerged to mirror the
two faces of the political order: the formal, measured economy with its
impressive statistics of economic growth, and the other, where the
majority of people live and work, the so-called informal economy. A
substantial middle class has developed out of the 'success' of the
measured economy; but its economic wellbeing has never been
guaranteed, and significant numbers of middle-class people have been
unable to match their aspirations with concrete economic gains.

The responses of the people forced to seek their own means of
survival is another thread in Colombia's contemporary history. For many,
these took a non-political form. Criminality in the cities was one means
of survival, and generated its own violent underworld. Colombia's crime
rate became legendary.

Population movements shifted to where sources of wealth opened
up, but rarely did the poor gain access to more than a small part of it.
Peasants sought to colonise the remaining public lands, but the battle for
the agricultural frontier was harsh and violent. Abandoned by the state,
peasant colonisers tried to make a living from nothing but their family
labour, while wealthy cattle ranchers seized every opportunity to expel
them.

In the emerald zones of eastern Boyacá, state incompetence and
neglect paved the way for a bitter fight for control of the mines, and
thousands of poor miners who headed for the region hoping to make
their fortune, helped to build the empires of a murderous mafia of
emerald dealers. Gold attracted thousands of poor prospectors to the
north-east of Antioquia, where they laboured for long hours with their
picks and shovels in the shadow of the great dredges of the mining
company, in a region which lacked the most basic infrastructure and
amenities. Untold ecological damage has been done by prospectors,
emerald miners and peasant colonisers in their frenzied search for a
livelihood from the forests, rocks and rivers.

The arrival of cocaine in the late 1970s added to the diverse forms
of survival, enriching a new elite, while coca growing provided a
heaven-sent income for a few peasant colonisers on the verge of
economic bankruptcy. It also brought the gang warfare and bloodshed
associated with drugs the world over. And the rise of cocaine corrupted
and destabilised political institutions, already vulnerable to partisan
influences.

The response of other people was to organise and protest at their abandonment by the state and their manipulation by politicians of the traditional parties. Lack of land, poor working conditions and lack of social provision, lack of water and sewerage, impassable roads, electricity projects that destroyed livelihoods and the ubiquitous corruption that oiled the local political machines, all generated organisation and protest. This popular response, varied in its political character except in one respect: the rejection of the two-party system which was the basis of the political order and which had hitherto ensured its legitimacy.

Yet another response was more overtly political. Guerrilla movements appeared in the early 1960s proposing the transformation of the ruling order. They were virtually destroyed by the 1970s, but rose again to put down deeper roots in society in the late 1970s and 1980s as the state failed to reform and continued to exclude the majority of Colombians.

The state's inability to look after the interests of society as a whole, to rise above the partisan interests of regional political bosses and the organised private sector, sowed the seeds of the violence of the 1980s. The failure of the peace initiatives in the first half of the 1980s revealed the fear of many in the ruling elite of relinquishing any control over political and economic life. An army, trained in US counter-insurgency techniques and with long experience of its own in the field, was prepared to lend its services to the preservation of the existing order.

Part Three deals with the counter-offensive of that elite against the pressure for change. It was not a unified counter-offensive; there were some who saw the need for reform and modernisation of the political order. But they were faced by an entrenched and militant conservatism. Although the popular movement was accustomed to repression, the ferocity of the right in the 1980s took many activists by surprise.

This counter-offensive initially took the form of diverse regional struggles by local landowners and business elites to regain control of areas where the popular movement had grown particularly strong or where the guerrillas threatened their monopoly of armed power. The armed forces and drug barons assisted them in the formation of dozens of paramilitary death squads, and the cocaine mafia grew stronger from this alliance of the powerful.

Amnesty International has gathered together the considerable information that now exists linking the armed forces, other members of the traditional elite and the drug traffickers in the formation of the estimated 140 paramilitary groups in the country:

> The Procurator-General's Public Ministry and civilian security agencies have initiated investigations into the composition of

paramilitary groups and the source of their financial support. Through such investigations, evidence has emerged that many paramilitary 'death squads' are financed by landowners, industrialists and alleged drug traffickers and operate in coordination with, or under the authority of, sectors of the Colombian armed forces. Armed forces units which have persistently been implicated in paramilitary 'death squad' activities include the intelligence unit of the National Police, F-2, the army's intelligence division, B-2, and the army's intelligence and counter-intelligence unit, BINCI. (Amnesty International 1989)

In addition to the paramilitary groups as such, civilians have been encouraged to form self-defence groups. There is a long history of such groups, which go back to *La Violencia*, and subsequently to their use as auxiliaries to the armed forces during the counter-insurgency campaigns of the 1960s and 1970s. These groups have become particularly active in key regions of the country, where important natural resources are at stake, such as the fertile lands, oilfields and natural gas reserves of the Magdalena Medio.

What began as regional efforts, soon began to look as if they had some level of national coordination. Belatedly, the state tried to regain control over the 'private justice' being meted out, and its own powers of repression were enhanced and given legal sanction. The armed forces have been strengthened, and civilian control over a number of areas (notably Urabá, Arauca and Caquetá) of the country effectively ceded to military commanders appointed by the President. The government has in this way encouraged the impunity with which the army operates in dealing with what it calls 'subversion' and what others call legitimate popular protest.

Galán's assassination brought to the fore both in Colombia and in the world at large the degree to which the cocaine mafia had built up their political as well as economic power, while the army, state and business elites were giving priority to dealing with the popular movement and the guerrilla armies of the left. The launching of a new right-wing political party, MORENA, based in Puerto Boyacá in the Magdalena Medio, a region now virtually controlled by the drug-traffickers and their local allies, led some to talk of the formation of a narco-fascist programme in the country. While the majority of Colombia's traditional elite may not favour such a programme, its ambivalence towards cocaine dollars and the anti-communist crusade they have helped finance has facilitated the consolidation of the mafia's political presence.

The Liberal administration of Virgilio Barco began its own offensive against the drug barons; property was confiscated, cocaine laboratories destroyed, lower-level dealers were arrested. The leading drug barons themselves at first escaped unscathed to organise their own counter-offensive. They threatened to kill ten judges for every Colombian extradited on drugs charges. The wave of violence which ensued showed that they meant business.

At the same time, the drug mafia and their allies in politics and business, began to exploit the banner of nationalism. Another thread came to the fore in the debate on how to deal with the drug problem. That thread was the role of the US in Colombia. The US has always had very close relations with the Colombian government and, in particular, the armed forces. The US has provided training and weapons to the army, and the Colombian government has been its loyal ally. Colombia was the only Latin American country to support Britain and the US during the Falklands/Malvinas war.

The strategic importance of Colombia as the gateway to South America, bordering on both the Pacific and the Atlantic, is very great. There is talk of building a canal to replace the Panama canal in the northern part of the country, around the San Juan river. Colombia's huge potential coal, oil and natural gas reserves and the country's proximity to the US make it an important source of energy resources and one which might reduce dependence on the volatile Middle East. The Pacific coast of the country is earmarked for major developments, and the Japanese are showing increasing interest in that part of the country.

The cocaine wars of the last half of 1989 have allowed the US to step up its presence and influence in the country. But many have questioned the efficacy and even the purpose of its intervention. General Miguel Gómez Padilla, director of the National Police, claimed that the weapons and equipment sent were 'more appropriate for a conventional war than for the type of struggle we carry out here against the drug traffickers . . . The National Police has carried out between 85 and 90 per cent of the anti-narcotic operations in Colombia, but 85 per cent of the emergency assistance approved by Bush is destined for the Colombian army and air force'. (*La Prensa* 11 September 1989). Many observers believe that the US government should pay more attention to dealing with the demand for cocaine in its own country from the estimated six million regular users.

By the end of 1989, the Colombian state was struggling to retain its authority and credibility, even though it enjoyed the propaganda coup surrounding the killing of cartel boss Gonzalo Rodríguez Gacha in December of that year. Right-wing paramilitary violence against the popular movement and political opposition, which had slowed down during the height of the cocaine war of August-September was being resumed with a vengeance at the end of 1989. The political elite was deeply divided on how to deal with a crisis and the country lacked direction as never before.

* * * * *

There is one thread which runs throughout Colombia's history which is clearer than any other. That is the way the country's ruling elite has always identified the fate of the nation with its own. 'But is the prosperity of a class really identifiable with the well-being of a country?', asks the Uruguayan writer, Eduardo Galeano (Galeano 1973:116). One of the more recent phenomena in this complex history is the response of other classes who say no. If the struggle of classes does not explain everything in Colombia today, it is the one thread without which it will never be possible to untangle Bolívar's knot.

PART ONE

The Birth of the Political Order

I believe that we are acting, thinking, conceiving and trying to go on making not a real country, but one of paper. The Constitution, the laws . . . everything in Colombia is magnificent, everything on paper. It has no connection with reality. In that sense, Venezuela is closer to Bolívar's thinking than Colombia. Colombia is a Santanderian country. The institutions, the legal and administrative organisation are Santanderian, but the country is Bolívarian. That is another thing. There is a democratic tradition, repressed a long, long time ago, which is the only hope for us, for Colombia. (Gabriel García Márquez, *Semana* 20 March 1989)

Chronology

1509	Spanish found San Sebastian de Urabá
1538	Spanish found Santa Fé de Bogotá
1781	Uprising of the *Comunero* movement against the Spanish bureaucracy
1810-16	Wars of Independence
1819	Bolívar's triumphal entry into Bogotá
1828	Conspiracy against Bolívar
1830	Bolívar dies. Confederation of Gran Colombia dissolved
1830-50	Republic of Nueva Granada
1849-53	Presidency of General José Hilario López inaugurates 37 years of Liberal government
1863	Federalist Liberal Constitution of Rionegro Republic, renamed the United States of Colombia
1878	Society of Colombian Farmers (SAC) established
1885-1930	Years of the Conservative Republic
1886	President Núñez's authoritarian centralist Constitution passed (still in effect today); Concordat restores the role of the church in state and society
1899-1902	Thousand Day War

1.1 Historical Threads

'. . . a kind of archipelago'

Geography and climate have had a decisive impact on the course of Colombian history. The country is dominated by three Andean mountain ranges separated by two broad river valleys, of the Magdalena and Cauca rivers. Beyond the mountains, on the Atlantic coast, the eastern *llanos* and the south-eastern Amazon basin, lie extensive plains of savannas and forest.

The Andean ranges create temperature changes at different altitudes, which have greatly influenced agriculture and settlement patterns. There are three main climatic regions: the cold highlands, the temperate slopes and the hot valleys. Most indigenous peoples settled on the cooler highland areas, as did the Spanish after the Conquest in the early 16th century. Bogotá, the capital, is over 2,600 metres high on a plateau in the eastern mountain range. Settlement on the warmer slopes and plains took place only through pressure of land concentration and population growth in the 19th century, and continues to this day. The great movement of colonisation is a thread that runs through Colombian history to the present.

The great size and physical barriers of the country have created tremendous transport and communications problems. Until the 20th century Colombia was a country of isolated regions, 'a kind of archipelago' as historians have called it. The high costs and difficulties of transport hindered the development of a national market and politically reinforced the regionalism which has been a basis of political power in Colombia to this day.

Colonial legacy

'Three centuries of colonialism left as a legacy... a generally impoverished ruling class, without imagination or great ambition' (Jaramillo Uribe 1978)

The Spaniards found no sophisticated empires in Colombia to match the Incas of Peru or the Aztecs of Mexico. Its indigenous population numbered three to four million according to some estimates, compared to 25-50 million for pre-hispanic Mexico and ten million in the Inca empire. This number was soon much reduced by conquest and disease and was down to 130,000 by the end of the 18th century.

Today, Colombia's indigenous population numbers about half a million. Most Colombians are the result of racial mixing. While the available indigenous labour was sufficient to encourage the rise of a Spanish landowning elite, it was insufficient to meet the demand. Poorer Spaniards settled as artisans or as small peasant farmers in Santander in the north-east, while African slaves were introduced into the gold mines of Antioquia and the *haciendas* of the Cauca Valley and some areas of the Atlantic coast. Indigenous, Spanish and African races mixed in Colombia and, by the end of the 18th century, nearly 50 per cent of the population was of mixed blood.

The Spaniards found gold in Colombia, but nothing like the fabulous silver riches of Potosí's Cerro Rico in present-day Bolivia. Gold became the main export of the New Kingdom of Granada (1564-1718) and the Viceroyalty of Nueva Granada (1718-1810) as it subsequently became, with production shifting from Antioquia in the late 16th and early 17th centuries to the Chocó in the 18th. Ownership of mines helped give the local oligarchy of merchants and landowners a preponderant role in the country's economic life, but was not a source of great wealth, and mining was already in decline towards the end of the colonial period.

Two Colombias emerged during the colonial period which lasted into the first decades of Independence. 'That of the west, slave-owning and mining, and that of the east, agricultural and manufacturing. The great river Magdalena is the dividing line between these two Colombias' (Nieto Arteta 1971). A landowning elite based mainly around Bogotá and Popayán dominated both Colombias. Its power lay in the great estates or *haciendas* which grew up everywhere except in Antioquia and Santander, where small farms and mining in the former and manufacturing in the latter characterised the local economy.

A labour supply was vital to the large estates. The *encomienda* was a system for drafting Indian labour to work on them as 'tribute' to the landowner, while the Indian communities were given collective land ownership in *resguardos* or reservations. But the continuous decline of the Indian population led to the transfer of much *resguardo* land to the landowners. The increasing population of mixed blood, the mestizos, did not qualify for land on the Indian *resguardo* and they became part of the *hacienda*, as tenants, sharecroppers or peons tied to the estate through debts. The expansion of the large estates versus the efforts of the rural poor to establish their rights to the land is another constant theme of Colombian history.

Agriculture remained backward throughout the colonial period. Farming methods advanced little technologically from pre-hispanic times.

The iron plough was still not used at the end of the 18th century, nor was irrigation or fertiliser. Plantation agriculture never developed, as it did in Mexico or other areas of the Spanish empire. Some historians have blamed this on the lack of entrepreneurial impetus of the local ruling classes. Indeed, some identify this as another thread in the country's history. But geography also played its role; transporting goods, which were mostly carried by mule, but also by humans over impossible terrain, was both costly and risky.

Colonial society was hierarchical and stratified and this generated many social tensions. The black population fought hard to escape slavery, either by running away and setting up *palenques* (rebel communities) or through open revolt. In 1781, the indigenous population played a considerable role (as many as half of the 20,000 or so people mobilised were Indians) in the *Comunero* uprising.

The *Comunero* movement was an uneasy alliance of all, poor and rich, who opposed the Spanish bureaucratic oppression and new taxation policies. It centred on the north-east of the country, which had a vigorous economic life based on locally-produced manufactures and agricultural production. The movement's leaders were modest property owners and businessmen, joined by members of the creole elite who wanted to keep demands within acceptable limits.

But the movement raised the hopes of poor mestizos and unleashed the anger of dispossessed Indians whose grievances were not just against the colonial authorities, but against all who had robbed them of their land. A leader emerged, José Antonio Galán, a poor mestizo, who tried to turn the movement into an expression of the interests of the popular classes. The creole elite quickly deserted it and helped the Spaniards to crush the movement. Its fear of the populace was ultimately much greater than its hatred of the Spanish authorities. The independence movement itself would be firmly in its control.

Independence but no nation

Between 1810 and 1816 the independence struggle was marked by fierce quarrels among the creole elite, some wanting a unitary regime, and others a federal alliance. This debate, fuelled by the deep regionalism and competing interests of the elite was to continue into Independence.

Conflict also emerged between the vision of Simon Bolívar, the first president of Gran Colombia, set up after his triumphant entry into Bogotá in 1819[1], and his vice-president, the great administrator, Francisco de Paula Santander. Some trace Colombia's inability to build a nation in the 19th century to the defeat of Bolívar, whose vision rose far above the particularist interests of the time, which so tore it apart. Colombia subsequently fell into the hands of warring landowners and merchants unable to build a coherent state, although they remained formally committed to constitutions, laws and even elections.

Santander and his followers, who had been less directly involved in the war and felt no particular loyalties toward Bolívar and his vision of a federal Latin America, intended to fill the political spaces emerging with Independence. But they could not agree on one political project and Bolívar's army was a serious obstacle to their ambitions. The army was the one centralising force, conflicting with the localised and regional mentality of the elite. With its many Venezuelan officers, the army had also become a vehicle for advancement for 'mulattoes' and mestizos, a rare democratising force in an otherwise rigidly stratified society.

Fearful that the discord among the ruling factions would threaten the newly-independent republics, Bolívar used his army to impose an authoritarian constitution in 1828. This experience left a lasting legacy of anti-militarism among Colombia's ruling elite. When Bolívar retired in 1830, following an attempt on his life in 1828, the army lost its patron and, starved of resources, it became one of the weakest armies in Latin America. Other state institutions remained in a similar condition. No sector of the elite succeeded in imposing itself for long and disorder and instability reigned.

The *República de Nueva Granada* lasted from 1830 to 1850, and was a poor and isolated country with a population of just over one million. Communication between the regions was based on coastal and river navigation and arduous Andean trails. Never a wealthy colony, the independence wars had further decapitalised it; it was the least dynamic of the three countries that had formed Gran Colombia. Venezuela had been Spain's most important agricultural colony and, like Ecuador, was a leading producer of cocoa.

The problem of reconstructing the economy after 1830 generated various debates, principally around the issues of protectionism and industrialisation versus free trade and the integration of the economy into the world market on the basis of agricultural and mining exports. By the mid-century, the weakness of manufacturing (under constant threat from cheap British products) and the influence of British ideas of free trade on the commercial elite had resulted in the predominance of the liberal economic school. Liberalisation was completed under José Hilario López (1849-53) who, among other things, broke the state tobacco monopoly. By the end of the 1850s, tobacco production had expanded to reach 28

1. Gran Colombia included present day Venezuela and Ecuador as well as Colombia. Bolívar hoped it would one day also include Peru and Bolivia, creating a federation of the Andes. But Gran Colombia only lasted until 1830.

per cent of exports while gold had fallen from 75 per cent of exports in the 1840s to 33 per cent. Hilario López also abolished slavery.

Party warfare

'In Colombia there was a national party politics even before there was truly speaking a national economy or a national culture' (Bushnell 1986)

The historian, Gonzalo Sánchez describes Colombia during the 19th century as a 'country of permanent war'. Following the 14 years of the Wars of Independence, there were eight general civil wars, 14 local civil wars, countless small uprisings, two international wars with Ecuador and three coups d'état. These wars never ended in decisive victories, but there were short breathing spaces before renewed fighting.

The two parties responsible for this warfare and which even today dominate Colombian political life, date officially from the late 1840s. The Liberal programme was drawn up by Ezequiel Rojas in 1848 and that of the Conservatives by Mariano Ospina Rodríguez and José Eusebio Caro in 1849. Some trace their roots back to the independence war and the two figures of Santander and Bolívar, the Liberals to the former and Conservatives to the latter. But clear distinctions between the parties either in origins or politics, are not easy to establish.

Economic issues did not colour party affiliation; the ruling elite was divided between both parties and there were supporters of free trade and protection in each. Federalism versus centralism caused divisions in the early years but not deep or lasting ones. It was a Conservative government that drew up the 1857 constitution with a clearly federalist intent. But it was the Liberals who in 1863, following one of the most destructive of all civil wars, took federalism to its ultimate with the constitution of Rionegro. Central government was left with no military or political powers except in the field of external relations. This constitution renamed the republic the United States of Colombia. It was, according to Victor Hugo, a constitution 'written for a country of angels'.

During the 19th century the church became the only issue through which the parties could be distinguished. For the Conservatives, more inclined towards the preservation of the status quo, the church was a guarantor of social order and authority. For the Liberals, seeking to modernise the state, the church was a bastion of privilege. It undermined its efforts through its political influence on the masses, particularly through its control of education and this helped to give the Conservatives electoral majorities in the mostly rural-based electorate of the 19th century. After the Liberal President, Tomás Cipriano de Mosquera,

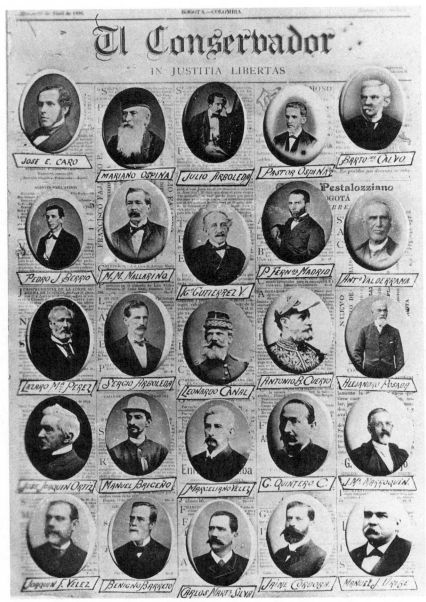

Photographic collages of politicians distributed during an electoral campaign, 1896.

Oscar Monsalve

Oscar Monsalve

expropriated church property in 1861, the question of compensation along with the issue of church control over education, fuelled years of inter-party hostility.

But the differences between the two parties can not in themselves explain the extent of the violence generated between them. Clearly, after a while people began to believe the differences really did exist, and this belief itself generated deeper divisions. But the penetration by the two parties into popular consciousness may have been the decisive factor. As the two banners became established during the 1850s, so the rural and urban poor were drawn in behind one or the other.

The wars of the 19th century were not between small armed groups, but mobilised the population into armies of thousands of men. Initially, for most people participation in the local landowner's army offered promise of some favour or reward. But as they engaged in battle and saw family and friends killed or wounded by the 'enemy', so loyalties and hatreds were born with deep personal roots. A Swiss professor, E. Rothlisberger, who witnessed the 1885 revolution wrote: 'The majority do not fight in one party or another out of conviction but because they must avenge some atrocity'.

Unlike in other Latin American countries at the time, the army itself was rarely involved in the fighting. The military coup of General Melo of 1854 was a rare event, not only because it originated in the army, but also because it reflected social conflicts in the country which had not yet been superseded by loyalties to the multi-class political parties. It brought together the officers who had risen from the ranks in Bolívar's army, angry at attempts to limit their already much diminished role and the artisans who sought a return to protection for manufacturing industry. Artisans were a solid social group by the mid-century, but badly affected by the flood of British manufactured imports. In 1855, 25 per cent of cotton goods were imported; this figure would rise to 70 per cent by 1890. They organised 'democratic societies', the earliest form of worker association, rallied around the slogan of 'Bread, Work or Death' and organised militias to defend themselves from repression.

Melo and his supporters were defeated by a bipartisan coalition led by generals from the landowning class. With the federalist constitution of 1863, a central army ceased to exist; regional armies and regional oligarchs now disputed power in almost 40 rebellions and uprisings in the 23-year life of the constitution and one 'national' war (1876-7), led by the Conservatives against Liberal attempts to introduce lay education.

Some, in attempting to identify a history and culture of violence in Colombia see continuity in the instability of the 19th century and the violent epochs of the 20th. But others have questioned the degree of violence of these civil wars. 'A poor country', notes the British historian,

Army General Staff officers c.1850s.

Malcolm Deas (1986), 'makes poor wars'. Despite the instability, the years of federalism were among the most culturally and intellectually dynamic in the country's history. Elections and electioneering were still a vital part of political life, despite the freqent recourse to arms, and a vibrant press covered them. Most governments came into office through elections and this also played a role in deepening people's party alignments and creating some national political awareness in a country otherwise torn by regionalism.

The years of party warfare must, nevertheless, have had some impact on the country's political culture. As the Jesuit, Francisco de Roux has said: 'It is a simplification to say that the Colombian people was an aggressive people from the beginning. Rather what you find is a country where the political customs of the ruling class have led the people into war from the very first days of the republic.'

The agricultural frontier

However much they were politically divided, the landowning elites agreed on basic economic issues, such as how to extend the agricultural frontier. The powerful landowners from Cundinamarca and Cauca, where the *encomendero-hacienda* system had predominated during the colonial period, aimed to extend the large estate to the new agricultural areas which were opening up. Only in Antioquia, where a sparse population had inhibited the establishment of the *hacienda*, and in Santander, where poor Spanish immigrants had settled as independent farmers, was the pattern different and a very different story unfolding.

There was an immense reserve of public lands in the new republic, an estimated 75 per cent of the country's land area in 1850. During the course of the 19th century a great deal of this was given out to a handful of private owners. Two concessionaries, for instance, were granted 150,000 hectares between them; 73 per cent of the two million hectares given out during the 19th century were granted in concessions of more than 1,000 hectares.

Both Conservative and Liberal governments were interested in populating the lowlands with a view to producing tropical crops for export, for it was felt that highland crops were insufficiently competitive on the world market. Labour was a major problem if landowners were to exploit their estates commercially. The mass of the population still lived in the highland areas, and if the peasants gained access to the ample land in the low-lying warmer areas they would no longer have any incentive to work on the large estates. Population movements were in fact beginning to take place from the densely-populated highlands to the slopes and intermontane valleys. But governments resisted giving title to their own peasants. Instead they offered large expanses of land to European immigrants, most of whom failed to respond. Those peasant *colonos* who tried to settle the public lands were expelled in a variety of ways.

Landowners could pay the legal costs of acquiring title to the lands, but just as often they usurped it and occupied it illegally, finding a friendly judge to confirm their ownership. Once the landowner had made claim to the land, accompanied by the police he would tell the *colono* who had settled there that he must leave or sign a contract to rent it. The rent was most often taken in the form of labour.

At first the *colonos* did little to protest against their situation. But after 1875 laws were passed which gave them some protection. These were ignored by landowners and violent conflict frequently broke out when the peasants invoked them in their defence. The landowners destroyed crops, brought down bridges to prevent peasants taking produce to market, formed vigilante groups to intimidate and terrorise, and imprisoned peasant leaders on false charges. The bloody struggle over Colombia's agricultural frontier was just beginning.

'Regeneration or catastrophe'

The roots of Colombia's instability lay in the country's poor and backward economic condition. While elites adopted ideological positions committed to the free-trade philosophies prevailing in Europe, for most of the 19th century they lacked the means to benefit from them. The Colombian state never developed a resource base in the 19th century sufficient to allow it to create a real nation out of an area that was federalist by nature. No one export crop was found during the 19th century to generate foreign exchange and give dominance in the state to those fortunate to produce it and control its export.

The ruling elite remained impoverished compared to its counterparts in Mexico, Lima and Rio de Janeiro, and no one group within it managed to dominate the rest for very long. Power rested on landownership rather than trade, and the traditional values and practices associated with the *latifundio* were unchallenged at the end of the 19th century when most other Latin American countries had strengthened and centralised the state and completed their liberal political and economic reforms.

The state depended mostly on customs duties in a country where imports and exports were still low. Tobacco and quinine provided short-lived export booms but, by the last quarter of the 19th century, both were in irreversible decline. Coffee began to contribute increasing amounts to export earnings from the 1870s, but its importance for the future was not yet recognised. Transport still inhibited commerce. Even when regular steam navigation was introduced on the Magdalena river in the 1850s and some rail lines had been laid, it still took four to six weeks to travel from the Atlantic ports to Bogotá.

As export earnings declined, so demand grew for stronger central government: 'regeneration or catastrophe' proclaimed the future president, Rafael Núñez. Those committed to technical progress and development found the constant war-mongering a main obstacle. In 1878, the Society of Colombian Agriculturalists (SAC)) was formed by such a group of farmers. In the end, the major thrust for change came from an independent sector of the Liberals, who sought to increase the authority of central government and to regularise relations between church and state. With the support of like-minded Conservatives, Rafael Núñez won the 1880 elections.

The ultra-centralist constitution of 1886 was as authoritarian as the 1863 constitution was Liberal and is seen by some as a first attempt at a national political project by the landowning class. It considerably strengthened the power of the president, and is the constitution in force today. A Concordat of 1887 restored the role of the church in state and society, referring to the Catholic Church as an essential element of social order. Whereas Liberal revolutions elsewhere in Latin America had stripped the church of its privileges, in Colombia it was given control of education and most civil ceremonies. A permanent army was created and in 1891 a military school was opened. The Liberal project was buried, and the era of the Conservative Republic (which lasted until 1930) had begun. Neither had in fact won a victory over the other; the old order was never defeated in Colombia, but incorporated into the new through political compromise.

In each of the political parties two tendencies had gradually emerged: the intransigents and the accommodators, with an ample measure of both in each party. The former were strong among aspiring bureaucrats, those unable to make good profits from the land, who saw the state as an economic resource and a political career a means of access to it. They demanded that no member of the opposing party be given government jobs. The accommodators were mostly businessmen seeking a stable economic environment in which to pursue their activities. Desirous of peace they would ally with those of similar disposition in the opposing party. Alongside the fanatical character associated with Colombia's two traditional parties there is also this conciliatory tradition, which has undoubtedly contributed to the survival of the parties into the 20th century.

But it was the intransigents who were to have the last word. World prices for coffee which, by the 1890s provided some 50 per cent of the country's exports by value, collapsed. Against the background of economic crisis, a group of Liberal leaders once more resorted to war in 1899, bringing the catastrophe Núñez so feared. One of the main motivations seems to have been the exclusion of the Liberal Party from government jobs. Peace could thus eventually be arranged without too much difficulty, but not before the level of destruction had made even the intransigents see the need for it.

'A gust of death had passed over the entire country'

The Thousand Day War (1899-1902) was the longest and most destructive of Colombia's civil wars. The devastation was exacerbated by the emergence of numerous, mainly Liberal, guerrilla armies in various parts of the country, particularly Tolima, Cundinamarca, Santander and the Cauca. Guerrilla warfare had been forced reluctantly onto the party leaders after the defeat of their army at Palonegro. The Conservatives, with their control of the state, had a strong army and the only way the Liberals could save their honour was through guerrilla warfare. The guerrillas were not easy to control. They were from the poorest social groups: mostly landless peasants, Indians and some urban poor. They wrought havoc on the large coffee estates of Cundinamarca and Tolima: 100,000 people died in the war.

Material destruction was devastating. The incipient development of the coffee economy in Cundinamarca and Santander was cut short, public finances and economic life in general were plunged into chaos. In 1903, Colombia could do nothing to prevent the separation of Panama under the encouragement of the US. 'A gust of death had passed over the entire country', wrote the Colombian politician Jorge Holguin, who lived through those years. But while the Thousand Day War was the last of the 19th century, it was only the first of the 20th.

Chronology

1903	US foments Panamanian separatism in order to build canal
1914-18	Indian rebellions in Cauca under Quintín Lame
1915-29	US investment expands, especially in the petroleum and banana sectors
1923	Central Bank (*Banco de la República*) set up
1925	First Union Central, National Workers Confederation (CNT) established
1926	Revolutionary Socialist Party (PSR) founded
1927	Federation of Coffee Growers, FEDERACAFE, established
1928	Banana workers' strike violently crushed
1930	Communist Party created from PSR ashes. Liberal Party once more hegemonic under President Olaya Herrera (1930-34)
1933	National Unity of the Revolutionary Left, UNIR, constituted; drawn back later to the Liberal Party
1934-38	President López Pumarejo's 'Revolution on the March'; favourable labour legislation passed
1936	Confederation of unions established, later to be known as the Confederation of Colombian Workers, the CTC
1936	First Agrarian Reform legislation; Law 200, recognised social function of land ownership
1938-42	Presidency of Eduardo Santos, member of family owning largest daily newspaper, *El Tiempo*
1942-45	Second Presidency of López Pumarejo
1944	National Association of Industrialists, ANDI, established
1945-46	Government of Alberto Lleras Camargo
1946	Union of Colombian Workers, UTC, set up
1947	Increasing levels of violence between the parties. An estimated 14,000 people die. General Strike results in wave of repression
1948	Jorge Eliécer Gaitán, Liberal Party populist leader assassinated. Uprising in Bogotá
1946-50	Government of Mariano Ospina (Conservatives once more head government)

1.2 The Oligarchic Republic

Coffee and Antioquia

Colombia entered the 20th century with one of the most backward economies in Latin America. In 1905 real exports per capita were hardly more than 30 per cent above what they had been at the end of the colonial period. The economy was still very closed and, along with Haiti, Colombia had the lowest indices in Latin America of per capita imports and exports, and of foreign investment.

It was coffee which provided the economic basis to forge a nation out of the fractured republic. There are three phases in the history of Colombian coffee production. Between 1870 and 1910, the centre of production was on the large estates of Santander and Cundinamarca. From 1960 onwards, production was dominated by large coffee entrepreneurs. In between, from 1910 to 1950, is the era of the peasant coffee farmer. During these years production shifted from east to west, in particular to the department of Antioquia. 'The Antioqueños are a strong, hard working and serious people; the future of Colombia belongs to them', wrote a European visitor to Colombia in 1880 (quoted in Le Grand 1986). By 1932 Antioquia and Caldas to the south, produced nearly 50 per cent of the country's coffee. In the first three decades of the 20th century, production rose from 40 per cent to 70 per cent of exports and, by the end of that period, Colombia was fourth in Latin America in terms of volume of external trade.

Antioquia has played a particularly important and much debated role in Colombia's economic development. Gold mining rather than agriculture was the basis of its colonial economy; the region produced 30 per cent of Colombia's gold in the 18th century. Small travelling merchants became key figures in the local economy, providing essential goods to an isolated region and acting as intermediaries in the legal and illegal marketing of the gold. Mining was largely in the hands of individual miners, who grew their own food. The colonial administration gave priority to the mining economy and carefully controlled concessions to large landowners so that the *hacienda* never dominated the economy of the region, as it did elsewhere.

With Independence the merchants found themselves in control of a large share of the nation's gold production and free to trade as they wished. They were soon providing the government with loans, receiving land and mining concessions in return. Their investment in European mining technology stimulated a new boom in gold production in the mid-19th century. They became a well-established and well-endowed regional elite in a capital-starved country. Interested in new export products to replace declining gold production, the merchants encouraged land settlement, much of which they organised themselves. For instance, they obtained tracts of public land for livestock production from the state in exchange for building roads. The construction workers received smallholdings along the new roads. In this and other ways, small farmers were able to settle in the region alongside the large estates, which still maintained a privileged position in many municipalities.

It was these small and medium-sized family farms which provided the basis for Colombia's coffee boom. Access to land enabled them to consolidate a subsistence peasant economy while waiting the four or five years for the coffee trees to give fruit. With no particular advantages of scale, coffee production flourished in the hands of the independent farmers who relied on family labour. The small farms proved highly productive and cost effective, able to ride out depressions thanks to the ability of the farmers to grow their own food. Large plantations, on the other hand, had constant problems of labour supply and cost.

Nevertheless, the small producers were vulnerable to the intermediaries who marketed their produce. Some were local traders who gave the peasants an advance on the harvest at high interest rates and at a low price, while the coffee bourgeoisie of large landowners, distributors and traders bought the harvest direct and supervised its processing and export, where the truly large sums were to be made from coffee production.

Coffee and the nation state

Coffee transformed the Colombian economy, made the fortunes of landowners and merchants, encouraged the formation of a national market and provided the basis for national industry.

Colombians managed to hold onto a large part of the wealth generated from coffee production by maintaining a share of the international coffee trade even when US import firms moved in to control it in the 1920s. The National Federation of Coffee Growers (FEDERACAFE), established in 1927, ensured Colombian participation, and subordination to the foreign exporters lasted only until 1940. The Colombian government owned most of the railway that transported the coffee, and Colombians also owned most of the coffee-husking plants.

With income more widely spread than in other coffee-producing countries, a market was created for other goods. Improvements in transport also helped the creation of a national market. The industrial processing of coffee beans together with the production of textiles, both based in Antioquia, formed the basis of the country's industrial growth in the first two decades of the 20th century.

But it was not until the second half of the 1920s that industrial production took off and a wide range of basic consumer goods began to be produced. Most industrial production was still very small in scale, but in Medellín, Barranquilla and Bogotá, some tobacco, beer, soft drinks and textile firms employed as many as 250 workers.

Improvements in road and rail transport to facilitate coffee exports were an important factor in stimulating the economy; the total length of railway track increased almost six times in the first three decades of the century. These and other public works were possible now that the Colombian state had a resource base, although it was still limited. Customs duties levied on the imports of goods, which increased considerably with the coffee boom, provided the greater part of government revenues, but US loans and indemnification for the loss of Panama were also important. In 1923 the *Banco de la República* was set up and began organising the country's chaotic monetary system, creating a single monetary unit and regulating credit.

US investment expanded from between US$2 million and US$4 million in 1913 to US$200 million in 1929. The United Fruit Company invested in banana production on the Caribbean coast near Santa Marta, Tropical Oil (an affiliate of Standard Oil) began to export oil near the port of Barrancabermeja on the Magdalena river after 1925. But the militancy of the workers in those sectors discouraged great expansion of investment.

Coffee provided the means to create the nation state. But economic growth and change had social implications and from these emerged early labour struggles and renewed peasant struggles for land.

The heroic years: urban labour (1919-29)

Public works created employment and attracted people to the towns, which grew rapidly in the 1920s. The urban population increased at an average annual rate of 5.9 per cent between 1918 and 1938, compared to 0.4 per cent in the rural areas.

The numbers employed in manufacturing industry were small; even in 1930 they were only 15,000, and many of these were women. It was not in the factories, but in the railways, ports and later banana and oil enclaves that the first labour struggles began. These workers were joined by artisans — tailors, masons, shoemakers — who formed the country's first recognised union, the Society of Artisans of Sonsón, established with Jesuit support in 1909. Artisans still made up the bulk of the unions as late as the 1940s. This radical, highly-politicised group (they had seized Bogotá for three days during the Liberal insurrection of 1893, influenced by the Paris Commune) played an important role in the labour struggles of the 1920s.

The government recognised the right to strike in 1919, but at the same time guaranteed the right of employers to hire contract workers to replace the strikers. The number of strikes grew over the next few years. Some were spontaneous, but many were influenced by socialist agitators, such as María Cano, Raúl Eduardo Mahecha, Tomás Uribe Márquez and Ignacio Torres Giraldo.

Excited by the Bolshevik revolution, Cano, Mahecha and other workers and radical intellectuals founded a socialist party in 1919. In the 1921 legislative elections they won 23 per cent of the vote in Medellín. The Liberals were concerned. Unable to challenge the Conservative hold on the rural vote they needed to capture the rising urban electorate. They began to incorporate some of the demands of urban labour into their programme.

A Liberal candidate for the 1922 elections told an interviewer: 'I don't see any reason for founding a third political party, when all the aspirations of workers fit within Liberalism'. Within the Liberal Party, a number of individuals were open to the new ideas, although none became a socialist as such. Among them was Jorge Eliécer Gaitán, who wrote a thesis as a student in 1924 on 'socialist ideas in Colombia'.

Some socialists agreed to collaborate with the Liberals, but a group of activists began to build a revolutionary workers' movement independent of both traditional parties. The Revolutionary Socialist Party (PSR) was founded in 1926 in the wake of the country's first oil-workers' strike and following the creation of the first union central, the National Workers Confederation in 1925.

Party cadres began to spread socialist ideas in town and countryside, mainly along the Magdalena river. María Cano was famous for her fiery speeches as she travelled through the region, encouraging the formation of workers' societies. In his study, *Los Bolcheviques del Líbano*, Gonzalo Sánchez describes the revolutionary socialism which took root during these years in the coffee zone of El Líbano in the department of Tolima. A revolutionary culture developed in the region, in which people baptised their children in the 'holy name of oppressed humanity'. Small peasant farmers, artisans and labourers from El Líbano would later be involved in what Sánchez calls, 'perhaps, the first armed insurrection in Latin America in which an army of peasants, with leadership from and in alliance with urban sectors, put forward the problem of the seizure of power in the name of socialist ideas' (Sánchez 1984:13).

Militancy grew in the labour force, particularly among the transport and port workers on the Magdalena river. There were also three important strikes in the foreign enclaves — the oil workers in 1924 and 1927 and the banana-plantation workers in 1928. The courts and the military were used to repress the workers' movement. In 1928 the army fired on a peaceful demonstration of banana workers in Ciénaga. In the massacre and subsequent hunt for strikers who had fled, an estimated 1,000 workers died.

The most active PSR leaders were now either arrested or forced underground and the leadership of the movement fell into the hands of what Torres Giraldo describes as 'intellectuals with no links to the workers'. The strikes had been seen as a possible starting point for the launching of an insurrection, but the defeats changed this perspective. An attempted insurrection did take place in July 1929 but with a confused and vacillating leadership. Localised uprisings took place in Santander and Tolima with the remarkable political experience of El Líbano. They lasted for about a fortnight before being put down.

Having lost its momentum, the workers' movement was then further demobilised by the onset of the depression following the great crash of 1929. The PSR fell into a crisis, to be reorganised by a new general secretary, Guillermo Hernández Rodríguez, who had recently arrived from Moscow and been charged with that task by the Communist International. The Communist Party was created in 1930 from the ashes of the PSR and, under the direction of the Third International, became increasingly isolated from the urban workers.

It abandoned efforts to build an independent revolutionary party in line with the Popular Front strategy emanating from Moscow. This called upon the party to ally itself with the Liberals who were seen as representing the rise of a progressive national bourgeoisie, and it was the Liberals who gradually took over the political leadership of the workers' movement.

'Real' country and 'political country'

In Colombia there are two countries: the *political* country which concerns itself with elections, its bureaucratic sinecures,

> its business interests, its privileges and influences . . . The
> political country or the oligarchy are one and the same. And
> the *national* country, the people who think of their work, of
> their health, of their culture . . . We belong to the *national*
> country, to the people of all parties who are going to fight
> against the *political* country, against the oligarchies of all the
> parties. (Jorge Eliécer Gaitán, quoted in Bermúdez Rossi
> 1982:60)

The years of the Conservative Republic (1885-1930) were years of
considerable social and economic change. In most Latin American
countries it was the Liberal parties which carried out these changes:
consolidation of the export economy, strengthening of the state,
extension of transport and communications systems, encouragement of
foreign investment, etc. They were often implemented by authoritarian
governments and involved a major shift in economic and political power,
away from the traditional landed elites towards the more commercially-
minded who controlled the export sector.

In Colombia, the birth of the export economy and the first steps in
the modernisation of the state were not only begun later than elsewhere,
they were carried out without the political destruction of traditional
forces. Traditional landowners had already established a stable political
hold over certain regions and the Conservative Republic rested on
authority, the army and the church. Economic changes were grafted on
to the existing social and political order and made possible by the coffee
boom in the 1920s, the so-called 'dance of the millions' when foreign
capital flowed into the country, and the fact that the economic elite as a
whole, Conservative and Liberal, were behind them.

Coffee production did not establish the overwhelming supremacy
of a coffee oligarchy over all others. The larger producers and those who
processed and exported the coffee came to constitute the most dynamic
and powerful economic group, but they were part of an oligarchy with
diverse economic interests based in a number of cities and regions. This
included commercial farmers, such as the sugar producers of Valle,
industrialists and bankers, as well as traditional ranchers. It was not a
solid, unified oligarchy like its powerful Brazilian or Argentinian
counterparts, but there were no major conflicts between its sectors. Its
economic and political predominance was such that, along with a few
well-established families who increasingly began to dedicate their lives
to politics, this elite represented the 'political' country.

While the state had been strengthened during the period of
economic change, it remained fragile and under-resourced. No sector of
the oligarchy organised itself through the state. From the beginning, the

coffee bourgeoisie controlled its own affairs. The Colombian state never became an agent of development (as elsewhere in Latin America) and a commitment to economic liberalism and the predominant role of the private sector went deep.

The two parties together helped to maintain the political and social order and excluded any third party. The greater strength of central government weakened, if by no means eliminated, the power of the regional leaders of both parties. Despite outbreaks of local party conflict, notably in Santander and Boyacá in 1930, they did not lead to generalised rebellions. Factions were inevitable within the parties, neither of which represented any one sector of the ruling class or particular regional interest. But the destructive potential of the factions could be minimised. While the parties could fight ferocious wars, they could also organise a 'gentlemanly' peace, and the Conservative presidencies during this period mostly governed with the support of a fraction of the Liberal Party. Under Carlos Restrepo (1910-14) a constitutional reform guaranteed the participation of the minority party in government with a quota of bureaucratic and parliamentary representation, although the majority Conservative Party would maintain control of the executive.

Rural politics and the cacique

In the malleable and fragmented political system of 19th-century Colombia, the *cacique* is the link in the complicated political relationship between city and countryside. Between a rural system which is technically and economically primitive, socially archaic, ideologically Catholic, superstitious and conservative, and the landowning and business classes, who live in the city and who, independently of how far they participate directly in politics, stand for a political model which is republican, representative and invariably given legitimacy by some voting system or other (direct, indirect, restricted, universal . . .). The *cacique* lives in the towns which are the peasants' main markets, together with other intermediaries.

Like the estate manager, the *cacique* is the political line of contact between different social sectors. Just like the coffee estates, the political country underwent constant readjustments which extended the autonomy of these intermediaries and allowed them to take initiatives and assume control of local affairs.

In spite of the social changes that followed the first world war *caciquismo* grew stronger in the countryside and flourished in the towns. For the movements of peasant protest, it was an obstacle when the hour of commitment came, or a tough enemy in moments of open confrontation.

Oscar Monsalve

Guajaro Indian *cacique* and wife, holding portrait of President Reyes as patron and icon, 1909.

From the point of view of the political leadership of the peasant movements, *caciquismo* tried to prevent the urban groups making direct contact with the rural masses and vice-versa. This role was even more marked in the case of groups which had no legitimacy in local life, such as UNIR, PAN[2] and the Communist Party. For this reason, when aspects such as the growth of *class consciousness* are analysed, we should not underestimate the means used by priests and *caciques* to strengthen localist tradition, to hold onto the subordinated and individualistic loyalties of the peasantry.

Specific elements in the agrarian structure served as deterrent to the formation of class consciousness among the peasants. We should emphasise family structures, the deep-rooted tradition of private property, the well defined notion about lines of stratification within the peasant community and their fatalistic and superstitious mentality. But when these peasants, with their idea of a Civil Code, discover after two or three generations that the estate structure blocks their aspirations for advancement, they organise themselves, protest and struggle to change their status.

The historical role fulfilled by the urban-based political groups which sought to extend links to the peasants and to voice their demands for social and

2. National Agrarian Party (PAN) led by Erasmo Valencia. This movement was the first attempt to build a national peasant party between 1935-6, though it grew out of the Sumapaz area.

> political change on a much wider scale, consisted in demolishing, even if partially, the wall raised by the regional oligarchies and the *caciques* between the dispersed peasantry and the national state. With the protest movement the peasant sector became a subject for the state to reflect on, an object for limited and partial policies . . . a key element in the analysis of the agrarian question and its role in economic development. For their part, the rural oligarchies, a weak and confused Church and the *caciques* each guarding his own view, had to yield slowly to the growing penetration by state institutions and agencies into the territorial limits of domination which had once been their own private, traditional domain.
> (Palacios 1979:382-3)

Conservative electoral success rested on the ability of local political bosses or *caciques* to mobilise the rural vote. Electoral manipulation and fraud were widespread, guaranteeing the political and economic future of a powerful political class which then gained control of the state budget. With the passage of time, clientelist practices were no longer based on the relations of servitude in the countryside, but came to include jobs in the bureaucracy, grants, and public services more attuned to the interests of urban populations.

The Liberals might have remained the Conservatives' junior partner without an independent political future had it not been for its radical wing, which began to court the emerging labour movement and make a bid for the urban vote. Its success in this enterprise helps to explain the survival and growth of the party and the failure of an independent worker-based party to challenge it.

The Liberals won the election of 1930 because of a split in the Conservative Party, in which not even the clergy could agree on backing a single candidate. The new government, and particularly the López Pumarejo regime (1934-8) which followed it, tried to modernise the political order to accommodate the social changes that accompanied industrialisation and the rise of the urban working class.

Alfonso López Pumarejo was as much a part of the 'political' country as his predecessors. A banker, he came from the country's financial oligarchy; the export business founded by his father had for a decade controlled almost half of Colombia's coffee exports. But he belonged to a new generation of political leaders, whose political ideas kept pace with economic change. In a frank open letter in April 1928 López Pumarejo argued that the Liberal Party should become more progressive in its defence of the status quo and acknowledge certain popular aspirations. In this way the party could avoid being eclipsed by the left and could gain national power for the first time since the 1880s. But he was also reflecting the views of certain sectors of the ruling elite who believed that the state should intervene in social issues, rather than leave this domain to the police and army. The massacre of the banana workers had shocked many.

This rare interlude of reform which López Pumarejo introduced was, however, not allowed to last very long or to go very deep. The ruling class's profound conservatism was soon aroused when it looked as if the process of reform would create dangerous precedents and allow too much power to social forces which might not be too easy to control. These social forces were the 'real' country, the mass of the population living in rural and increasingly urban, poverty and excluded from genuine political participation. This 'real' country of the people was a different world to the 'political' country of the oligarchy and political elite. Political loyalties kept both worlds in touch, but were sectarian and potentially violent. They did not reflect the material reality and experience of the mass of the population and, beneath them there was little holding the social fabric together.

The 'Revolution on the March' (1934-8)

In Colombia, the 1929 crash and its aftermath were mainly felt in the early 1930s. The fall in coffee prices affected the capacity to import and to finance the debt burden (29 per cent of export earnings in the first half of the 1930s) which had helped pay for the expansion of public works. But the crisis did not affect Colombia as badly as elsewhere and, by 1936 coffee exports had recovered their value.

It is at this time of economic depression that, from a narrow base of recruitment, a new ruling elite took office with the election of the Liberal, Rafael Olaya Herrera, in 1930. There were great expectations. Alberto Lleras Camargo, one of the 'new ruling elite' declared in his memoirs, 'it was a world which was coming to an end, not an election which was won . . . The priests observed a terrified silence in their parishes. The Middle Ages had just died.'

It was Olaya Herrera's successor, López Pumarejo, who really attempted the modernisation implied in Lleras Camargo's remark. A 'Revolution on the March' was the chosen theme of his first presidency (1934-8). Amid heated debates about state intervention in the economy and various other social issues, López Pumarejo attempted to use the state to create stable conditions under which capitalist (particularly industrial) development could take place. His project was to turn Colombia into a modern bourgeois democracy, breaking with the authoritarian centralisation of Conservative rule dominated by traditional catholicism. The models were British liberal democracy and Roosevelt's welfarism.

He strengthened the state through the tax reform of 1935, which gave it a larger and more secure resource base than ever before, freeing it from exclusive dependence on external trade, though it never gained the economic basis for a serious intervention in economic and social life. The state did not actively promote industrialisation, as in Brazil or Mexico, but provided conditions under which entrepreneurs could take initiatives. Industrialists, as well as the coffee bourgeoisie with whom they had close personal and financial ties, were strong supporters of economic liberalism. Devaluation (backed by both) proved more important than protection and, through price increases for imported goods, gave industrialists a captive market. And, indeed, industry made qualitative advances during the 1930s. Between 1933 and 1938 it grew at an average annual rate of 10.8 per cent.

Among the favourable conditions for industry was a cheap and cooperative labour force. Labour had great expectations of the López Pumarejo government. The Communist Party pledged its support; believing that class struggle was only appropriate in the economic sphere it was ready to make varied alliances in the political sphere. Some favourable labour legislation was introduced: the eight-hour day in 1934; the right to unionise was made part of the constitution in 1936.

The government began to intervene in labour disputes, often to moderate the intransigent positions adopted by employers. The number of unions grew, although there were still only 42,678 unionised workers in 1935. A confederation of unions set up in 1936, which became what was later called the Confederation of Colombian Workers (CTC) came increasingly under the influence of the Liberal Party, with which the Communist workers' leaders were in an electoral alliance. Its main base was among workers who depended directly or indirectly on the state. It had little impact among private-sector workers, where the union movement remained weak.

The experience of the López Pumarejo government turned out to be disastrous for the workers' movement. Support for the government began to replace workers' own interests as the main objective of their organisation and their political disorientation was manifest. The workers now looked to the government to solve disputes rather than rely on their own struggles. And they gained little in material benefits from their faith in the Liberal Party. Many of the urban labour force's income advances in the 1920s were lost during the Liberal Republic. Real wages fell between 1935 and 1950 and many rural workers saw an absolute decline in their already miserable standard of living. Social expenditure was virtually stagnant between 1930 and 1950.

But despite the frustrations and disappointments, workers' loyalty to the Liberal Party was perhaps the most lasting legacy of the first López Pumarejo government, and it ensured him support for his second. The workers believed they had won 'political citizenship' under López Pumarejo and their faith remained unshaken. The Communist Party put theoretical flesh on the bones of this faith. They believed that, in supporting him, they were taking their place alongside the bourgeoisie to modernise Colombian capitalism.

It was this 'social pact' that characterised the first López Pumarejo government, rather than its pragmatic nationalism or limited interventionism, which was soon to be reversed in favour of the economic liberalism favoured by the economic elites. In the end, neither the workers' movement nor the state had the strength to take on the latter: 'What draws the one towards the other, trade unions and the state', writes Daniel Pécaut (1987b), 'is in the end the common weakness they share in the face of the bourgeois-oligarchic alliance'.

Peasant struggles

'The land problem is the capital problem among us and the men of the State will have to give it priority if we are to avoid a social revolution of great significance.' (*Acción Liberal*, October/November 1932)

Liberal administrations faced a wave of peasant unrest which had been in gestation for the previous decade. While the economic progress of the 1920s greatly increased demand for agricultural produce and enhanced the value of land, bringing prosperity to many landowners, the peasants gained very little. They toiled under various labour or sharecropping arrangements, living in poverty and servitude. Unable to pay taxes because their backward agriculture left no surplus, they were forced to carry out personal services for the local authorities, acting sometimes as human pack horses. A law prohibiting the levying of road tolls from people carrying goods of any sort on their shoulders was presented to Congress in 1916 (but was not debated because of its shameful implications).

A widespread peasant reponse to the exploitative conditions in the countryside began in the 1920s. Disputes grew over land rights and tenancy agreements and, in the Cauca and Nariño departments, Indians mounted resistance to attempts to dismantle the remaining *resguardos*.

Oscar Monsalve

The capture of Quintín Lame (centre, seated, with cigar), 1930.

Resistance was led by Quintín Lame who organised a rebellion in the Cauca between 1914 and 1918, and later in Huila and Tolima.

But it was in the large coffee estates of the east that struggles were most intense. Peasants sought the right to grow coffee on their own plots in order to take advantage of the opportunities it was offering small farmers elsewhere. Landowners feared that once coffee was established on their land, the tenants would press for ownership and they would lose control of the labour force on which they depended. Already, the boom in public works had led many peasants to head for the cities.

Towards the end of the 1920s as the economic crisis deepened and the end of the boom in public works sent people back to the land, militancy grew. Between 1928 and 1937, 20,000 peasants participated in rural struggles in some 18 areas of the country, 11,000 of them in Cundinamarca alone.

Peasant activity was most militant in the south-west of Cundinamarca and parts of Tolima, an area where powerful families owning vast expanses of land had dominated since colonial times. The epicentre of the former was Viota and Fusagasuga, and of the latter, Chaparral and Villarrica. In Sumapaz and Tequendama nearby, conditions were particularly servile, and the landowners dominated the personal and family lives of their tenants as well as their economic activity.

The response of the Liberal government of 1930 was to try to institutionalise the movement and bring it under government control, as had happened in post-revolutionary Mexico. In 1931 peasants were granted the right to unionise. Numerous peasant leagues were registered. The Liberal Party disputed the leadership of these movements with the Communist Party and the Committee for Regional Inter-union Unity, UNIR, an organisation of intellectuals, students and professionals founded in 1933 under the leadership of the radical Liberal, Jorge Eliécer Gaitán.

UNIR was comparable to APRA in Peru and the PRI in Mexico in its anti-imperialist and radical populist politics. It gained most of its support during the peasant struggles of the 1930s, particularly in the coffee zones around Sumapaz and in parts of Tolima. Gaitán eloquently denounced the peasants' situation in the region, called for the destruction of unproductive *latifundia* and the creation of a society of small independent peasant farmers. He was supported by the legendary peasant leader, Juan de la Cruz Varela, who established an influential agrarian movement in Sumapaz. But UNIR was not a revolutionary movement, and its legalistic and gradualist character drew it back into electoral politics in 1935, from which it had initially abstained, and from there back into the Liberal Party.

The Communist Party was much more radical, calling for 'revolutionary land seizures' and 'expropriation of landowners without compensation'. It established enduring support in Tequendama and in 'red' Viota in Cundinamarca, bastions of the Liberal guerrillas of the Thousand Day War. But the party did not break the localism of the peasant movement, a movement that had been disconnected from the struggles of urban workers elsewhere in the country, following the defeats of the 1920s and the collapse of labour militancy with the Depression. This disconnection of urban and rural struggles is a thread which runs through Colombian labour history. Politically, too, the party suffered from the disassociation of political and social struggles in the rural areas. This was established during the 19th century, when landowners drew their peasants behind them to fight their party battles, establishing loyalties which cut across class antagonisms.

López Pumarejo's response to the rural protest was Law 200 of 1936, which recognised the social function of ownership and allowed for the distribution of land that was not exploited productively by its owner. It gave ten years for this process to begin and many landowners began dividing up their land among their families to avoid expropriation. The landowners mounted a fierce resistance and it was never implemented in most areas, but the huge coffee estates of Cundinamarca and Tolima were bought up by the government, with full compensation to their owners, and the land broken into small parcels and sold to the coffee workers. This process was uneven, however, and struggles continued in some areas such as Chaparral where the Communist Party took over leadership from UNIR.

The decline of peasant militancy in Colombia has been traced to this transformation of combative coffee workers into conservative freeholders. Its regional character also weakened the peasant movement. Although the level of organisation stands out, no national movement came out of the peasant struggles of the 1930s. The strategic sector of the economy was coffee, and that was in the hands of small farmers.

Another factor is the shift in strategy of those claiming political leadership of the movement. The return of Gaitán to the Liberal Party is not so surprising, but the Communist Party also remained subservient to a strategy which made its alliance with the Liberals more important than the demands of the peasantry. 'Our post', the Communist Party declared in its newspaper, *Tierra* (Land) in February 1937, 'is at the side of the reformist government of López . . . Today we are not subversives. The only subversives are the falangist Conservatives. We Communists aspire to become the champions of order and peace'.

Retreat and 'reconquest' (1938-45)

The counter-revolution to the López Pumarejo 'revolution' began to be organised seriously in 1935, and had seized the initiative by the end of the following year. The president himself declared a 'pause' in his reforms in 1937, the year a crisis in the international coffee market badly hit export earnings, and moved to assuage the discontent of the ruling elite. His successor in the presidency, Eduardo Santos (1938-42) would have preferred an alliance with the as yet politically insignificant middle class rather than with organised labour, to which the government was increasingly hostile. López Pumarejo's second presidency (1942-5) once again rested on the support of the unions, but it was his government which paradoxically now reversed the process of state interventionism and paved the way for the ascendancy of economic liberalism. His second government was plagued by political crisis as party cleavages grew more virulent and the right organised what its arch-representative, Laureano Gómez, called the 'reconquest'.

López Pumarejo's limited reforms had aroused hostility in most of the conservative bastions of Colombian society. The Catholic Church was one of the most extreme of these. It had viewed the modernisation process in the 1920s and 1930s with suspicion, if not hostility. Mgr Miguel Angel Builes, Bishop of Santa Rosa de Osos, complained that, although the roads and railways that went through his diocese represented material progress, they resulted in a 'terrible spiritual regression', as the workers forgot God and dedicated themselves to dancing, gambling and fornication. Builes was also one of those who bitterly opposed trade unions, only 'enemies of Christ, the soldiers of Marxism' joined them, he said.

The church campaigned ferociously against the Liberal government, which aimed to secularise the state and to limit the clergy's influence over political and electoral life. The constitutional reform of 1936 suppressed explicit reference to the church's rights in the field of education and its and the seminaries' exemption from taxes. The bishops proclaimed that the constitution was no longer Christian but atheist.

The Conservative Party was just as virulent in its attacks on the proposed reform. It had declared a 'purifying' abstention in the elections of 1934 and 1938, its anger fuelled by the dismissal of Conservatives from the state bureaucracy. Extreme right-wing currents within the Catholic-Conservative axis began to proliferate after 1935. Paramilitary associations appeared in Antioquia and Caldas, in particular, with the support of local bishops and businessmen. The party was influenced by intellectuals with openly fascist views and members sympathised with Hitler and Mussolini, particularly during World War II. Laureano Gómez, who had risen to prominence within the party, openly supported Franco's Spain and promoted the concept of 'hispanidad', or pro-Franco 'Spanishness'.

The army was also antagonistic to the López Pumarejo administration. Like the economy and the state, the Colombian army was a late developer. Professionalisation began in the early 20th century and was not completed until 1943, when the highest ranks of the army were finally occupied by graduates of the military school. During the López Pumarejo government, the army became embroiled in the party conflicts of the epoch. The president reinforced the police force as a means of countering the Conservative army, paying little attention to the army except to intervene in promotions, to the resentment of the officer corps.

Being middle-class in origin, this officer corps identifed with the 'nation' as it had been defined by the oligarchy and politicians in the early years of the century. López Pumarejo's attempts to reform and to renovate were viewed with great distrust. This was fuelled by the Conservative Party's own hostility. In July 1944 an isolated group of officers attempted a coup. This failed, but heightened the tension mounting in the country at the time.

The 'bourgeois-oligarchic' alliance was the main enemy of López Pumarejo's project of greater state intervention and social responsibility. The large industrialists (the owners of small businesses were often recent immigrants and tended not to get involved in national politics), the coffee producers and the landowners, all opposed state regulation on social questions and interference in their affairs. And they certainly wanted nothing to do with alliances with worker or peasant organisations.

With support from bankers and industrialists, Liberal and Conservative landowners set up a violent opposition movement, to organise against Law 200 of 1936. This included attacks on peasants who demanded the right to land. Between 1944 and 1946 many of the labour and agricultural policies of the first López Pumarejo government were reversed. Law 100 of 1944 protected landowners from the claims of sharecroppers and opened the way for the landowners' violent revenge on peasant organisers in parts of Tolima and Cundinamarca. It was in these areas that Communist-led peasant self-defence groups came to predominate during *La Violencia*.

This, too, was the beginning of the rise of the *gremios*, the associations of landowners and businessmen. State regulation had been extended between 1940 and 1942 during the disruption to international commerce caused by the World War II, convincing many that, even in the most liberal of economies, some regulation was inevitable. The *gremios* were the institutions that guaranteed the private sector's ability to monitor and direct state intervention within acceptable limits. They gained key positions in economic decision-making during López Pumarejo's second presidency, restricting the autonomy of the state and ensuring its commitment to economic liberalism.

The most powerful of the *gremios* was the National Federation of Coffee Growers (FEDERACAFE). It reorganised itself in the wake of the crisis of the early 1930s and, from an association of small and large producers with poor resources and uncertain orientation, became a closed and hierarchical body in which large producers and exporters carried most weight. Firmly bipartisan in its leadership and strongly independent, it managed to ward off all government intervention, but to benefit from the Brazilian government's price-support efforts. It gradually gained control over the marketing of coffee from the US companies.

In 1940, the first quota pact in the history of the industry, the Inter-American Coffee Agreement, was signed to try to force prices up through withholding supplies from the market. A National Coffee Fund, based on special coffee taxes, was set up to finance the buying up of the harvest and the storage of that part to be witheld. The management of these funds turned the federation into a financial power.

The National Association of Industrialists (ANDI) was another powerful *gremio*, which was set up in 1944 by industrialists from Antioquia; it was followed a year later by the National Federation of Traders (FENALCO) and a number of others. This was a period of economic prosperity. There was a marked process of industrial concentration; two Antioqueño textile companies, Coltejer and Fabricato, represented 44 per cent of the total capital invested in the sector and began to diversify. Coltabaco, also based in Antioquia, controlled 77 per cent of the capital in the tobacco industry. The numbers of industrial workers increased from 100,000 to 150,000 between 1938 and 1945 and the sector was recognised as the key to economic development.

Towards *La Violencia*

Economic progress was accompanied by institutional and social crisis, a phenomenon which was to repeat itself several decades later. Poverty in the rural areas was leading to large-scale migration to the towns, and the urban population grew from 30 to 40 per cent of the total between 1938 and 1951.

Mounting opposition and a financial scandal involving his son, led López Pumarejo to resign in 1945. His successor, Alberto Lleras Camargo (1945-6), included three Conservatives in his cabinet. The Liberals approached the 1946 elections still traumatised by the conflicts generated by the 'Revolution on the March' and divided between two candidates, Gabriel Turbay and Jorge Eliécer Gaitán. The right, led by Turbay, was dedicated to the building up of the party machine and the conservation of power. On the left, Gaitán was mounting a challenge which went far beyond party politics. His populism found itself enmeshed in several cross-cutting social tensions: class conflict between the industrialists and the unions, conflicts between the traditional parties, and the conflict between the 'masses' and the oligarchy.

The split in Liberal ranks enabled the minority Conservative Party to take the presidency under Mariano Ospina Pérez, who also governed in the name of 'national unity', and divided cabinet posts between the parties. The era of reform and state intervention was truly over; the Liberals had lost their monopoly in government, which worried the people but not the *gremios* and party notables, who collaborated irrespective of party in a government dedicated to free enterprise and economic progress.

But the elections had demonstrated Gaitán's growing appeal to the people. Gaitán had attracted a large vote in towns with a popular Liberal tradition and solid worker presence, notably Bogotá, Barranquilla, Santa Marta, Cartagena and Cali, clearly defeating his Liberal rival. His message was simple and broadcast throughout the country in this new age of radio. While a bipartisan oligarchy monopolised wealth and political power, the mass of the people lived in poverty. He spoke clearly of uniting the 'people' against the 'oligarchy', the 'real' country against the 'political' country.

He was hostile to the CTC which he saw as a bureaucratic apparatus dominated by the Communist Party and inextricably linked to the oligarchic government of López Pumarejo. It fought for the privileges of the organised workers and left the rest of the people behind. The CTC gave its support to Turbay, but the rank and file turned to Gaitán.

Gaitán sought to make capitalism socially responsible, not to abolish it, and his appeal was as much to the shopkeepers and professionals of the petit-bourgeoisie as to the urban and rural dispossessed. As such he had two faces, that of social agitator and that of the man who had taken high ministerial office in the López and Santos governments, seeking reform through the 'proper channels'. The constitutionalism and legalism of 'formal' Colombia had true meaning for Gaitán; unlike most Colombian politicians he sought to put them into practice and create a genuinely participatory democracy.

This mass politics was a real challenge to the elitism of Colombia's 'oligarchic republic'. López Pumarejo had aroused hostility with what was a very cautious attempt to persuade the oligarchy to adapt to the social realities of the modern world, and to build a state with a 'national vision', above that of narrow sectional interests, with channels for participation of the workforce. Infinitely more threatening was Gaitán's mobilisation of the masses to force their entry into the political system.

Union demonstration, Medellín, c.1945

For the oligarchy populism equalled revolution. Gaitán was giving social mobilisation a political shape.

Industrialists were already highly concerned about the spread of unionisation to the private sector. The number of unions multiplied between 1944 and 1947. Most were based in individual enterprises and in a wide range of sectors, not just industry. They did not join the CTC, whose base remained in the public sector and in some strategic areas such as the river and oil workers, but whose credibility with its rank and file had been seriously eroded by the years of collaboration with the bourgeoisie and by the effect of inflation and falling incomes during the war. The defeat of the powerful river-workers' strike in 1945 at the hands of a resolute government and vacillating union leadership had been a major setback for the movement.

The employers went on the offensive against the independent unions. It was the church which took the initiative. A shift in position had led it to see the wisdom of intervening in the workers' movement itself to halt the spread of communist influence. The Union of Colombian Workers (UTC) was set up in 1946 under Conservative Party and church control and rapidly established itself particularly among the industrial workers of Medellín. The Conservative Party now had access to the workers' movement, and the employers could control the unions which were tied to their firms with no state interference.

But there was no halting the social mobilisation already in motion, which escalated during the last months of 1946. Demonstrations, street protests and strikes by many sectors of workers took place; between August of that year and the end of 1947 there were 600 conflicts involving factory workers, state employees, transport workers and artisans. But it was Gaitán's populism which was taking hold of the movement, giving it identity and uniting it against the oligarchy. The Liberals won control of Congress in the March 1947 legislative elections. Gaitán became the recognised leader of the Liberal Party soon afterwards, and it was as leader of that party that he now led the masses, whose economic demands were linked with the Liberal Party's return to power.

The CTC failed to understand this mood of the people when it tried to remove the political content from the general strike organised in May, and centre it on purely economic issues. Gaitán failed to support it and the trade union movement fell victim to repression, which saw 1,500 workers arrested on the day of the strike and the CTC deprived of its legal status for three months. It was a grave defeat for the organised working class and the politics of the Communist Party.

Meanwhile, open violence broke out, particularly in Boyacá and Santander North and South where a sector of the clergy gave strong support to Laureano Gómez. Gómez was now counterposed to Gaitán. His right-wing populism and Catholic fundamentalism were stirring up deeply felt emotions in various parts of the country and, after the March elections, the career politicians close to Gómez replaced the Conservative notables in the government.

The widespread politicisation of the country was reflected in the big increase in electoral turnouts — 63.7 per cent of those eligible in the 1947 Congressional elections compared to 39.4 per cent in those of 1945. Elections further exacerbated polarisation, because they meant a different carve-up of state and local council jobs, which middle-class sectors now saw as their path to social mobility. Even the police forces would change according to the politics of the mayor or governor. In Boyacá a Conservative-led para-police force was set up and was used to threaten and murder likely Liberal voters. This force became the basis of recruitment for the *chulavitas* (named after a hamlet in the small municipality of Boavita in Boyacá), a Conservative police force sent by the government into various departments where its acts of violence against Liberals became legendary. Political violence had claimed 14,000 victims by the end of 1947.

On 7 February 1948 Gaitán led a silent protest of 100,000 people through the streets of Bogotá, and delivered his speech for peace: 'All we ask, Mr President, is guarantees for human life, which is the least that a nation can ask'. Two months later, on 9 April, Gaitán was assassinated.

The roots of 'barbarism'

In rejecting state mediation and regulation of social conflicts, which had given the state considerable popular legitimacy under López Pumarejo, the ruling class had exposed the weakness of civil society. In the words of the French sociologist, Daniel Pécaut (1987b), it revealed 'something which threatened the entire social order: an undercurrent of social and political barbarism'. Gaitán's populist appeal to the marginalised coincided with that discovery. With the collapse of the organised labour movement, his was the only remaining force to bring the urban and rural poor together on the basis of their real material interests against the system of oligarchic rule. With the destruction of *gaitánismo*, the way was open for party loyalties to reassert their hold over the dispossessed and social struggles to degenerate into local party feuds. The country began its catastrophic slide towards *La Violencia*.

Chronology

1948-53	Worst years of *La Violencia*, estimated 200,000 dead
1949	Conservative government and landowners unleash violence against Liberals in countryside. First Liberal guerrillas organised in Santander under command of Rafael Rangel, followed by those in the south of Tolima under Gerardo Loaiza, and 36 fronts in the eastern *llanos*
1949-53	Government of Conservative, Laureano Gómez
1951	Laureano Gómez, sends Colombian troops to the Korean War
1952	Mutual Defence Agreement with the US signed; Colombia is the site of the first Latin American counter-insurgency training school
1953	General Gustavo Rojas Pinilla chosen by Liberal and Conservative Party politicians to lead a coup d'état
1953-57	Military government; Rojas Pinilla develops his own political movement, Movement of National Action (MAN). Amnesty offered to Liberal guerrillas, but many leaders subsequently assassinated
1955	Communist guerrillas and zone of self-defence attacked by army
1958	National Front of Liberal and Conservative Parties established; Alberto Lleras Carmargo (Liberal) becomes the first President (1958-62)
1958-65	Second stage of *La Violencia*
1960-62	Revolutionary Liberal Movement, (MRL), under López Michelsen, increases electoral support
1962	MRL negotiates with the National Front government and gains access to office
1964	16,000 troops attack Communist guerrillas in *Plan Lazo*
1966	The Revolutionary Armed Forces of Colombia (FARC) 1961-67 officially formed Colombia is a showcase for US Alliance For Progress programmes

1.3 La Violencia (1948-65)

The background to the civil wars of the 19th century is very different to that of *La Violencia*. Between the two periods of party conflict arose the challenge to oligarchic rule from the urban labour movements, from the organised peasantry and finally, and most seriously, from the populism of Gaitán. The premature collapse of the popular movement provides the fertile terrain for the country's degeneration into sectarian violence. While this violence did not take the form of class conflict, not far below the surface were a host of social antagonisms without appropriate political expression.

At one level *La Violencia* appeared as a political problem between the Conservatives in charge of the state and the Liberals mobilising their majority support to overthrow them. But party conflict unleashed in certain regions a host of other conflicts — social, political, economic and even personal. According to the Colombian social scientist, F. Leal Buitrago (1984:141-2), 'the strength of the parties was such that they were essentially acting as a channel for a cumulation of small social and economic processes originating in the provinces; the parties managed to convert isolated problems into a great political aggregation of national character, which came, at a given moment to endanger the very stability of the regime'.

The *Bogotazo* and its aftermath

The people responded to the assassination of Gaitán with a spontaneous uprising, now referred to as the *Bogotazo*. They took over the city in a wave of collective fury, looting and destroying everything that symbolised the power structures which excluded and impoverished them. It was not just the lumpen of the city who rioted, but workers, small traders and the lower middle classes. And Liberalism gave them their political identity.

In the provinces the response lasted longer and was more organised. In Barrancabermeja, Rafael Rangel headed a 'revolutionary council' for 14 days; Eliseo Velásquez in the *llanos* and Hermógenes Vargas in the south of Tolima began organising armed resistance, provoking further Conservative reaction. During 1948 more than 43,000 people died and the theatre of political action shifted to the rural areas. The urban populace was politically neutralised. Gaitán's movement did not survive his death. Repression fell heavily upon the union movement;

under the 'state of siege' now in force, meetings could only take place with the permission of the military and strikes were forbidden. Union leaders were arrested for organising meetings and replaced by government appointees. Union headquarters were occupied and thousands of workers dismissed in the private and public sector. In one sugar mill in Valle, Riopaila, 900 workers were sacked.

Party leaders, meanwhile, tried to resurrect a coalition government, but in May 1949 the six Liberals in the cabinet were replaced by three Conservatives and three military, including General Gustavo Rojas Pinilla. The Liberals tried to pass a law bringing elections scheduled for 1950 forward to November 1949, but this created such an uproar that two Liberal members of the Chamber of Representatives were shot and one was killed in the Chamber itself. Right-wing youths roamed the streets celebrating the murders. When the law was passed, because of the Liberal

Aftermath of the *Bogotazo*, 1948

majority, the Liberals refused to participate in the elections for lack of guarantees. The president responded by closing Congress, banning public meetings and imposing press censorship.

'The month of October', write the authors of the classic text, *La Violencia en Colombia* (1986, 1:44), 'marks one of the most abominable in the history of the decomposition of Colombia. The hamlet of Ceilán in Bugalagrande (Valle) is attacked, set on fire and sacked; the bandits leave about 150 dead, some of them burnt. Immediately afterwards, 27 citizens of San Rafael are murdered; their bodies thrown into the river, stain the waters a pure scarlet'. Massacre followed massacre; 112 people were shot in one day in Belalcazar in the Cauca. Anyone not supportive of the government became a potential victim, while the opposition formed resistance committees to avenge them.

La Violencia: the hurricane unleashed

The violence began with a confrontation between Liberal and Conservative parties, but the dynamic of class hostilities steadily sharpened its class-struggle character. The Liberal leader Jorge Eliécer Gaitán — known half-contemptuously and half-fearfully to his own party's oligarchy as 'The Wolf' or 'The Idiot' — had won great popular prestige and threatened the established order. When he was shot dead, the hurricane was unleashed. First the spontaneous *bogotazo* — an uncontrollable human tide in the streets of the capital; then the violence spread to the countryside, where bands organized by the Conservatives had for some time been sowing terror. The bitter taste of hatred, long in the peasants' mouths, provoked an explosion; the government sent police and soldiers to cut off testicles, slash pregnant women's bellies, and throw babies in the air to catch on bayonet points — the order of the day being 'don't leave even the seed'. Liberal Party sages shut themselves in their homes, never abandoning their good manners and the gentlemanly tone of their manifestos, or went into exile abroad. It was a war of incredible cruelty and it became worse as it went on, feeding the lust for vengeance. New ways of killing came into vogue: the *corte corbata*, for example, left the tongue hanging from the neck. Rape, arson, and plunder went on and on; people were quartered or burned alive, skinned or slowly cut in pieces; troops razed villages and plantations and rivers ran red with blood. Bandits spared lives in exchange for tribute, in money or loads of coffee, and the repressive forces expelled and pursued innumerable families, who fled to seek refuge in the mountains. Women gave birth in the woods. The first guerrilla leaders, determined to take revenge but without clear political vision, took to destroying for destruction's sake, letting off blood and steam without purpose.

> The names adopted by the protagonists of violence — Gorilla, Evil Shadow, the Condor, Redskin, the Vampire, Black Bird, Terror of the Plains — hardly suggest a revolutionary epic, yet the scent of social rebellion was in the couplets sung by their followers:
>
> > I'm just a campesino,
> > I didn't start the fight,
> > But if they come asking for trouble,
> > They'll get what's coming to them.
>
> (Galeano 1973:116-7)

With no opposition, the man who had done most to stir up sectarian hatred, Laureano Gómez, ardent foe of 'communists, masons and Liberals', was elected President in 1949. The darkest moments of Colombia's history had begun. Gómez tried unsuccesfully to erect a corporatist state in Colombia, along the lines of Franco's Spain, in which political liberties would be restricted and the liberal parlimentary model replaced by a form of government based on representation of the church, the *gremios* and professional associations. In the rural areas, the government pursued a policy of overt terrorism organised by local political bosses and landowners, in its crusade against communism and liberalism.

La Violencia (1949-53)

The first phase of *La Violencia* was its most violent. Three-quarters of its estimated 200,000 victims were killed between 1948 and 1953, more than 50,000 in 1950 alone. In these years the violence was generated mostly in the name of the parties; rural bosses mobilised their peasant clients in bloody vendettas against neighbouring villages; Liberal landowners organised peasant-guerrilla armies which engaged the Conservative forces of the state in 'hit and run' actions. A great mobilisation of peasant armies took place, with an inherent ambivalence. While they were led politically by sectors of the dominant classes through the traditional parties, the military leadership was in the hands of the peasants themselves.

Direct confrontation was rare; Liberal guerrillas carried out an act of sabotage and revenge was exacted on any Liberal household. Paramilitary groups of civilians and police, such as the *aplanchadores*, the fearsome *chulavitas* and the infamous *pájaros* or assassins, carried

Levels of Violence 1946-57

NORTE DE SANTANDER

ANTIOQUIA

SANTANDER

CALDAS

CUNDINAMARCA

TOLIMA

VALLE

META

HUILA

KEY

≡ c4,000
▨ 5,000-6,000
▥ 10,000-20,000
✿ 20,000-30,000
■ c42,000

out indescribable acts of violence which Liberals met with atrocities of their own. Decapitations, mutilations, sexual crimes and, with them, robbery and destruction of homes and land characterised *La Violencia* and earned it its name. Criminality and senseless violence intermixed with political and social violence. The barbarism unleashed was multifaceted and defies easy explanation. The army, reflecting the weakness of the state, was caught unprepared to deal with the guerrillas, but by 1951 it, too, was drawn into the conflagration.

Los Pájaros

The guerrillas hold sway over the *llano* (plain) and Tolima: half the country; the crime rate has taken on abysmal proportions. The Liberal fighters are called guerrillas, *bandoleros, chusmeros, cachiporros,*. A '*Patiamarillo*' is someone who has dealings or connections with the Liberals. '*Collarejo*' is the name given to the lowest category of Liberal.

On the other hand, *godos, chulavitas, chuvalos, chunchullos, guates, concos patones, indios, tombos, chulos* are all names given to the government forces. Now, suddenly a new and previously unknown name has appeared that embodies the response to the guerrillas: *Los Pájaros* (the birds).

Originating in western Caldas and refined in the Valle, they form a fraternity, a mafia of bewilderingly lethal effectiveness. They are intangible, ubiquitous, essentially urban to begin with. They work alone at first, with incredible speed, and leave no tracks. The group has at its disposal fleets of cars and motorbikes, all part of the grisly operation, and chauffeurs who are both accomplices to the crime and share in the spoils. They most closely resemble the hired assassin.

At first they don't assassinate the poorest groups, but well known people, alleged to support the revolution or landowners, especially of coffee plantations, whose harvests might finance the organisation. Here they talk of the 'organisation'; in Liberal ranks, they talk of the 'movement'. To assassinate someone is to do a 'job'. You can contact the *Pájaros* to do a 'little job'. A price is set and the deal is arranged.

The political machinery is pitted against the committees and municipal councils. The Liberal members of these bodies regularly fall into the hands of the *Pájaros*. There is no respect for places or persons, and no worry about punishment as nobody would dare to report such crimes. In the church of Belén de Umbría a well known citizen was shot while taking part in a service. The crime went unpunished.

They will be famous: the *Cóndor*, León María Lozano, *Pájaro Azul, Pájaro Verde, Pájaro Negro, Lamparilla, Turpial, Bola de Nieve*. They all had incredible criminal records. It is enough to recall that they have systematically killed many Liberal leaders . . .

Of course, they relied on the collaboration of the authorities, the police, the security police and the venality of the judges. Some even managed to get jobs in local government and on councils. *Lamparilla* had free access to the Valle government offices. The sectional head used to meet the head of the Dovio *Pájaros* at the Roldanillo Experimental Farm, for macabre conversations. There they talked about the 'work' they had carried out: methods, future victims, progress plans all in the presence of a completely reliable witness they believed at the time to be an accomplice and one of their number.

In the towns, they gather in special cafés; they rely on influential protectors; when necessary, they have ambulances at their disposal; they set up rest homes, like the one that used to operate around the Anacaro bridge on the Cauca river (via Anserma); they know of hideouts to which they can retreat after committing their crimes. They are a kind of home-grown Ku Klux Klan of interchangeable parts, always 'flying' from one place to another.

The *gamonales* (bosses) and middle men get rich in Valle and Caldas buying coffee stolen by *pájaros*, whom they sustain, nurture and protect. 'Feeding the birds' means providing them with arms, drugs, money . . .

It is worth noting some points made in a memorandum sent by Dr. Julio Alberto Hoyos on 9 March 1959 to the President of the Senate of the Republic, containing information that very clearly describes the *Pájaros* and how they operate.

'Some people who had been victims of *Cóndor* came to visit me at the Central Hotel in Tuluá. I remember a young tailor who took off his coat and shirt and showed me his chest and abdomen with various scars. Hè told me: these are the wounds inflicted by León María Lozano in the La Pampa café, when he arrived drunk and shooting.

I urged the informants to denounce him, but they refused, saying that if they did so, they would be assassinated along with their wives and children.' (Guzmán Campos 1986,I:165-6)

La Violencia by no means affected all of rural Colombia but was confined to certain regions. It affected the coffee-producing regions with particular intensity, as well as Valle, the *minifundia* areas of Boyacá and the Santanderes (which had long histories of partisan violence) and also the cattle lands of the eastern *llanos*.

Within the coffee-producing departments, the region of Cundinamarca and Tolima became the centre of brutal partisan violence, as well as the place where landowners settled old scores against the local peasantry who had organised against them in the 1930s. The *chulavitas* spread terror and forced thousands to flee to the south of Tolima.

Juan de la Cruz Varela armed his surviving peasant leagues around Sumapaz, while in other areas the Communist Party helped reorganise the peasants and their resistance. This initially took the form of peasant self-defence, but gradually the dynamics of events led peasants to take up arms and form their own guerrilla forces. In El Davis, peasants organised a guerrilla enclave and a self-sufficient community under the political leadership of the Communist Party, which, till it had a population of 5,000, attracted people fleeing from other areas. Agreements were made with Liberal forces nearby to carry out joint actions.

Among the Liberal guerrilla leaders who came to fight alongside the Communists were Pedro Antonio Marín (an agricultural labourer from Quindío, who later took the name of Manuel Marulanda Vélez), Jacobo Prías Alape and Ciro Trujillo. They drew closer to the Communist Party and had joined it by 1952, while by the end of 1953, most of the Liberal guerrilla chiefs were collaborating with the army against the Communists.

Elsewhere in the coffee-producing departments, complex developments took place. Many richer landowners chose to absent themselves. Liberals often fled on receiving the sinister *boleteo*, warning

Abandoned headquarters of Pedro Antonion Marín (*Tijo Fijo* 'Sure Shot') approached by army patrol.

them to leave the region or face death. Thousands of poorer peasants, as well as richer landowners, were dispossessed of their land or forced to sell it very cheaply. Land changed hands in a variety of ways; peasants were disposessed by other peasants as a result of party conflict and some peasants gained access to land abandoned by landowners as well as *vice versa*.

In the coffee areas, some land was bought by traders who made fortunes during *La Violencia* buying the coffee at very low prices and getting it to the processers and exporters. They were part of the economy of *La Violencia* which emerged in the coffee zones, which, through a variety of mechanisms, including theft, ensured the continued supply of coffee for export and, in the midst of the bloodshed, a healthy economy.

It has been estimated that in the country as a whole, at least 200,000 plots of agricultural land changed hands and one million people migrated, 150,000 of them to Venezuela, during *La Violencia*. Others headed for the small towns and later the large cities, while many began extending the agricultural frontier towards Upper Sinú, Magdalena Medio and the *llanos*. The displacement of the peasantry was great, but precisely how this related to the expansion of agrarian capitalism is still a subject of intense debate. Commercial agriculture began to develop during the 1950s, in the valleys which were less affected by *La Violencia*, but also in Valle, which was the scene of much violence.

In the eastern *llanos* during 1951, Liberal peasant guerrillas began to break from the Liberal ranchers who had initially helped to create them. The landowners resented the guerrillas' demands for money and supplies, although they had happily used them to defend their property and interests. When the army began to move against the guerrillas, they put their property before their partisan loyalties and formed a special paramilitary group, the 'guerrillas of peace' to hunt down the peasant guerrillas. Under the leadership of Guadalupe Salcedo, Franco Isaza, the Bautista brothers and others, the guerrillas reorganised. Resentment was growing against the conciliatory policies of the national Liberal leadership, not one of whom had taken up arms. That leadership had remained ambivalent towards the guerrilla armies. Forced to respond to the Conservative bid to exclude them permanently from control of the state, they had backed the formation of guerrilla armies, but were ready to disassociate themselves as soon as necessary.

Representatives from the region and other fronts attended a national conference of guerrillas in Boyacá in 1952, organised by the Communist Party, but the bid to coordinate the disparate bands of guerrillas ideologically or strategically never got off the ground. But social issues were creeping into many of the struggles. In 1952 and 1953 the guerrillas of the *llanos* produced two documents in which they referred to the land issue. Pressure on land in the region was mounting with the number of refugees. In the second of the documents they called for land expropriation irrespective of party affiliation. At this point, the guerrillas were still organised in local movements, which were often competing with each other and violent in the resolution of their conflicts. But the guerrillas' potential for greater coordination and to take up social issues was very threatening. It was not perhaps coincidental that the Liberal leadership now opted to use its armed strength to force negotiations on the Conservatives, despite the burning down of the Liberal newspapers, *El Tiempo* and *El Espectador* and the homes of Carlos Lleras Restrepo and López Pumarejo in 1952.

The Conservatives meanwhile were split between Laureano Gómez and Mariano Ospina Pérez, who had the backing of the industrialists and others in the economic elite who opposed the corporatist project of Gómez. With the acquiescence of the Liberal leaders, Ospina conspired with Conservative army officers and General Rojas Pinilla was chosen to lead a coup d'etat in June 1953. A period of military rule seemed the only way to save the social and political order.

Blood and accumulation

Throughout the period of *La Violencia*, the process of capital accumulation was so great that Alberto Lleras Camargo concluded in his writings that blood and accumulation went together. 'The Colombian situation is the best we have ever known', declared the president of ANDI in 1949, the year 18,500 people died. 'Social peace reigns' wrote the minister of labour in a report in 1951, a year in which 10,300 people were killed.

For the urban bourgeoisie, particularly the industrialists, the situation could not have been better. The ruling elites had moved swiftly to destroy the urban popular movement and all independent political expression after Gaitán's assassination. The UTC was strongly promoted by the government and the church in the wake of the virtual collapse of the CTC. By 1954 wage levels were 14 per cent below their 1947 level, despite the fact that 1949 heralded a period of great prosperity. Between 1948 and 1953 industrial production increased by 56 per cent.

The value of coffee exports, if not the volume of production, reached record levels. Worth US$242.3 million in 1949, they leapt to US$492.2 million in 1953. As long as production kept up and reached its market, it did not seem to worry anyone that people were dying in their thousands in the coffee regions.

The *gremios*, whose power and influence had grown since the mid-1940s, were a dominating force. Operating as if their interests were those of society as a whole, they maintained a bipartisan executive and counterposed their own unity and coherence with the chaos of the political world.

Political solution: military arbitration (1953-7)

At the end of World War II, the Colombian army had only 8,000 men and took 10.2 per cent of the government's budget. The situation changed on 9 April 1948. A year later, the army was receiving 19 per cent of the budget, and its numbers had substantially increased, nearing a target of 20,000 men.

In 1951 Laureano Gómez decided to send a battalion to fight in the Korean War. Needing US support, he wished to counteract the negative effect of his previous sympathies for the Axis powers. Colombia was the only Latin American country to send troops. The effect on them was very great. The true professionalisation of the Colombian army began,

Students returning from a memorial service die on a Bogotá street corner after soldiers open fire, 1954.

according to some, with the return of the battalion from Korea. There they had come in touch with modern warfare and established close relations with the US. The officers who fought in the war subsequently rose to high rank in the Colombian army.

General Rojas Pinilla had the support of both parties, who chose him as president for the 1954-8 period. He began by declaring an amnesty, with the objective of disarming and demobilising the guerrillas. Many, lacking clear political leadership or organisation, responded.

But Rojas Pinilla's 'peace' inaugurated a new period of official violence, in which an estimated 16,000 people died. Many of those who had accepted the amnesty were later killed, though some of the most legendary leaders were in fact killed after Rojas's downfall, such as Guadalupe Salcedo, murdered in 1957 a month after Rojas was overthrown, and Hermógenes Vargas, who was killed in 1960.

The amnesty did not include the Communists, even though they would have readily accepted it. Their areas were essentially refuges for peasants and their families who longed to resettle their land. The party was declared illegal in 1955 and the regions in which the Communists were supported were declared war zones. During the Villarrica War, as it was called, the region around Sumapaz and Villarrica was attacked by large numbers of soldiers, backed by aerial bombardments.

Subsequently the Communist guerrillas regrouped in the south of Tolima and the north of Cauca, where they set up what came to be called the 'independent republics'. Another group of about 3,000 peasants, many women and children, were evacuated from Sumapaz in a dramatic march. Defended by Communist guerrillas, hungry, cold and constantly attacked by the army, they marched out of the area to colonise the piedmont of Meta and beyond, a process of 'armed colonisation' which was to have important implications for the future. 'The same organisation', writes the historian Alfredo Molano (1987:46), 'which saved them from being killed by the *chulavitas* in 1950, which enabled them to confront the army in 1955, which defended their lives during the marches, allowed them in the 1960s and 1970s to limit the advance of the *latifundio*'.

The military government was seen as a transitionary period by the ruling class, but Rojas Pinilla had other plans. He began to build up his own base of support among the military, public-sector workers, labour and the urban poor. In 1954 he set up his own political movement, the Movement of National Action (MAN). He envisaged an army/people alliance, but, in trying to create it, pushed the traditional parties into closer unity against him. In fact he never succeeded in gaining the support needed to generate a third political force.

Even the church, which had earned the wrath of Gómez by supporting the 1953 coup, soon lost patience. Repression and censorship lost Rojas more friends, as did his attempts to increase taxes on coffee and his threats to do so on land and agriculture. All producer groups were worried about the increase in state intervention. The fall in coffee prices in 1955 had signalled the end of the bonanza with which he had entered office, and the onset of a phase of austerity. The opposition began to organise.

In 1956 Alberto Lleras Camargo and Laureano Gómez (Ospina Pérez had still not broken with Rojas) met in Spain and agreed the basis of a pact between the parties, in which they would alternate in power every four years during a minimum period of 16 years. A 'civic front' was formed to oppose Rojas and, under pressure from a widely-supported general strike by industry, the banks, commerce and the church, he was forced to resign in favour of a military junta. The junta called a plebiscite to ratify the party pact and, in 1958, Alberto Lleras Camargo became the first president of the National Front (FN).

La Violencia (1958-65)

[In the context of] the popular movement's continual setbacks and faced with the dominant classes' strong attempt at realignment within the National Front, banditry emerges, understandably, in wide areas of the countryside, as the peasantry's anarchic and desperate response. And as for the desperate, the only logical programme is destruction for its own sake; terror not only becomes an integral part, but in most cases, is the dominant element of their actions. (Sánchez and Meertens 1983:52)

Although the formation of the National Front officially brought *La Violencia* to an end, it did in fact continue in a different form, namely that of banditry, in which over 18,000 people lost their lives, 75 per cent of them in the departments of Tolima, Valle and Viejo Caldas.

The bandits of this second phase of violence were peasants who had been called guerrillas in its first phase, but who lost their political legitimacy in the new era. These bandit/guerrillas had either not accepted the amnesty offered by Rojas, or had done so and found themselves still under attack by the army. They had subsequently refused to accept either the amnesty offered by the National Front in 1958 or the party pact and peaceful coexistence which was then established.

They were joined by large numbers of revenge-seeking adolescents who, had grown up during the terror and seen their homes burned down and their families brutally murdered. No longer dependent on national political leadership, they now looked to local bosses who began to use them for local political purposes. Banditry flourished in areas where official terrorism had been widespread but where the peasants had not developed their own forms of resistance — in the north of Valle, north of Tolima and in Viejo Caldas, mostly coffee-growing areas where small and medium property coexisted with large estates. Here there were ample mountainous regions in which to hide and rich pickings from the estates from which to live. Some day labourers on the estates were 'part-time' bandits.

The local peasants gave active or passive support to the bandit chiefs. 'Chispas', 'Capítan Venganza', 'Desquite', 'Sangrenegra' 'Pedro Brincos' and others were mythical and heroic figures. Once in a while the bandits would identify with the social antagonisms of rural Colombia, as, for instance, when they even began to attack property belonging to landowners in their own party. Although potentially a radical social force, they mostly remained loyal to their Liberal Party affiliation. Their enemies were peasants of the other party as well as landowners, and they carried out violence against both. They accepted the patronage of local party bosses while standing out against the national political project of the ruling class.

This ambivalence was exploited by a rising political leader, Alfonso López Michelsen, son of López Pumarejo. He had set up a faction within the Liberal Party, the Revolutionary Liberal Movement (MRL), in opposition to the National Front. The bandits had considerable influence over the rural electorate, and the MRL began to court this nucleus of dissident votes, registering large numbers of voters in bandit-controlled rural areas. As the bandits drew closer to the MRL, local political bosses loyal to the National Front withdrew their support from them, seeking their power base more in their political control of the institutions of the state.

With the parties riven by factions, the MRL presented a coherent option and won 20 per cent of the Liberal vote in the 1960 legislative elections. It doubled this vote in 1962 when it presented a symbolic candidacy to the presidency which, under the terms of the party pact, fell to the Conservative, Guillermo León Valencia. In 1962, debates in parliament referred to the existence of two republics in Valle, one where only the Conservatives could enter, and the other where only the MRL faction of the Liberals was safe.

The MRL presented itself as the inheritor of the democratic tradition within Liberalism and was prepared to form an alliance with the Communist Party, as López Pumarejo had done. It opposed the anti-democratic nature of the National Front and argued that *La Violencia* had roots in socio-economic structures which demanded agrarian reform, not increased repression. Repression was the solution put forward by those who saw *La Violencia* as a public order problem, and even blamed the recently victorious Cuban revolution for the persistent disorder. The US and its cold-war ideology were becoming increasingly influential in the country.

The significance of the MRL vote in the 1962 elections led the new president to negotiate with it. The MRL seized the opportunity to institutionalise itself and gain access to government office. The National Front showed its capacity to deal with the problem of opposition within its ranks. The MRL accepted the ministry of mines and broke with the Communist Party. 'We shall not permit', López told a party convention in 1962, 'the discontent and frustration which the National Front is incubating, to take refuge under the hammer and sickle'.

Without the protection of urban politicians or local bosses, the bandits were left as a force of peasants alone, more clearly associated with the rural poverty and discontent which nurtured them. Increasingly, they were identified by the army as an element of 'subversion' linked to the 'communist menace' which now preoccupied it.

In 1960 General Alberto Ruiz Novoa had taken over the high command of the army, which was now firmly under the influence of the US. Not only had it sent troops to Korea, but Colombia was one of the first five Latin American countries to sign a mutual-defence assistance agreement with the US in 1952 and, in the same year, became the site of the first Latin Ameican counter-insurgency training school.

Ruiz Novoa had himself fought in Korea and a growing number of officers were now being trained by the US. He was also influenced by French colonels who had fought in Indo-China and Algeria. Under his command, the army began to think systematically about its role in modern society and about problems of national security and internal subversion. A series of US-sponsored inter-American military conferences emphasised the danger of communism. The poor, partisan institution of the 1940s was gaining a new identity and sense of purpose. Between 1961 and 1967, Colombia received US$60 million from the US in military assistance for counter-insurgency and 'economic development', all administered by the army, and a further US$100 million in military equipment.

General Ruiz Novoa became minister of war in the new Conservative administration of Valencia in 1962. He began by drawing up a comprehensive plan to deal with the violence. This involved strengthening the armed forces technically and creating an Eighth Brigade based in Armenia, with jurisdiction across departments. The Administrative Security Department (DAS) was set up to organise intelligence gathering for the counter-insurgency effort. Repression was to be combined with civic action, to change the positive image of the bandits among the peasants and to improve that of the army. Such action was in line with the military teachings of US counter-insurgency experts.

During 1963 and 1964, the main bandit chiefs were killed. Leaderless, many of their followers and supporters were killed or captured in a series of massive arrests. There followed a campaign against the so-called independent republics. The Communist Party had, in fact, been prepared to cooperate with the National Front. An extraordinary document signed by Marulanda, Ciro Castano and other former guerrillas, as they described themselves, made this clear:

> As patriots, who have struggled during the years prior to 10 May 1957 against the despotic dictatorships which sowed ruin in the countryside and towns, we are not interested in the armed struggle and we are willing to collaborate in any way we can, with the task of pacification which the present government of Doctor Alberto Lleras Camargo is prepared to implement. (*Tribuna*, Ibagué, 6 September 1958)

Verbal attacks on the 'independent republics', led by Alvaro Gómez, son of Laureano, had been mounting. These areas — Marquetalia, Riochiquito, El Pato, El Guayabero — were inspired by the experience of El Davis. Peasant colonisers farmed the land and organised their own defence. There was no broader political project, and indeed the Communist Party was fighting elections in alliance with the MRL at the time. But in the minds of the army, an offensive against the 'republics' was its first direct confrontation with 'communist subversion'.

With US advisers, it launched what would become one of its most infamous and consequential operations, the *Plan Lazo*, in 1964; 16,000 troops encircled the narrow valley of Marquetalia, where a small group of peasants (42 according to the testimony of Manuel Marulanda who led them) were working, while the airforce dropped bombs. Almost all the peasants from here and the other 'republics' escaped and formed mobile guerrilla groups. They came together in September 1964 in a conference of the *Bloque Sur* (bloc of the south). At its second conference in 1966, the Revolutionary Armed Forces of Colombia (FARC) was officially founded. *La Violencia* was over, but a new era of guerrilla warfare was beginning.

The bi-partisan state

The same elite that had been in charge before *La Violencia*, emerged, in full control, after it. The challenge from below had been defeated before it took hold, and this enabled the economy to function and prosper through most of it. The peasants meanwhile, rather than concentrate on their own class interests which might have turned them against the ruling elite, instead killed each other on its behalf, fighting its party battles and other parochial conflicts that divided them from one another.

The state was now exclusively the domain of the elite. It was literally carved up by the traditional parties. In addition to alternating the presidency between them for 16 years, all legislative bodies and public corporations (senate, house of representatives and departmental and municipal councils), cabinet offices, judicial posts and posts at all levels of public administration were to be distributed by agreement between the two parties.

No expression of social conflict was permitted outside the control of the two traditional parties. The state could play no role in the mediation of such conflicts and, indeed, had no independent role of its own to enable it to look after the interests of society as a whole. Reforming impulses generated from time to time by more enlightened members of the ruling elite were blocked. And, if the state had been unable to deal with the country's changing social profile before *La Violencia*, it was even more woefully inadequate faced with the rapid process of urbanisation, rural modernisation and industrialistion of the ensuing decades and their social consequences.

But the National Front began with high expectations. Not only dislike of the Rojas Pinilla regime but also the deep desire for peace added to its credibility. The US was keen to back the new government and offered financial support. Colombia became a 'showcase' for the Alliance for Progress of 1961, which sought to offset the radicalising effect of the Cuban revolution on Latin America with aid programmes.

A World Bank mission in 1949 established a close relationship between the institution and the Colombian government and it played an important part in the modernisation of the country in the 1950s and 1960s. Colombia became the World Bank's fourth largest borrower and the World Bank played a central role in financing infrastructural development and encouraging more coherent economic planning.

The mission had found that inadequate transport facilities, particularly roads, were the greatest single obstacle to Colombia's economic development. At that time, traffic between central Colombia and the Atlantic ports still depended largely on the Magdalena river, with a few supplementary rail and road links around the main towns. The World Bank helped to finance the Atlantic railway, built between 1952 and 1961, which cut the journey from Bogotá to the coast from several days to 24 hours. This opened up previously inaccessible but fertile agricultural regions, such as the Magdalena Medio, and stimulated commercial agriculture (IBRD 1967) The World Bank also funded a road-building and road-rehabilitation programme and, by 1961, although large parts of the country still lacked roads, it had a network of all-weather highways.

These developments helped pave the way for economic modernisation and growth, but similar efforts were not put into the social consequences of economic change. Social antagonisms may not have been the moving force in *La Violencia*, but they never disappeared. The second half of the 1950s had ushered in serious economic problems. Industry was seeking to advance beyond the production of basic consumer goods, but low coffee prices affected its ability to import the machinery to do this.

Migration to the cities was already producing strains. Between 1951 and 1964 the urban population more than doubled as people fled *La Violencia*; by 1964 half the total population, just over nine million people, lived in urban areas. Only a little more than a quarter of a million people had jobs in manufacturing. The informal sector became the economy for the majority of the urban poor, and criminal as well as legal activities the means of survival in the city. Growing urban discontent in search of a political expression was apparent by the early 1960s.

In the rural areas the government directed its attentions to the areas affected by *La Violencia*. An agrarian reform law of 1961 set up the Colombian Institute of Agrarian Reform (INCORA) and, with Alliance for Progress funding, assisted a few families to settle in the areas of colonisation, but otherwise achieved very little. Meanwhile, the late 1950s and 1960s saw a huge expansion in commercial agriculture. A growing urban population increased the demand for food, while agricultural exports were needed to finance industry's import requirements. The expansion of commercial agriculture created serious rural tensions as peasant farmers were forced off their land to make way for it, resulting in further migrations to the cities.

Political exclusion led many urban intellectuals to seek alternatives outside the bipartisan state. Influenced by the Cuban Revolution, the early 1960s saw the first guerrilla *focos* appear. Other movements challenged the two parties from within. By the mid-1960s, the reincorporation of the MRL had strengthened the attraction of Rojas Pinilla's attempt to make a political comeback with a new urban movement, the Popular National Alliance (ANAPO). The ruling elite needed ingenuity as well as armed force to deal with these challenges. But in failing to deal with their roots, it merely postponed the day of social and political reckoning. Much more blood would flow.

PART TWO

The Crisis of the Political Order

The tasks and responsibilities of the Colombian state have bowed under the weight of a decadent elite . . . Was it not the task of the ruling class to carry out urgent reforms in the agrarian, urban, university, banking and financial sectors, in foreign trade, in income distribution, in work and in business, to do all these things which could spare the country the bloodshed to which it now knows it is condemned? . . . Enormous are the costs of all kinds which a society must pay for the decay of its ruling class. (Carlos Jiménez Gómez, former Attorney-General, Introduction, Avila Bernal 1987:37-9)

Chronology

1966-70   Liberal government of Carlos Lleras Restrepo introduces Agrarian Reform legislation to modernise agrarian sector and administrative reforms to increase efficiency of state

1967   National Association of Peasants, ANUC, set up by Lleras Restrepo government

1970-74   Conservative government of Misael Pastrana Borrero and economic *gremios* launch offensive against peasantry (Pact of Chicoral). New concessions granted to large landowners

1974-78   Liberal government of Alfonso López Michelsen initiates plan to make Colombia the Japan of Latin America

1978-82   Liberal government of Julio César Turbay Ayala launches period of severe repression

1982-86   Conservative government of Belisario Betancur begins peace process with guerrilla movements. Army storms Palace of Justice in November 1985 to end M-19's occupation

2.1 Colombia's Two Economies

The political order forged in the last years of *La Violencia* remains the basis of the Colombian political system to this day. Social and economic reality, however, changed profoundly. The roots of the crisis of the 1980s lie in the incapacity of the political order to address the process of change.

Between 1964 and 1985 (census years) the rural population grew by less than 10 per cent and the urban population more than doubled, from 9 million to 19 million. This increase was not accompanied by matching increases in employment opportunities, in the provision of fundamental services or of housing.

The economy came to mirror the duality of the political order, between the formal and the real. At one level it modernised over the years and enjoyed growth rates which made it one of the most successful examples of economic management in Latin America. At the other level, a 'people's economy' emerged, in which the majority of the population live and work, the so-called 'informal sector'. These two economies are by no means separate, but are distinct in many ways.

The intellectuals and professionals who achieved advancement during these years of change and growth have formed part of one of Latin America's most significant middle classes, which, according to some studies, may account for as much as one-third of the population. A sector of this class has undoubtedly acquired real prosperity (see Table 1); a more substantial group, however, is neither prosperous nor impoverished, but lives in some insecurity of losing its tenuous access to opportunities and wellbeing. In effect, the majority of the so-called middle class may merely be those in waged employment rather than members of professions or a highly-paid salariat.

Many are baffled by the story of Colombia's formal economy and consistent performance compared to its Latin American neighbours. Colombia was the only Latin American country to sustain growth through the debt crisis of the 1980s. The very same factors that help to explain its success also explain the other side of the story, its failure to meet the needs of the majority of the people (see Table 2). Colombia's formal economy, like its 'formal' political order, is an exclusive realm reflecting the extreme concentration of wealth and power in the society.

The Colombian economy has been managed relatively free from political pressures. Populism had been swiftly dealt with in the 1940s. No industrial entrepreneurs had broken ranks to form alliances against the traditional oligarchy. The National Front pact brought political peace

Table I. Distribution of wealth

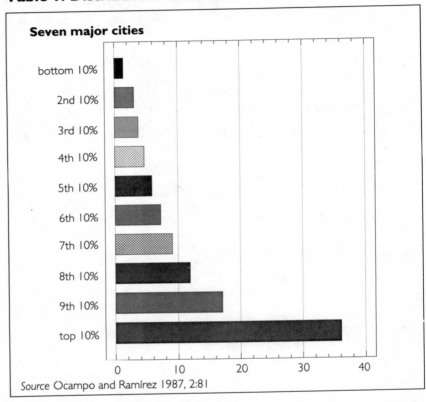

Seven major cities

Source Ocampo and Ramírez 1987, 2:81

to the ruling elite. Left-wing parties were very weak and the traditional ones dominated both the state and popular organisations such as trade unions, at least until the 1970s. Even the armed forces remained subordinate to civilian politicians, only gradually establishing an area of political autonomy. Functional political stability was maintained through the clientelist practices of politicians.

The danger of economic policy-making falling prey to these same practices was lessened by administrative reforms in 1958 and 1968. These created a series of decentralised agencies, which proliferated in all areas of the economy — agriculture, industry, housing, banking and natural resources. By 1980 there were 164 national agencies. Despite their name, these agencies are responsible directly to the president, in an attempt to move them from the partisan influences of congress and clientelist

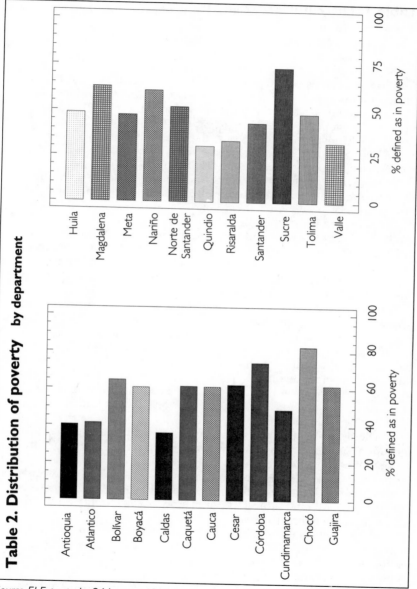

Table 2. Distribution of poverty   by department

Source *El Espectador* 24 January 1988

DANE defines poverty according to five criteria: inadequate food supply, poor living conditions, insufficient access to public services, low family income, and lack of education.

politics. But they were also removed from departmental and local levels of government.

This enabled government institutions to become more technocratic although they were to be by no means immune to political manipulation. It also enabled nationally-organised pressure groups to influence policy making. Sometimes private-sector groups were brought on to the boards of decentralised agencies, sometimes relationships were more informal. Bogotá became the location of these relationships, as the head offices of most of the agencies were there. Regional or local governments had little or no say in investment decisions, they were starved of resources and unable to respond to local needs. The Colombian state had been modernised, but only at the centre (Helmsing 1986:173).

The private sector wielded enormous influence over policy making. Over the years it had organised itself into a large number of producer associations or *gremios*, each careful to include representatives of both traditional parties in their executives. These included FEDEMETAL (industry), ACOPI (small and medium industry), FEDEGAN (livestock), FEDEARROZ (rice), ASOCANA (sugar), FEDEALGODON (cotton), CONFECAMARAS (commerce), CAMACOL (construction), ANIF (finance), ASOBANCARIA (banking), and FASECOLDA (insurance) as well as ANDI, SAC and FEDERACAFE.

These organisations have ensured the state's responsiveness to the private sector's interests. State intervention has been kept to a minimum, providing the conditions for private-sector activity and working according to their sector's interests. The private sector has played a large role in blocking reforms that might have enabled the state to look after the wider interests of society. Economic policies have been pragmatic rather than ideological; Colombia has avoided the sudden swings from radical-populist to radical-monetarist policies, which have characterised many Latin American economies.

The fundamental rules of economic management have mostly remained unaffected by the pressure for political change, although decentralisation was accepted as an economic as well as a political necessity by the 1980s. But social changes which have accompanied economic growth have sown the seeds of rebellion. One of these is the emergence of a better educated population, for whom life on the streets is less acceptable than to their parents.

Table 3 illustrates the growth in population by age group for the census years 1964, 1973 and 1985. The largest increases over the last twelve years occurred in the groups aged between 15 and 35, precisely those groups coming into the labour force.

Between 1973 and 1985, the total population increased by 7.3 million. Those of working age (15-59) increased by 5.61 million, of which

Table 3. Shifts in age structure

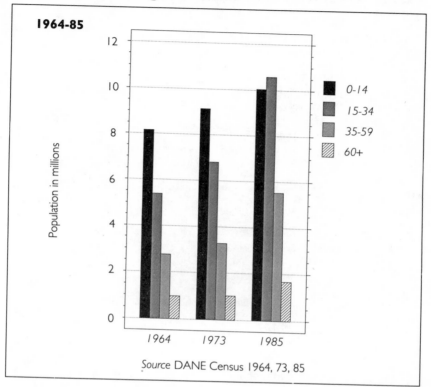

1964-85

Population in millions

Legend:
- 0-14
- 15-34
- 35-59
- 60+

x-axis: 1964, 1973, 1985

Source DANE Census 1964, 73, 85

3.76 million were aged 15-34. A substantial qualitative shift took place among the younger workers entering the labour market. Over the same period, the numbers with at least secondary education increased by 4.54 million. Younger men, and the increasing numbers of women in the labour market, now had access to educational levels formerly only found among workers in the formal sector of the economy. But that sector has failed to provide matching increases in jobs for these better-educated workers. By 1988, 72 out of every 100 people looking for work in the four main cities (Bogotá, Medellín, Cali and Barranquilla) were under thirty and, of these, over 70 per cent had at least some secondary education and 14 per cent had attended university for at least a term (*El Espectador* 24 October 1988).

Over broadly the same period (1973-85), those counted as in employment, including the informal sector, increased by 2.9 million. Very

Table 4. Employment by sector

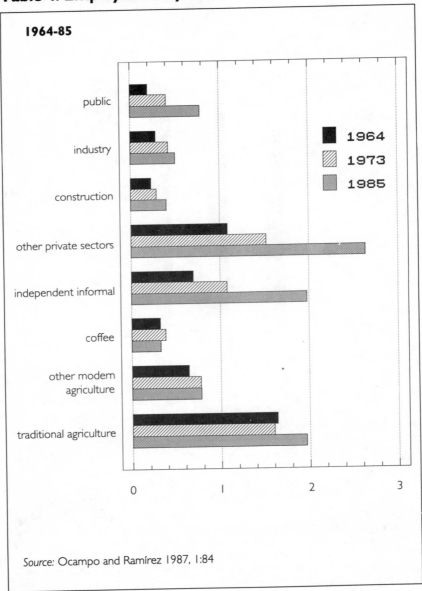

1964-85

public
industry
construction
other private sectors
independent informal
coffee
other modern agriculture
traditional agriculture

■ 1964
▨ 1973
▨ 1985

0   1   2   3

Source: Ocampo and Ramírez 1987, 1:84

few of these found employment in the formal sector. Just under one million became 'independent' informal workers, 1.1 million went into private non-industrial employment, over half of which is in the informal sector. Employment in modern manufacturing (more than ten workers per workplace) grew by only 80,000 jobs between 1973 and 1984. The construction sector, seen by some as central to solving Colombia's problems, added only 110,000 jobs during the period. The informal sector earns just under one third of industrial wages (see Table 5).

A better-educated population, seeking more dignified livelihoods, began to make itself heard in the 1970s, thus contributing to the crisis of the political order, which reached its most acute phase in the 1980s at a time when economic recession also hit the industrial heartlands.

Table 5. Real wages in Colombia

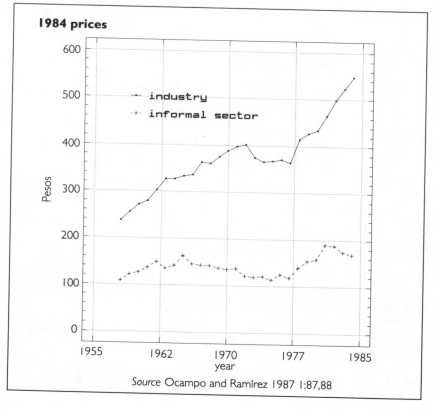

Source Ocampo and Ramírez 1987 1:87,88

Table 6. Rising Educational Standards

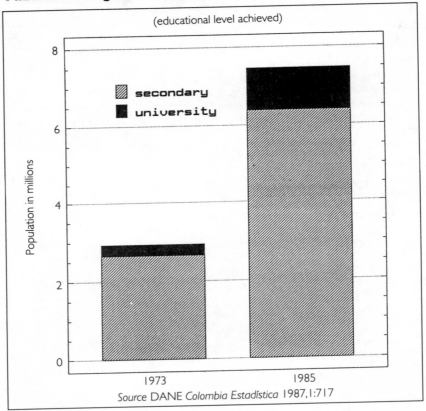

(educational level achieved)

secondary
university

Population in millions

1973   1985

Source DANE *Colombia Estadística* 1987,1:717

The people's economy

The informal economy covers a wide range of activities, both legal and illegal, all unregulated by the state. By 1984, 56.6 per cent of employment in the urban areas was in the informal sector, involving 3.5 million people compared with 2.7 million in the formal sector.

The informal economy includes workers who earn their living on the streets doing odd jobs, washing cars, shining shoes, collecting rubbish for resale, the hopeful providers of services who will leap out at a traffic light to wipe car windscreens. It includes casual sellers of artifacts, cigarettes, newspapers and flowers and also prostitutes and thieves.

Rubbish

Few statistics horrify as much as the 'spectacle' of the dirty streets and rivers: the great majority of Colombian municipalities don't collect the rubbish, two and a half million tons of waste are left in the open air each year, 30,000 Colombians live from what others throw away . . .

The world of rubbish is a national problem which isn't limited to the mountains of rubbish in the dumps, streets and highways of Bogotá. And it doesn't end, either, with discussion about the efficiency of the bodies charged with the service in that city. Waste isn't collected in Ocaña and Girardot, nor in Montería and Florencia, nor in a good part of the thousand and nine municipalities of Colombia.

But it is in Bogotá where the urban nomads who live by collecting the rubbish are most numerous. According to the anthropologist, María Teresa Salcedo, a collector in the capital can cover over twenty kilometres a day in his small wooden cart. They become street sweepers *ad honorem* and help clean the 2,300 tons of waste that the District Public Services Corporation fails to collect. . . .

Scavenging on the rubbish dump, Bucaramanga.

But the rubbish collectors face competition from the rats, mice and all sorts of micro-organisms which teem amongst the waste . . . Colombia has approximately 120 million rats which, according to the World Health Organisation, contribute to 26 of 999 classified causes of sickness and death . . . flies, too, proliferate among rubbish left in the sun and rain. One kilogram of organic material, according to the Ministry of Health, guarantees the life of 70,000 flies. These have a wide radius of activity and carry more than one virus.

When waste doesn't feed the rats or the flies directly, water runs over it to 'feed' Colombians in another way. A study by the engineer Hernando Rodríguez Herrera, of the environmental health division of the Health Ministry, confirms that in 612 municipalities of Colombia, 20 per cent of the rubbish ends up in *quebradas* (brooks), *riachuelos* (streams) and rivers. This water is drunk by Colombian children, and then the peasant mothers don't know what to do with the gastroenteritis of their children . . . also the industrial waste which firms deposit in our rivers generates residues of mercury. Consumption by a pregnant women of this water causes deformities on birth. In March of this year seven deformed children were born in Mariquita, who later died. Their mothers had drunk contaminated water which feeds the town.

The waste reduces the levels of oxygen and destroys the ecosystem of the rivers. Almost 700 tons are thrown into the Magdalena river each day which runs for 1,531 kilometres through the country.

That the problem of rubbish continues like this is due to the bureaucratisation of the government bodies charged with that service. In general, these bodies are political targets of so-called 'clientelism' and that's the reason for their ineffectiveness, which is costly in money and health. (*El Tiempo* 6 June 1988)

Also belonging to the informal sector are those employed in small enterprises outside the ambit of government control and regulation. About half the construction industry is in the informal sector. All are characterised by the precarious nature of existence. Long-term employment contracts, employment- and social-protection schemes, safety and health provisions are all absent, as is the payment of taxes to the authorities.

The sector operates at the margin of the formal economy of modern capitalist production and state provision. Certain parts of overall production may depend on the informal sector, and indeed, larger companies are often happy to depend on unregulated smaller firms for cheap inputs. Meanwhile those working in the informal sector still consume the products of industry and depend on the spending of those in the formal economy.

The informal sector also acts as a buffer to the formal sector in times of recession. Between 1979 and 1983, there was a loss of 53,600 jobs in manufacturing, and unemployment in the urban areas rose from 8.10 per cent in 1978 to 13.20 per cent in 1984. Many of those who lost their jobs had to survive in the informal sector.

But the low incomes generated in the sector make it difficult for informal workers to earn enough to provide the basic elements of life. A Department of National Statistics (DANE) survey in 1988 of 13 towns with a population of 11,419,378, found that 32.02 per cent of the population lived in poverty, and 4.36 per cent of these in absolute poverty, a total of 3,655,973 people (DANE 1988a:164).

The World Bank's economy

Colombia is in many ways the World Bank's favourite child. It has accepted the economic adjustments thought necessary by the international institutions and managed to pay its debt and interest payments even through the troubles of the 1980s. This is the world of the formal economy, the measured economy. But it lives inside and, to some degree, feeds from (and passes on costs to) the larger economy, including the informal sector.

In 1985 Colombia had a measured GDP of US$31,000 million, or US$1,000 per head of population, compared to a UK figure of US$10,000 per capita and a US figure of $20,000 per capita. This average is not, of course, spread evenly over households. In 1985 the richest 10 per cent of urban families received a little less than 40 per cent of the total income, while 50 per cent of families received less than 20 per cent. The poorest 20 per cent gained less than 5 per cent of the total (DANE 1987:81).

Colombia sustained reasonable growth rates in the 1960s and 1970s, suffering a recession in the early 1980s from which it emerged by the middle of the decade (see Table 7). By the end of the 1980s, there were renewed fears of recession. Birth-control programmes, vigorously promoted by the US, succeeded in slowing population growth. While in 1960 women had an average of seven children, by the end of the 1970s the average was about 3.5. Together with large-scale emigration, this resulted in a population growth of only 1.6 per cent a year between 1973 and 1985 (see Table 3). Colombia now has a relatively 'modern' demographic profile to accompany its urbanised society. A substantial, well-educated middle class has also grown up and a technocratic elite of

Table 7. Growth in measured GDP

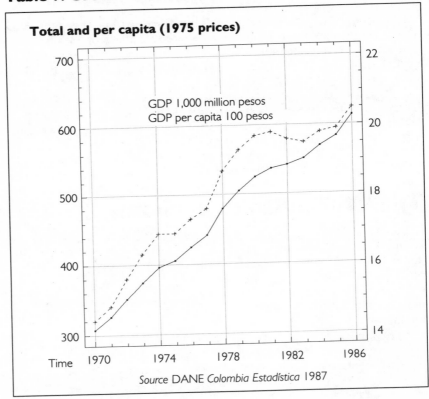

Total and per capita (1975 prices)

GDP 1,000 million pesos
GDP per capita 100 pesos

Time

Source DANE *Colombia Estadística* 1987

professionals, many trained in US universities, adds to formal Colombia's appearance of modernity and progress.

Successive administrations have faced the problem of improving economic performance. This includes speeding up the rate of economic growth, creating higher incomes for individuals, more employment opportunities, and a revenue base to enable governments to provide essential services and deal with social problems. Each Colombian president has attempted to deal with these in different ways and with different priorities. They have been hampered by the vulnerability of export earnings to fluctuations within the international market, the low level of government revenue and the difficulties of generating the levels of capital investment needed to increase labour productivity and to stimulate growth.

Presidents and policies

1966-70 Carlos Lleras Restrepo (Liberal). Attempted the most serious package of reforms of the National Front. His government was nevertheless also authoritarian, and the army and police were used frequently against the urban and rural unrest which grew during these years.

He sought to strengthen the state, rationalise decision-making and build an alliance against the traditional landowners. The 1968 constitutional reform strengthened presidential authority, notably in economic matters, and increased his control over a growing sector of decentralised agencies. Articles 121 and 122 of the reform distinguished between a State of Siege for political purposes and a State of Emergency for economic ones. He encouraged increased professionalism in the state agencies and improved national planning. He had public differences with the World Bank and IMF, but remained acceptably orthodox in his policies, and they welcomed his administrative reforms. Lleras was a prime mover in the creation of the Andean Common Market (1969) which controlled the extent to which foreign companies could take advantage of the common tariff barriers. He established a new framework for trade and foreign exchange which shifted policies partially away from import-substitution towards export promotion. He tried to accelerate the agrarian reform programme which was blocked or circumvented by landowners; Law 1 of 1968 granted potential rights to tenants and sharecroppers but provoked landowners to expel them on a massive scale. He set up the peasants organisation, ANUC, to try and pressure the landowners for change.

1970-74 Misael Pastrana Borrero (Conservative). Pastrana oversaw the adoption of some parts of the development strategy, known as 'Operation Colombia'.

The so-called 'four strategies' were housing construction, export promotion, increased agricultural productivity and redistribution based on progressive taxation. Administration attention focused on the first two of the strategies. Under Pastrana, a system was introduced which guaranteed investors a real rate of return on savings which were used for housing development. The construction sector was seen as the main motor of development, which would employ those coming in from the countryside, a process the plan sought to encourage. The construction sector grew by 12.6 per cent in 1973 compared to 1.8 per cent in 1972, but this did not result in housing for the poor nor did it create the jobs needed for those flooding into the city from the countryside. And in the rural areas, the Pastrana administration was noted for 'counter-reform'. New legislation in 1973 was drafted which made it virtually impossible to expropriate land without the landowner's consent.

1974-78 Alfonso López Michelsen (Liberal). The López government created expectations of another reforming presidency, and began by introducing a tax reform. But most of López's presidency involved dealing with the effects of the 1975 world recession and the bonanza in legal and illegal dollars earnings.

His vision was to turn Colombia into a South American Japan, and he emphasised export diversification and increased competitiveness in domestic industry. He liberalised imports and reduced protection while trying to maintain the system of mini-devaluations which helped exports. He made some attempts to encourage industrial decentralisation by setting up industrial parks in smaller towns, but with little success; and in the rural areas he launched a programme to support peasant agriculture. The increase in the money supply led to growing inflation, and the government's neo-liberal responses of a tight monetary policy and cuts in public expenditure hit the popular sectors hard. Food prices rose by 49.7 per cent between May 1976 and May 1977 according to DANE figures, while real wages fell. His presidency saw increasing social unrest, culminating in the heavily repressed National Civic Strike of September 1977.

1978-82 Julio César Turbay Ayala (Liberal). Based his National Integration Plan on an expansion of spending for basic infrastructural projects, particularly transport, communications, mining and energy which required long-term borrowing.

But Turbay's presidency coincided with a deteriorating external situation following the second oil price rise, the fall in coffee prices and industrial recession at home. He also liberalised imports to avoid inflationary pressures generated by his costly projects. Colombia's external debt was US$103,000 million when he left office. State imports grew and the balance of trade worsened. Turbay's presidency is noted as the most repressive in the country's recent history.

1982-86 Belisario Betancur (Conservative). 'Change with Equity', announced a year after his government came to power, remained a list of worthy intentions. Betancur inherited the worst economic crisis of all the administrations.

Betancur began by reintroducing exchange and import controls, mini-devaluations and protection, aiming to combine external adjustment with economic growth. By the end of 1984 he was forced to turn to more orthodox stabilisation policies. He refused for political reasons to negotiate a formal deal with the IMF, urged by producer groups and private banks, but he did introduce an austerity plan that the IMF would have approved, involving public expenditure cuts and an increase in the rate of devaluation. In the spring of 1985, the IMF was given 'enhanced surveillance' rights as the World Bank increased its disbursements of funds to the country. Unemployment in the major cities reached 14.1 per cent in 1985. The country's external debt was a little under US$15,000 million by 1986.

The developed countries have a wide range of saving methods available; the public have sufficient confidence in government bonds to buy these on a long- or shorter-term basis, providing funds for long-term investment. In Colombia there is no such long-term market for the government to attract funds. But it takes many years for a project such as a large-scale electricity plant to begin to repay its total cost and Colombia, like other Third World countries, is forced to finance these projects in a short number of years.

International loans have been on terms that are neither long enough nor cheap enough. But that is where Colombia had to turn to finance its large-scale energy projects of the late 1970s. As a result, Colombia's foreign debt reached US$16,500 million by 1988, of which US$13,100 million was owed by the public sector, about 40 per cent by the electricity, coal and oil sectors alone. This was manageable by Latin American standards, but nevertheless a large drain on scarce resources; servicing the debt cost 7 per cent of GNP that year (World Bank 1989:210).

Government revenues have remained low, limiting social expenditure and its ability to deal with the pressing problems of low-income sectors. With so many outside the formal, taxable economy, the government has relied for 50 per cent of its revenues on indirect taxes. Business elites have fought tooth and nail against increased direct taxes, and tax fraud is a national hobby of the business class.

The private sector has dominated economic growth and diversification in Colombia and has resisted reforms that might have ensured a more equitable distribution of the fruits of that growth. This growth has been uneven not only between individuals but also between regions and between town and countryside. The coffee sector has been the most dynamic and entrepreneurial and at times of high export earnings, has invested considerably in social provision in the coffee-growing areas. In modern Colombia, the relative prosperity of these regions stands in stark contrast to the absolute neglect of other areas.

By the 1980s regional disparities were extreme. The incomes of the rich regions of Bogotá, Valle and Atlántico could be double those of the poorer regions of Chocó, Cauca and Nariño. Industrialisation is concentrated in the 'golden triangle' of Bogotá, Cali and Medellín. Towns and cities have grown spontaneously through land invasions and illegal settlements and there is a huge housing deficit. Provision for drinking water and sewerage is woefully inadequate outside the main cities, and even within some of them. Rural areas everywhere suffer neglect and, in some, the state is virtually absent.

The formal economy has grown without the redistributionist pressures that have created inflation and crisis in other Latin American countries. It has more than met the needs of a minority, who live just as opulently as the elites of the industrialised world. But it has changed the lives of everyone. The advance of capitalist modernisation has been highly uneven; it has dispossessed peasants in rural areas, but failed to provide for those forced off the land. Manufacturing industry has grown but by 1985 had created only half a million jobs. The formal economy has generated both growth and poverty.

The politics of water

Lack of an adequate supply of water has generated huge protests throughout Colombia. Typical is the town of Sincelejo, capital of the department of Sucre. The following report was written by Bernardo Basco for *El Tiempo*.

'These days Sincelejo has the unpleasant smell of dirty lavatories . . . It hasn't had water for two weeks. Not a drop. And no solution to the problem is on the horizon. The situation is serious because already a total civic strike is being organised that could be tragic. The 140,000 inhabitants of this town won't tolerate any more..

The proof? The protest demonstrations have degenerated into violence: last Friday about 500 people attacked public buildings with stones and sticks. They set fire to huts, they burned tyres and they blocked the eastern highway. There were many arrests.

The association of *gremios* of Sucre, made up of the Chamber of Commerce and other employers' associations, called all firms to close down for fifteen minutes at 11am and 4pm, and, if the crisis isn't solved, to close altogether.

On top of everything, it is one of the most severe summers in many years. It doesn't rain and the people on the periphery gather with buckets at the gulleys, but with no luck. The small streams are drying out and only give water with earth, almost mud. The little water available has to be bought from lorries with tanks, at speculative prices. A gallon can cost 30 pesos when the authorised price is 18 pesos. 'Either we eat or we buy water' is the phrase repeated again and again amongst the people of the shanty towns.

There are laughable paradoxes: of the 150 litres a second which are supplying the town, 50 are lost due to the cracks in the old pipes which carry it. But that's not all. Some neighbourhoods take the water secretly from the mother pipe, which goes under their houses and that complicates the problem as the liquid loses pressure.

The consequences of the lack of water couldn't be more evident. The regional hospital has postponed all surgery; the schools and colleges cancelled all classes yesterday; business and the hotel sector face losses. . . .

Sincelejo has never had an adequate water supply. Thirty years ago, it got a water pipe because its inhabitants organised a civic strike, they stopped all activities and blocked the eastern highway. An emergency piping system was built, several wells were brought into use and a little later the government created a body to manage public services (EMPOSUCRE). Nevertheless, twenty years after becoming the departmental capital of Sucre, Sincelejo has no water. Although 90 per cent of the 126 neighbourhoods are connected to supply, in reality the service doesn't even cover 45 per cent.

Meanwhile, while the town dies of thirst, everyone, without exception — economic *gremios*, civic leaders, trade unions etc — blame the politicians for the disaster of EMPOSUCRE. EMPOSUCRE, says the population, became from its beginning a bureaucratic fiefdom of the group of Gustavo Dager Chadid. All its managers have been followers of the Liberal politician. Its budget has been used by his supporters to finance political campaigns and buy votes. The corporation is bankrupt, and not even the regional prosecutor knows how much its deficit is, a sum of about 500 million pesos is estimated. There is another problem: EMPOSUCRE under Law 12 of administrative decentralisation, must be taken over by the municipalilty. But Sincelejo cannot afford to take on its deficit.

In the neighbourhoods on the outskirts of the town, all created by land invasions, the problem is more serious. The pipes don't even reach and there are no little streams. The inhabitants asked the local government of Sincelejo to approach the water tank lorries to stop the speculation, because "they have enriched a few at the cost of the thirst of the many".'
(*El Tiempo* 16 February 1988)

The economic sectors

Table 8 shows the various sectors' contributions to the measured economy in terms of output. The dominance of manufacturing is clear and contrasts sharply with the small numbers of workers employed by that sector. The economy has diversified over the years and is now less dependent on coffee. By the late 1980s, Colombia was not only the second largest coffee exporter in the world (after Brazil), but was also the world's second largest cut-flower exporter, the third largest coal exporter, the fifth largest banana exporter, and Latin America's second largest gold exporter and fourth largest oil exporter.

Industry: the golden triangle

By 1968, Bogotá, Medellín and Cali were responsible for over 68 per cent of national value added and over 60 per cent of industrial employment; the fourth industrial centre, Barranquilla, had declined over the years. Together they were called the golden triangle. Foreign investment in the 1960s reinforced the regional concentration; 65 per cent of it was in the same three cities in 1979. During the 1970s Bogotá emerged as the pre-eminent industrial, financial and political centre of the country.

Industry grew at an average rate of 8.5 per cent a year between 1967 and 1974, with continuous diversification favouring intermediate goods (textiles, wood, paper, rubber, chemicals), consumer durables and, to a lesser extent, capital goods. Industrial exports were encouraged during this period and reached a peak of 46 per cent of total exports in 1974.

State protection had encouraged many administratively and technologically backward industries, which were run by old oligarchic

Table 8. Contributions to the measured economy

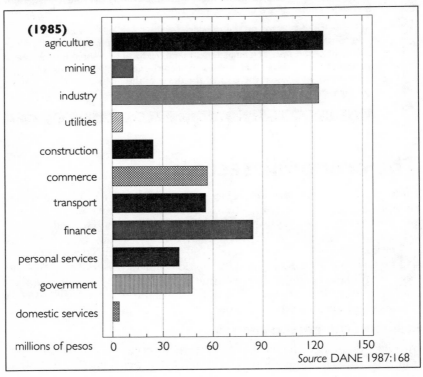

Source DANE 1987:168

families who controlled their workforces through paternalism, religion and manipulation.

Ownership was highly concentrated. By 1968 over half of industrial value added was in sectors that could be classified as oligopolies, either highly concentrated (over 75 per cent of production in the hands of three firms) or moderately so (50-75 per cent in the hands of four firms). The Bavaria company, for instance, controlled 70 per cent of the brewing industry; Postobón controlled 57.3 per cent of the soft-drinks industry (Silva Colmenares 1977:48-54). As firms bought up or created industries producing inputs into their production process (vertical integration) and then invested in new sectors, related or not to their existing production (horizontal integration), huge and powerful conglomerates were created.

A study by the *Superintendencia de Sociedades* of the linkages between 3,102 limited companies registered in 1975 found that 24 conglomerates encompassed 300 limited companies and their manufacturing activities accounted for 20 per cent of output. There were also two 'superconglomerates', the Medellín-based SurAmericana Group, which incorporated eight conglomerates, and the Santodomingo group, which incorporated four (Helmsing 1986:166).

Below the conglomerates, a medium-sized industry had become consolidated in the hands of immigrants (who had mainly come from Europe and the Middle East in the 1930s) and local entrepreneurs, who had risen out of the professional middle classes. Foreign investment was significant but not preponderant in Colombian industry. It grew in the 1960s and was concentrated in the intermediate and capital-goods sectors, such as paper, chemicals, rubber, glass, non-ferrous metals and transport machinery. In these years, foreign companies bought into Colombian-owned firms which retained overall control. In the 1970s, the multinationals came to control the enterprises themselves. An estimate in the 1970s suggests that firms with majority control by foreign capital were responsible for about 25 per cent of industrial value-added (Ocampo 1987:287).

Industrial growth began to slow down in 1974 and, between then and 1980, averaged 5.63 per cent a year. During this period Colombia's economy was liberalised and cheaper foreign goods were allowed in to force greater efficiency on the intermediate and capital-goods sectors. At the same time contraband was undermining the consumer-goods sector. Industrial exports slowed down with the partial ending of subsidies in 1975 and, during the world recession of 1979, fell to 29 per cent of total exports. They were also hit by inflation and the distortion of the currency by the influx of dollars from the coffee bonanza and the illegal drug trade.

Also, by the late 1970s the industrial firms had developed a fragile dependence on a financial system that had grown prodigiously and with insufficient regulation after interest rates were freed in 1974. Firms took on high-cost short-term loans and became dangerously indebted. When the recession hit they found themselves unable to repay loans and this created a major crisis in the financial system in 1982.

The crisis exposed poor and fraudulent management in the banking sector, and the state intervened on a massive scale to bail it out. It spent over US$500 million in soft loans, loss write-offs and fresh injections of capital and, ironically for a state committed to non-intervention, was forced to intervene directly in five private commercial banks. Overnight, the state found itself in control of eight commercial banks (not four as before) representing 65 per cent of the system's capital. The rest of the banking sector was controlled by foreign banks (10 per cent) and private Colombian interests (25 per cent), three quarters of which is controlled by three large economic groups.

The government also bailed industry out of the recession. Import restrictions and new export subsidies were introduced and industrial restructuring took place. Firms modernised their practices, renovated their machinery and introduced new technology and automation. Labour was increasingly employed on temporary contracts, which avoided protective labour legislation and weakened the mostly independent unions that now dominated industry. The number of temporary workers in private employment increased from 10.5 per cent of the labour force in 1980 to 16.5 per cent in 1987 (Kalmanovitz 1988:28).

Concentration of ownership was more acute than ever. By 1987, 0.01 per cent of shareholders (fifty shareholders) from the ten biggest companies on the Bogotá stock exchange controlled 36.5 per cent of all shares (*El Tiempo* 12 December 1988), a concentration of economic power repeated in most sectors of the Colombian economy.

Industrial recovery was under way by 1984, with a period of sustained growth after 1986, though it did not repeat the high levels of growth of the early 1970s. The Chenery report (1986) on the labour market had estimated that the Colombian economy had to grow by no less than 6 per cent a year to deal with the unemployment problem, and industry would have to make a major contribution to that growth. Economists estimated, however, that industrial production in the 1980s was unlikely to reach even half the growth experienced in the 1970s (*Economía Colombiana* January/February 1989:44).

In any case, Colombia's industries had to compete in an era of technological sophistication, which did not generate employment in manufacturing. Job opportunities were most likely in the service sector, as in the industrialised world of the 1980s, but that world did not have the huge informal sector and its associated mass of urban poor. The pattern of Colombia's industrial growth would not solve the people's need for jobs.

Agriculture: changing landscapes

Throughout the 1960s and 1970s the age-old battle continued between the peasants and large landowners to determine which kind of rural economy should predominate: a more democratic peasant-based economy or one dominated by large-scale entrepreneurs and *latifundia*. The battle had shifted through the centuries from the highlands to the slopes and now reached the warmer lower slopes and lowland regions, the so-called areas of colonisation: Caquetá, Putumayo, Ariari (southern Meta), Carare (Arauca), Urabá (Antioquia) and the middle Magdalena valley.

Those dispossessed by *La Violencia* fled, not just to the towns, but to these regions to open new agricultural frontiers, seeking a means to life in Colombia's still considerable expanses of unsettled land. Capitalist modernisation, particularly in the Magdalena and Cauca valleys, forced others to seek the same solutions. A battle commenced among cattle ranchers and peasant colonisers for Colombia's remaining fertile lands, which was gradually being won by the former. By 1984, it was estimated that half the area of colonised land was in *latifundia* and half in medium or small farms (*Economía Colombiana* October 1986)

The battle for the frontier

There are forms of colonisation, just like there are forms of violence . . . the most simple form is, of course, peasant colonisation. It is a product of a broader process, the decomposition of the peasant economy, but at the same time, it prolongs it and reproduces it. Without exception, sooner or later peasant colonisation reaches a critical point and tends to be replaced — not transformed — by entrepreneurial colonisation. The speed of this process depends on two factors. On the one hand, the quality of the land, and on the other the degree of peasant organisation. The most favourable conditions for replacement are in zones where the land is of excellent quality and peasant organisation non-existent . . .

Usually, the *colono* is a ruined or persecuted peasant who heads for areas where ownership of the land doesn't exist or is incomplete, zones which scarcely exist now in the country. There are public lands in the plains of the Pacific, in the Amazon, few in the Orinoco and very few in the highland areas of the mountain ranges. This means that the peasant must go further and further in search of the land of his dreams, where the cost of transport is very high. The *colono* has only his labour power, when he arrives at the promised land, he is dispossessed . . .

Without any capital . . . the form of production is extremely precarious. He slashes and burns, just as the Indians did and still do. He throws the maize seed on the ashes. He is ruled by natural cycles. He cannot burn in July nor sow in January. He is completely at the mercy of the weather. While he awaits the harvest, he manages to subsist and builds a place to live. In order to eat, he hunts, fishes and eventually goes out of the area to find temporary work or shares work with *colonos* who preceded him and have established a minimum stability. The next year, he returns to uproot another different plot of jungle, while he lets the first grow over again. Thus it goes on. In two or three years, he has stubble growing of different ages and he can burn the oldest to sow again. As he cannot use fertiliser he makes use of the ashes; the capacity of recovery and fertility of the stubble to a large extent determines the output of the harvest. There is a natural tendency for productivity to decline, as the stubble gets poorer and less abundant each time. This is why the *colono* fells a new plot of jungle each year and the less productive land is planted with pasture. This segment of his work is in fact the only possible form of accumulation.

In the market the *colono* falls into the sinister web of the traders. Invariably, the *colono* is selling along with hundreds of others. Agreements exist amongst the traders to buy at a certain fixed price which allows high rates of profit. But as if this wasn't enough, the traders have another source of power over the *colono*: debt. The *colono* asks the trader for goods on account for the future harvest. When he finally hands this over and settles the account, it is rarely favourable to him. The traders charge very high interests for the service and produce complicated accounts and the *colono* emerges having paid more than he owes.

Those who control local transport, the traders and those who give credit are usually the same person. Or different but associated people. There is rarely competition between them, but where there is, it is to the death . . . the rivalry between traders is very intense because the profits are so extraordinary . . .

The *colono* is absolutely defenceless in this situation. Alone, isolated, disorganised, unsociable, shy, usually illiterate, he cannot impose himself nor develop the power to negotiate with organised opponents who use all the influences, tricks and lack of scruples imaginable. In synthesis, when the *colono* manages to generate a narrow margin of surplus it is transferred to commercial capital . . . peasant colonisers don't manage to accumulate as capital the surplus they produce. In this way, any accident, any problem, can accelerate a crisis which is chronic in itself.

In this extremely fragile economic situation, the *colono* must also bear the pressure of the *latifundio*. As he improves the land, builds roads, and 'civilises' the region, the land acquires a price, it becomes marketable. The *latifundista* waits expectantly for this result. He knows of the advances of colonisation. He is associated with the transport owners, the intermediaries and the traders, with whom he is used to doing business and having common interests. He also knows the local authorities and the politicians. Together, these people form the local power elite, they are associated in one way or another. The economically strongest sector determines who are the local authorities and their links with the political sector are close and supportive. They finance the political campaigns, they maintain and renew their relations with the parties and with the regional or national public administration. The price of support which they give the politicians is charged when they take over the administration. They can do favours because they all possess an economic 'clientele'.

When the *colono* becomes bankrupt, he has no alternative other than to call on his 'accumulated capital', that is the 'improvements' he has made, the pasture he has sown. The credit he has obtained, the advances they have made to him, all his economic activity is backed by the land he has improved. So that when he is ruined, he is forced to give it up as a form of payment or to sell it to pay his accumulated debts. In reality this has been the deliberate, if silent objective of the trader, the loan giver and the transport owner . . . they destroy the *colono* in order to take over his improved land . . .

In reality, the process of bankruptcy is accelerated by the *latifundistas* who follow behind the colonisers. They call upon a thousand tricks to destroy the *colono*. They take away his water, they loan him money, they invade his property or simply, they liquidate him. The *latifundistas* can do what they like, because they know that 'justice' is always on their side. That is why they help to elect the politicians, why they have influence in administration, why they are associated with the traders, why they manage their gangs. The *colono* is alone before such power; he has no alternative than to sell to the *latifundista* in order to pay his debts . . . The weakness, sometimes calculated, of the central state, allows the local machinery to work. But it is a relative weakness. Central power does not dare to contradict regional or local practices because in general it is made up of the same and fulfils similar functions . . .

What did coca represent for the peasant coloniser? . . . For the coloniser it simply represented the possibility of obtaining that additional economic impulse that his land does not produce and without which he would be on the verge of ruin. It represented the opportunity to make the transition to ranching and perhaps towards an agricultural enterprise, and, as such, the chance of not losing the accumulated work of years. In other words, coca prevented the decomposition of the peasant economy.
(Molano 1988 and 1989)

Elsewhere capitalist modernisation began transforming Colombia's rural economy. Lauchlin Currie, who had visited Colombia as part of the World Bank delegation in 1949, had argued for the more rational use of land and labour in agriculture. Extensive cattle raising occupied fertile land, while labour was absorbed in inefficient subsistence agriculture. A more modern productive agriculture would free labour to move to the cities where it could be absorbed in labour-intensive urban construction. 'Operation Colombia', as Currie's programme was called, though it was not implemented as such, was influential among economists and governments in the 1960s and 1970s.

Large-scale commercial farms expanded dramatically in the 1960s to meet the food needs of a growing urban population and to generate export earnings for industrial expansion. In the fertile lands of the Cauca valley, Tolima, Cesar and parts of the Atlantic coast, traditional *latifundia* were transformed into highly-mechanised modern enterprises. Decree 444 of 1967 gave credit and other incentives to agriculture, and sugar, cotton and rice production soon had exportable surpluses. Law 1a of 1968 resulted in a massive expulsion of tenant farmers and sharecroppers and, by the end of the decade, farms under ten hectares had diminished substantially in number and size.

This process generated many rural conflicts, and sensitivity to the social and political dangers of rural modernisation fuelled the debates about agrarian reform in the 1960s. Carlos Lleras Restrepo (1966-70) was president during these years of peasant unrest, which also saw the rise of a new generation of guerrilla movements in the rural areas and the political challenge of ANAPO in the growing cities. One of Colombia's most far-seeing and innovative presidents, he questioned the wisdom of Operation Colombia and instead advocated keeping peasants on the land. In a letter to the 'operational committee' of the Ministry of Agriculture in 1967, he wrote:

> During the coming years urban demand for labour for industries and services will not surpass supply, but on the contrary, the latter will have an excess that will be extremely difficult to absorb . . . In such conditions, whatever contributes to bind the peasant population to the land can be considered as socially and economically useful, even though in some cases it may imply the prolongation of an economy of simple subsistence. (quoted in Zamosc 1986:48)

He had been greatly frustrated by the intense opposition to his 1961 land reform. But landowners were heavily represented in Congress. A Liberal congressman at the time, he had tried to drive it through Congress, only to find that an emasculated version could make it to the statute books after a compromise transaction between the two party leaders. As president, Lleras Restrepo proposed to create a force outside the parties which would press for better services and land reform. The intention was to strengthen the landless peasants in areas of traditional *latifundia* by setting up an organisation that would be outside the control of the traditional parties but not autonomous. It would be a direct link between the peasants and the state.

The National Association of Peasant Users (ANUC) was set up in 1967, but it soon broke free from state patronage and became a combative movement, which organised the peasants to demand the right to land through marches and land invasions. The early 1970s saw the mobilisation of thousands of peasants in an attempt to halt the expansion of cattle ranchers and commercial farmers and to preserve a peasant economy.

Under Lleras Restrepo's Conservative successor, Misael Pastrana, the government and rural *gremios* launched their counter-offensive against the peasantry. New legislation in 1973 gave major concessions to large landowners, and the Agricultural Financial Fund gave large amounts of cheap credit to commercial agriculture. Between 1968 and 1977, there was an increase of 40 per cent in the harvested area for the seven main crops of capitalist agriculture: sugar cane, barley, soybeans, rice, cotton, sorghum and sesame.

In addition to these agricultural cash crops, banana exports expanded during the 1960s and 1970s in Urabá, with its good soil and cheap, mostly black, labour force; cut flowers found a favourable climate and a cheap, largely female, labour force in the Bogotá 'savannah'. By 1975, non-traditional agricultural exports made up 12 per cent of total exports.

The expansion of commercial agriculture was uneven and did not eliminate peasant agriculture. In the Andean departments of Nariño and Cauca in the south, Antioquia and Caldas in the west and Cundinamarca, Boyacá, Santander and Norte de Santander, peasants tried to survive on diminishing plots of land alongside modern, mechanised agriculture and traditional *latifundia*. In 1984 there were 1,504,215 *minifundistas* with an average of 2.14 hectares of land; 636,255 of these had less than one hectare. INCORA estimated that each family needed a minimum of 22 hectares. A further 157,691 families were landless (Arango 1988:31).

These peasant farmers lacked credit and the means to improve productivity, but still produced 55 per cent of the country's basic foodstuffs, such as maize, cassava, plaintain and potatoes. The Integrated Rural Development (DRI) programme of the mid-1970s sought to support this sector. In nine years of investment (1976-85) the DRI dispensed 40,000 million pesos; but the Agricultural Financial Fund dispensed nearly

81,000 million pesos to large farmers in 1985 alone (*ibid*:37). Export subsidies, credits, devaluation and all sorts of government policies favoured commercial agriculture.

In other areas, particularly the plains of the Atlantic coast (departments of Córdoba, Sucre, Bolívar, Atlántico, Cesar and Magdalena) and in the eastern *llanos* (departments of Casanare and the north of Meta), traditional, usually inefficient, cattle *latifundia* still dominated. In 1984, ten million hectares of land were in estates of more than 500 hectares each owned by an estimated 12,000 landowners, most of whom were cattle barons (*Economía Colombiana* October 1986). The peasants' demand for access to land created violent conflicts in these areas throughout the 1970s and 1980s.

The unresolved struggle for the land in Colombia generated some of the most violent of the conflicts of the 1980s. A serious agrarian reform, however, was never put on the agenda, 'only a strategy of land redistribution based on the criteria of preserving public order' (Arango 1988:35). In 25 years, from 1961 to 1985, INCORA bought up 4,009 farms totalling 472,470 hectares and expropriated only 254 farms totalling 66,035 hectares. This land was distributed to just 30,000 families. The majority of acquisitions were made between 1971 and 1973, the years of maximum peasant organisation; 200,000 hectares were acquired in that period, 42 per cent of the total (Quintero Latorre 1988:39).

A further 350,000 hectares were 'ceded' to INCORA, but were largely unusable land. INCORA also distributed just over five million hectares of public lands and gave out 190,480 titles of private ownership between 1970 and 1987, mainly in the areas of colonisation. But a certain amount of land in each adjudication was free to be resold, from 1,000 to 3,000 hectares in the eastern *llanos*, and this facilitated the concentration of land (*ibid*:44).

By the 1980s, the drug mafia was investing its immense resources in land and, in many areas, reversing the small steps towards reform. In the Magdalena Medio it bought an estimated 180,000 hectares of fertile land, compared with the meagre 12,605 hectares INCORA bought in the region under the National Rehabilitation Plan between 1983 and 1988 and 101,564 in the country as a whole (*El Tiempo* 31 July 1988; Quintero Latorre 1988:45; *El País Internacional* 5 November 1989).

'Colombia is coffee or it is nothing'

Coffee was of great importance to the economy throughout this period. Given that it is the main source of export earnings, fluctuations in international coffee prices have had a significant impact. In 1980, coffee provided over 50 per cent of total exports, but in the following year its export earnings fell by 30 per cent to US$1,500 million. There was another boom in 1986 (with a similar share in total exports) and an accompanying fall in coffee earnings of 43 per cent in 1987. This is important because it helps to explain not only the past but also the likely role of coffee in the future — the 1989 collapse of the International Coffee Agreement led to a sharp fall in coffee prices (a 40 per cent fall from peak to trough in 1989).

This source of economic instability should, however, be seen in a historical perspective. In the 1950-4 period, coffee provided almost 79 per cent of all export earnings, a figure that had dropped to 61 per cent by 1965-9 and had fallen to less than 50 per cent by 1980-4. This is despite the fact that between the late 1950s and the first half of the 1980s coffee production broadly doubled.

This expansion of production was due, not to an increase in land cultivated for coffee, but to the arrival of more modern methods and the introduction of the Brazilian *caturra* plant in the 1960s. Modernisation was promoted by FEDERACAFE and taken up with particular vigour by the commercially-minded larger estates. The small coffee farmers, the 'heroes' of the first half of the century, had become the 'villains' of the second half because of their traditional methods of cultivation which were extremely time consuming (Palacios 1983:464). It was calculated that 83 per cent of total costs in the 1950s were accounted for by labour,

Joe Fish

Sorting coffee beans on an Indian *resguardo*, Tierradentro, Cauca.

14 per cent by taxes or transport and only 3 per cent by tools and other inputs, with labour productivity only half that of El Salvador (Ocampo 1987:287).

Between 1960 and 1964, only 1 per cent of coffee land was devoted to modern production; by 1980-4 it had risen to 38 per cent (*ibid*:288). Over the years the number of small family producers declined and swelled the ranks of the coffee proletariat of the region. In Valle, for instance, the number of farms fell from 23,975 in 1955 to 17,116 in 1970 (Palacios 1983:449). Some of these could get access to credit from the Federation to modernise production, but the Federation encouraged the most inefficient producers to plant other crops.

According to a study by the Economic Commission for Latin America in 1987 (Arango 1988:36), peasant farmers still contributed 30 per cent of production and over half of the 320,000 private growers operated on smallholdings of less than 15 hectares. But it was the medium and larger growers who were able to take most advantage of the new production methods.

By the mid-1970s increased production and severe frosts in Brazil (which affected the supply of coffee on the international market) helped Colombia to recapture the position it had lost in the world market after 1950. During the second half of the 1970s Colombian coffee experienced a bonanza in earnings. The government refused to tax the excess profits which resulted and FEDERACAFE reaped the benefits. While other sectors entered a recession in the late 1970s, the coffee sector was thriving. By the end of the 1970s, the sector was providing 200,000 people with permanent employment and a further 400,000 with seasonal work; some estimates suggest that as much as 10 per cent of the labour force was indirectly or directly dependent on coffee by this time.

FEDERACAFE has proved very effective in defending the interests of the coffee sector both within Colombia and internationally. Although a private organisation, it carries out many public tasks. It determines all important coffee policies, oversees the purchase of coffee for export and represents Colombia in international negotiations. Through managing the Coffee Fund, income from coffee taxes, coffee exports and sales of coffee for domestic consumption, FEDERACAFE has been able to expand its interests into finance, shipping, construction and other areas of agriculture. By the 1980s it owned two banks, a merchant fleet, warehousing companies, cooperatives, an insurance company and savings and investment funds, and was one of the biggest economic enterprises in the country.

FEDERACAFE has also funded development projects in the coffee-growing regions, where health, education and service provisions are noticeably higher and social unrest noticeably lower than in almost any other region. It was also a strong backer of President Barco's 1987 plan for rehabilitating some of the country's neglected rural areas where guerrilla movements had established roots.

In 1985 the comptroller-general investigated the Coffee Fund and found that many of its investments had nothing to do with coffee and that it was being used for purposes other than those for which it had been set up: 'The activities of the enterprises [in which the fund invests] are not aimed at meeting the needs of the coffee producers and cannot easily be considered, as a whole, as complementary to the coffee industry, a requirement established in . . . the present contract between the Federation and the national government' (quoted in Atehortua 1986:80).

Further questions were raised about the Coffee Fund when an agreement between the government and the federation about the administration of the fund came up for renewal at the end of 1988. Another study commissioned from the National University also questioned the management of the fund and some congressmen even spoke of nationalising it. The federation reacted so intensely that the government moved quickly to reassure it, renewing the contract for a further 10 years, with minor modifications, while publicly recognising the validity of the comptroller-general's report.

The Federation is the most powerful *gremio* in the country. A study of Colombia's *gremios* by Miguel Urrutia in 1983, sponsored by the Ford Foundation, defined it as a parallel state and concluded that:

> After the President of the Republic, the most powerful person in Colombia is the manager of the Federation, given that he has a place as of right on the most important decision-making bodies in the country . . [The Federation] is without doubt the largest industrial conglomerate in Colombia, and if anyone added up the balance sheet, it would comparè with a medium-sized transnational. (Urrutia 1983:116-17)

It is not a homogeneous body, but represents exporters, large-scale enterprises and peasant producers. It has been controlled by the first two of these since the 1930s. One study concluded that because of restrictions on membership for the smallest producers, the federation represents only 135,000 producers, 44 per cent of coffee growers and, of these, only 26,000 participate in elections to its committees (Atehortua 1986:76). The departmental and national committees are run by the large producers, who elect one another on the basis of family and friendship ties.

Over the years the gap between modernised and unmodernised farms, and between large and small producers has widened. The future of the small farmers became more uncertain in the 1980s. International prices fluctuated considerably in the first half of the decade and internal prices were low. This created severe problems for the smaller producers who had modernised on the basis of credit and were highly indebted. When prices are low, the producers use less fertiliser and this exposes the plants to disease. Many plants were reaching the end of their productivity in this period. In 1983, the roya coffee pest reached Colombia. The most effective solution was to replant with the new Colombia variety of coffee, but this entailed high costs and a period of at least two years for the new plants to grow.

The collapse of the coffee agreement in 1989 and the disruption of price was a serious blow to coffee growers and the thousands who depended on coffee for employment, as well as to government spending plans. Although Colombia produces the best-quality, most sought-after coffee and is considered a very efficient producer, it will be badly affected by the price fall. The end of the stockpiling system meant a stormy period ahead for the international coffee market, a period of readjustment with an uncertain outcome. But by the end of the 1980s Colombia was no longer synonymous with coffee.

Energy: a national debate

Energy is an issue in Colombia, not only because of its role in the national economy and its significance in international trade, but also because of its importance to the basic needs of the population.

Many Colombians are without access to adequate energy sources, either for cooking or for electricity's many other uses. This is especially true in rural areas where the cost of extending electric cables is high relative to the number of additional users. The provision of electricity is important considering how much is dependent on it — lighting, water and sewerage pumps, cooling, refrigeration and heating.

For this reason the energy debate has become a popular issue in Colombia, both at the domestic level (the need, for example, for housing, water and sewerage) and at a national level (questions of energy policy and the contest for control over Colombia's oil and coal resources). Different perspectives are evident in the demands of the majority for better access to energy resources, while the government sees the exploitation of oil and coal resources as a source of foreign exchange.

From 1970 to 1986 the total generation of electricity grew from 7.5 gigawatt/hours to 27, and current plans would push this to more than 33 by 1990. In the period from 1970 to 1983, consumption of electrical energy by the domestic sector grew from 2.5 gigawatt/hours to 8.2, an increase of 350 per cent (DANE 1986). Despite this growth in consumption, electricity is still not the main source of domestic energy. The 1985 census showed that fewer than 30 per cent of households cook with electricity, the same percentage as use wood; as many again use kerosene or propane gas. A particular feature of Bogotá is the use of paraffin (*cocinol*), which is a notoriously dangerous form of domestic energy that has caused many injuries and deaths in Bogotá's poor neighbourhoods.

Although the vast majority has not benefited from them, Colombia is rich in energy resources. It has one of the world's largest sources of hydro-electricity and hydro-power represents around three-quarters of installed electrical-generating capacity; for a long time it has been a significant oil producer and, by the 1980s, had become an oil exporter and was developing its giant coal resources.

The inability of the country to make good use of all this and the fact that much of the foreign debt is related to energy projects, has given rise to internal debate. In particular, the country's large investments in hydro-electric power have not been matched by investments in transmission and distribution, leading to a situation of excess supply of generation capacity but unmet demand by the consumer and substantial energy losses (around 25 per cent). This creates further difficulties in that revenue from consumers is needed to help pay off the large international loans undertaken to finance the project. The result is that existing consumers have to bear the heavy burden of higher electricity charges. Many urban protest movements have developed around this issue.

Colombia has played host to a number of large-scale energy projects undertaken with multinational energy corporations, particularly oil projects but, more recently, the giant CARBOCOL-Intercor (EXXON's Colombian offshoot) coal project at El Cerrejón. Oil has been extracted in Colombia for many years. After a period of falling production when Colombia became a net oil importer, it has picked up in recent years and today Colombia is once more an oil exporter. Most of this production has taken place in conjunction with foreign oil companies. Oil output fell from 218,000 barrels a day in 1970 to 123,000 barrels in 1979. By 1986 this had increased to 302,000 barrels with a planned production of 500,000 barrels a day by 1990. Natural gas output rose from 88,000 cubic feet per day in 1970 to 382,000 by 1986.

In 1980 coal output stood at 4 million tonnes, while by 1986 this had risen to 11.5 million, almost all of the increase coming from the Atlantic coast, where El Cerrejón is located. Projections for 1990 indicate output of 22.6 million tonnes. Other areas of Colombia are also thought to be promising sites for large-scale coal production, such as the huge La Loma deposit in Cesar department, whose development is planned by the US Drummond Corporation. But transport to the port is a major problem for the inland mines.

Many of these energy projects are in Colombia's most neglected regions, such as the Caño Limón oil field in Arauca. According to a 1988

DANE study on poverty in Colombia, 62 per cent of the region's 21,000 people live in poverty and 32 per cent of these in absolute poverty. Roads are unpaved, housing and water supplies are inadequate and there is no sewerage. Local people feel they gain nothing from the wealth below their soil.

There have been intense debates over the terms of the contracts signed with multinationals to exploit Colombia's resources. Relations with the powerful transnational oil companies have always been controversial in Colombia. In the early 1960s the Minister of Mines, Enrique Pardo Parra, criticised their operations and sought to limit their profit remittances. President Valencia was then told that he would have to get rid of him if he wished to continue to get US funds from the Alliance for Progress (Kline 1987:35).

Oil exploration and development and operating a high-technology coal mine, such as El Cerrejón, involve huge costs. With insufficient capital and technical expertise, the Colombian government is in a weak position, and powerful multinationals can use this vulnerability to their advantage. The estimated cost of the El Cerrejón project is US$3,400 million, with oil exploration estimated to cost US$3,500 million by 1990. Oil reserves by the end of the 1980s are anticipated to give Colombia self-sufficiency only in the short run and Colombia is therefore eager to attract foreign companies to contribute to the costs of exploring for new reserves. Mining became the main area of foreign (particularly US) investment in the 1980s, replacing manufacturing.

The government was forced to borrow much of its share of the exploration costs, which represented a considerable burden of debt given the high interest rates and low energy prices through most of the 1980s. It entered into association contracts with multinationals to provide the rest. Under this scheme, output is split fifty-fifty with a 20 per cent royalty; where risks are low, the state oil company, ECOPETROL, has negotiated a larger share of production.

The energy debate: the workers' view:

'We are an immensely rich country in natural resources, in gas in coal, in oil and water. But by the end of the century there will be a million peasant houses without light; 40 per cent of energy consumption in Colombia is wood. If we developed electrical energy on the basis of coal, we could produce much more employment and it would be ten times cheaper to produce than present energy. We must use our natural resources not in terms of how many dollars it will generate for us, but in terms of how many jobs and how much industrial development they will bring. We have such a quantity of natural resources that we could say to countries like England, the USSR, West Germany and the US itself, how many tons of coal do you want in exchange for the technology to develop our carbo-chemical industry? We could say to another country, how much oil do you want in exchange for the technology to build our own steel industry?

We can't go on thinking in terms of this dance of dollars, without thinking about Colombia in the year 2,000. We have concentrated the people in the towns, but we have no industrial development. We are part of Latin America, but we live from the poverty of our neighbours; when there are frosts in Brazil, we are happy because we are going to sell more coffee. But the development of Colombian industry, when? We cannot continue looking to the suffering of the Central American people or Brazilians, so that the price of coffee is raised in order for us to import manufactured goods . . .

The Association Contracts which we have signed with the multinationals to develop our coal and oil contain elements which harm our national sovereignty. In the case of coal, specifically El Cerrejón, we made a deal without knowing what it was worth. According to the contract, half the coal is for the foreign partner, EXXON, and half for the country, for the most productive 30 years of the mine. They bear the risks of exploration for the first six years, although exploration isn't really necessary as the coal of La Guajira was discovered in 1862 and the French even offered to buy the peninsular from us at the time.

They told us that the deal was worth US$3.2 billion, that is twice the national budget of Colombia at the time. EXXON's assets are worth fifteen times the national budget and its sales round the world, twenty three times our GDP. Our problem is that we cannot contribute our fifty per cent of the total costs because that's the value of our national budget. If we don't, we are fined according to the contract. We have to go to the IMF and promise to pay with coal, as we did with the World Bank. The financial organisations of EXXON, Chase Manhattan, the Bank of Japan, Lloyds Bank of Britain, are willing to lend the money and we have to borrow it.

EXXON brings us the plans and costs of the project. We don't have the technological expertise to question them or put forward our own within the thirty days specified, so we are obliged to borrow the money according to the costs they have worked out. The University of Antioquia carried out a study on El Cerrejón and found that similar projects in the world have a maximum cost of US$1.5 billion, but ours cost US$3.2 billion.

We also have to pay EXXON to take out "our coal". We pay them so much to move it from the mine, so much to put it on the train, so much to move it to the port. If EXXON sells each ton for US$30 on the international market, we receive only US$23 after these expenses have been deducted.

What do we have as a result? We are not obtaining new technology, we do not have a coal products industry, we do not have a research programme, the 150 kilometres of railway line which have been built is no great extension in transport facilities and the project has generated only 3,000 jobs. In 1988 the price of coal is low: the US$27 a tonne should be balanced against Colombia's share of production costs, which are US$35 a tonne and the financial cost of the debt, US$46 a tonne, giving total production costs of US$81. We operate at a loss of US$50 even if the price stabilises at US$30. And after thirty years, we get a mine dug 200 metres deep and we will have to begin again with new technology to exploit the coal beneath that. In addition, a study has shown that this kind of open cast mine puts the workers at risk from a particular disease which attacks the lungs and the blood. There have been 32 deaths in the mine in three years, and sixty workers have had to retire with unidentified illnesses.

The contract for oil exploration is the same as for coal. In the case of oil we produce at present about 400,000 barrels per day. We consume 200,000 barrels, but the state enterprise, ECOPETROL, only processes 80,000. Every day we have to buy 120,000 barrels on the international market of the refined product. After 67 years of our oil industry we haven't been able to develop self-sufficiency in refining. In 1986 the foreign oil companies invested US$168 million, while Colombia bought from them (its own oil), oil worth US$531 million. In 1987 the figure was about US$230 million in investment against US$600 million in purchases, despite the low oil prices.

Oil and coal have a geopolitical value. Colombia is well placed geographically for the market of the year 2000. Already the struggle is for the Pacific, not the Atlantic markets. We could take real advantage of that for national development. We believe that the energy policy of the country has to be redesigned in its entirety. We believe that the Association Contracts harm national sovereignty; there is no technology transfer, no social gain either in coal or oil. We believe energy policy can be redesigned to meet social needs, to make a social profit.'
Source: interview with Pedro Galindo, representative of FEDEPETROL, the oil workers' federation, March 1988.

Some of the criticisms of the government's oil and coal policy, in particular the association contracts signed with the transnational companies, are presented in the interview above. In 1986, the issue leapt into the headlines when guerrillas launched a policy of blowing up the oil pipelines and kidnapping foreign oil executives. This has not stopped investment but has cost considerable amounts in repairs to installations and loss of foreign-exchange earnings, and has made the use of its vast energy resources one of the most controversial issues in Colombia. By the end of the 1980s, there was an increasing level of debate, even among government circles, over the country's control of its natural resources.

The underground economy

Illegal activities of all kinds flourish in Colombia and have done so for many years. They range from bribery and corruption of public officials to tax evasion and smuggling, to drug trafficking and petty theft. They involve many sectors of society, though crime has become a means of survival rather than a source of enrichment for a sector of the poor, with its own violent culture and underworld.

Colombia's hungry children

'No country can survive like this', says the director of the Colombian Institute of Family Welfare, Jaime Benítez Tobón. 'Malnutrition is a time-bomb which could destroy anyone'. In Colombia, four and a half million children under 14 years are hungry. That is to say one in every two children. 'Painful figures', says Benítez, 'because, according to the last census -in which it was calculated that the Colombian population had risen to 28.5 million people — 17 per cent were under seven years old, and another 20 per cent between seven and fourteen. That means that more than ten million Colombians are under 14 years old.

'Unemployment or underemployment of 40 per cent of parents, with incomes below the minimum for a basket of goods, are the main causes of malnutrition. And this, in turn, is the origin of the great vices which ensnare Colombian children.' Gaminismo (the phenomenon of street children), prostitution, delinquency are just some of these evils. Colombia also has one of the highest indices of truancy. 'Children who go to school hungry. Or who don't go because they are hungry. Or who are thrown out of school because they don't learn and are badly treated when in fact they are hungry. A hunger which doesn't allow them to understand and doesn't let them learn.' Paradoxically, perhaps the street children suffer least hunger, because in the streets there is always something to eat. 'Nevertheless, gaminismo is the great cause of delinquency. All the problems of the child are born there. Often, gaminismo is permitted by parents as a means of protection; the unemployed or underemployed, sick or incapacitated worker sorts out his problems in that way.' But these children who live in the streets, who begin selling cigarettes and fruit and then go into prostitution and delinquency, and who must number about 3,000 in Bogotá and in the country as a whole many thousands, do not really reflect the problem of malnutrition.

'Lucky the children of Biafra', says Jaime Benítez Tobón, 'at least they are thrown food from an airplane. Some of our children are less fortunate because the country doesn't even know they exist.' Few people know, in

> fact, that in Bogotá, malnutrition isn't dramatic. Nor in Boyacá, where agriculture and the prevalence of *minifundia* give the children something to eat. But it's different in Córdoba, a department with the highest figures of hunger. Also different is Bolívar, in the suburbs of Cartagena, where in 1985, when the minimum wage was 13,557 pesos, 73 per cent of families earned less than ten thousand pesos.
>
> (*El Tiempo* 27 July 1988)

At the higher levels of society there is fraud of all kinds:

> It is corruption alone that accounts for the catalogue of 19,358 fraudulent transactions in foreign exchange, committed by such a broad section of Colombians that it ranged from bishops and ex-ministers to generals and football players . . . Corruption alone (confirms the Comptroller-General) ensures that each year 65,000 million pesos (about US$350 million) is handed out in this country in the form of bribes and kick-backs. 'Bribes', says the Comptroller, 'are like the Holy Spirit: they are everywhere, but nobody sees them. The crisis of corruption is rampant. There is still a long way to go in preventing the flow of public money into private pockets'.
>
> (Avila Bernal 1987:220-21)

'White-collar' crime, that is crimes against the public administration (such as embezzlement, extortion, bribery, illegal contracts) increased considerably in the 1980s — according to 1986 DANE statistics from 2,956 in 1981 to 4,129 in 1984 (Thoumi 1987: 38).

Tax evasion is endemic, though the level of direct taxation is among the lowest in Latin America. Successive administrations have usually declared a tax amnesty on assuming office, which is now expected and has encouraged rather than discouraged evasion.

Business groups have mobilised strong opposition to tax reform. In 1974, López Michelsen, backed by the World Bank and using his presidential authority rather than Congress, enacted a reform which included a capital-gains tax, but the outcry from the private sector forced him to present a modified version to Congress. Following the passage of the new law, between 1975 and 1981 taxes on income and wealth fell from 4.3 per cent of GDP to 2.7 per cent. Between these years there was no substantial change in income distribution, and inflation was insufficient to account for the lowering of the value of the tax collection. It seems likely that tax evasion was responsible (*ibid*:43). When President

Julio César Turbay Ayala took office in 1978, he owed a strong political debt to the industrialists' *gremio*, ANDI, for electoral support in Antioquia and, consequently, the law was further modified.

Smuggling is also widespread and has a long history in Colombia. Coffee, cattle, consumer goods (from cigars to computers), gold and emeralds are among the goods smuggled. Smuggling of coffee and cattle has often been indirectly encouraged by government exchange controls and other barriers imposed on international trade at different times. Coffee was smuggled during the boom years after 1976 when the International Coffee Agreement imposed limits on exports. One estimate put the value of illegal exports of traditional products, of which coffee and beef were the most important, at 13.8 per cent of officially-recorded goods and services in 1977 (*ibid*:39).

That the blackmarket in smuggled consumer goods thrives in Colombia is aided by the corruption of the customs service. Customs officers can earn twenty to fifty times their salaries in bribes from smugglers (Varón 1988). Often the smugglers have close ties with local politicians whom they support at election time; in turn, government moves against them are blocked by their congressional friends. Contraband is alleged to cost the government US$400 million a year in lost tax revenues. According to the merchants' federation, FENALCO, nearly a quarter of the imports sold in Colombia are smuggled into the country at a value of US$1,000-1,250 million a year.

Most Colombian towns contain a blackmarket shopping centre, which they call *Sanandresito* after the island of San Andrés where much of the contraband enters Colombia. Bogotá has at least three large markets of this sort and many smaller ones selling TV sets, cameras, radios, perfumes, clothing and other goods. According to one journalist, nearly all watches, foreign cigars, cassettes and video equipment sold in Colombia and half of the marketed micro-computer equipment is contraband (*ibid*).

Gold and emeralds, which have been smuggled for many years, are both associated with violence of one sort or another. In the 1980s the government tried to regularise these two activities. It adjusted the price policy for gold so that it became worthwhile for prospectors to hand their findings to the Central Bank rather than to smuggle them to Panama. Output doubled between 1984 and 1986, but the poor prospectors, who work long back-breaking hours in conditions of neglect and deprivation, found that gold prospecting brought them much more hardship than wealth. Their protests, along with those of the many peasant colonisers who were lured to the region by gold fever, have been accompanied by much violence.

Emeralds and *La Violencia*

Eighty per cent of Colombia's emerald riches are found in the area of Muzo and Coscuez, about 100 kilometres north of Bogotá in the east of the department of Boyacá. The region has a population of 62,000 in 11 municipalities, and a floating population of another 35,000. The extraordinary levels of violence in this region are rooted in the uncontrolled rise of its mining economy, which has developed a code of living and dying all of its own. For five decades, since the 1930s, armed groups have disputed the region, initially for party political reasons, later for emeralds and most recently for cocaine.

During *La Violencia*, the situation was explosive; this was the birth place of the infamous *chulavita* police, who became a national phenomenon. The town of Chiquinquirá itself, the epicentre of the region, was polarised between the two political parties and a centre of daily armed conflict.

It was in the wake of *La Violencia* that the seeds were sown for a new wave of violence which would hit the region between 1966 and 1970 and again from 1971 to 1979, the so-called Emerald Wars. Its origins lay in the way the state tried and failed to manage the emerald mines.

In 1946, it delegated this task to the *Banco de la República*. The emerald market had been badly hit by World War II and only began to recover in the 1960s. But administrative mistakes in the management of the mines and the marketing of the emeralds opened the way to corruption and left some mines, such as Peñas Blancas, open to anyone who worked them. Many came to the region when they learned about the possibility of making a fortune. The result was a process which overwhelmed the institutions resulting in generalised delinquency and a virtual collapse of the local peasant economy as young people in particular left their family plots to mine emeralds.

An economy emerged which paralleled the state mining monopoly, ECOMINAS and contracted companies of the 'official' emerald economy. It was clandestine and illegal, but tolerated. The legal activity used modern technology and methods, the other used poor prospectors, *guaqueros,* who sifted through the material discarded by the official mining sector, or who dug illegal tunnels, using primitive tools.

The *guaquero* usually arrived at the region with a prior contact, the *plantero*, to whom he had to sell his finds at a fixed price. The relationship with the *plantero* created ties of loyalty and dependency, and gradually, as violence grew in the region, the *plantero* had to protect himself and his 'men'; this became the basis of local private armies. A new regional bourgeoisie emerged from the fortunes made by the *planteros*. This class made its bid to control not only emeralds but all aspects of local life. In particular a group of traders of Syrian-Lebanese origin together with some older *planteros*, formed a clan known as the Muzo Group. This group rivalled that of Efraín González, a Conservative bandit of *La Violencia*, who had captured a large part of the clandestine emerald market during the 1950s. Both groups courted local politicians. The Muzo group made links with various politicians who took up their bid to legalise their activities. Efraín cultivated the Conservatives and later, ANAPO, gaining a reputation as a 'social' bandit who helped the poor.

Efraín's death in 1965 was followed by the outbreak of the Emerald Wars. His role was taken by another legendary figure, Humberto Ariza, *el Ganso*. But it was the Muzo group which emerged victorious with support from a section of the army, and some stability emerged in the region of Muzo on the basis of the group's predominance. The man who came to rule the region, the so-called Godfather of Emeralds, was Gilberto Molina. With the rise of Molina, the emerald world divided into two, those who were with him and those who were against him. Some considered him their benefactor and saviour; he virtually built the municipality of Quipama, whose inhabitants called him 'papa'. There he built a municipal palace, an airport, two convents, and planned a five star hotel. He solved all local problems, maintained order out of the barrel of the gun, and decided who worked in the emerald mines.

Amongst those against him, were the people of Coscuez. Here, *guaqueros*, mostly urban and rural unemployed in search of a living, squatted in permanent settlements near the mines, demanding the right to prospect. Molina stood in the way. The conflicts generated in this area were acute, particularly after 1983 when the minimal level of regional organisation by local *planteros* broke down. Armed groups sought to maintain control over local mines against neighbouring municipalities, in particular the Muzo group which sought to control Coscuez.

Meanwhile, a new factor intervened in the late 1970s. With their accumulated capital from emeralds, local *planteros* began to spread the coca seed, particularly to the eastern *llanos* and beyond as well as in the region itself, using the same methods of contracting out production and the same violence as was the custom in the emerald regions. Molina himself was frequently associated with the Medellín mafia bosses. He was also involved in the paramilitary groups which began murdering peasants and suspected members of the FARC in the 1980s. Molina himself was assassinated in February 1989.

FARC faced problems in winning support in the region among individualistic mining communities, but in some areas it gained legitimacy by solving some of the many disputes within the population that custom had resolved through assassination, and by sorting out some of the social problems. But organised delinquency was a more widespread phenomenon than the guerrillas. The region is a centre for arms trafficking and crime of all sorts. The rule of law is completely absent. One study showed that this region, which represents 6.9 per cent of the population of Boyacá, accounts for over 20 per cent of the crimes, of which nearly 58 per cent are against life and personal integrity, and 38 per cent are economic crimes.

The figure of the assassin, or *sicario* is particularly notorious in the region. The *sicario* emerged during the Emerald Wars, as those who were defeated sought their revenge through hiring assassins to kill the leaders of enemy groups. Entire families were wiped out in this way. By 1970, there were a number of professional killers around; 'el Chimazo' had seventy assassinations to his name by the time he was twenty. Many of the murders are carried out by adolescents; in 1986, a Conservative politician lost his life by mistake in an assassination attempt by a child of twelve or thirteen. Other politicians did not die by mistake; among those who lost their lives in the first half of 1988 were a deputy to the Assembly of Boyacá, the mayor of Briceño, the mayor of Muzo and a deputy, representative to the House.
Source: Buendia 1988 and *Semana* 7 March 1989

The association of crime and violence with emeralds dates back to the 1930s and some members of the cocaine mafia began their criminal lives in the emerald trade. Gang warfare has often broken out between groups of *guaqueros*, poor prospectors, over diggings, even causing the so-called 'Emerald Wars' in the late 1960s, which cost more than 500 lives. In the 1980s the government attempted to rationalise methods of exploring for and mining emeralds and the quantity (by carat weight) more than doubled between 1984 and 1987, though the greater part of the value added is generated at the distribution and retail stage in the US, which is the main market (*Financial Times* 24 June 1988).

Gold and poverty

Gold production is undertaken mostly by poor prospectors, *barequeros*, using primitive and arduous panning, shovelling and digging methods, in the forested lowlands around El Bagre, some 300 kilometres north east of Medellín. A mining company, Mineros de Antioquia, formed in 1974 when the US-owned Pato Consolidated Gold Dredging was 'Colombianised', also mines gold in the El Bagre area, using giant dredgers and employing about 600 men. Another company, La Frontino Gold Mines, mines in the nearby municipality of Segovia.

The region provides about three-quarters of national gold production, but is another of Colombia's virtually abandoned areas. The company compound of Mineros de Antioquia is an oasis of progress in a desert of neglect, with schools, hospitals, clubs and all basic services. Until 1985 when some improvements began after a series of civic protests, the country around it lacked all basic amenities: electricity, drinking water and sewerage, and despite its resources, roads and communications were appalling. With an urban population of 12,200 people and growing rural population of peasant colonisers, the region had only one doctor, one dentist, and two nursing auxiliaries to deal with a multitude of health problems, from malaria, anaemia, malnutrition and bullet wounds from armed conflicts which have taken place. In 1988, a journalist described the life of the miner:

> The imminent gold wealth of the Antioqueño north-east contrasts sharply with the life of those who daily head for the municipal capital to sell their gold dust. With no formal organisation, the miners subsist between riches and poverty — the riches when they have a 'find' or 'guaca' followed by poverty. Because the money of the miner is 'pocket money', when there's a lot, they spend a lot, and when there is nothing they put up with hunger for as long as necessary . . . The improvised camps of the miners along the banks of the river change location according to where it is thought that gold can be found. In this type of pilgrimage, following the path of the precious metal, rarely can they offer their children access to education. The little ones take on the role of their fathers (*El Espectador* 26 September 1988)

When the government gave incentives to boost production in the 1980s, people flocked to the area and began to colonise the land which they worked in between prospecting for the gold. But the land was both poor and in short supply. Tensions mounted in the area between the poor prospectors and the companies, particularly as the region's gold reserves were only expected to last another fifteen years. But also over ecological issues. The company dredges caused floods from working the rivers and other damage. Despite some improvements in 1985, service provision remained poor and as the people became more organised, the region became the centre of some of the worst violence in Colombia.
Source: Rodríguez Solano and García 1988

Violence is very much a feature of a country where so many people make a living outside the law. In 1973, with 19.8 murders for every 100,000 inhabitants, Colombia was one of the most violent countries in the world (compare, for instance, Thailand, 15.6, Mexico, 13, US, 9.7, France 0.8). By 1978, the figure was 53 per 100,000. The conclusion of a DANE study (1986) on criminality in eleven towns in 1985-6 concluded that the 'poverty in which the majority of the Colombian people live is the main cause of delinquency. In 1985, over 60 per cent of reported crimes were economic, the majority of which were petty theft'.

In 1987, a study by the National University on the high level of violence in Cali and Medellín found that, 'rather than delinquency, these two towns suffer a syndrome of violence, manifested in the physical liquidation of citizens'. In Cali, it found that the number of murders with firearms grew from 51 per cent of all murders in 1980 to 85 per cent in 1986, and in Medellín from 40 per cent in 1979 to 76 per cent in 1985. The authors make the point that there is a qualitative difference between murders using firearms, which suggest planning and calculation, and traditional knife murders associated with bar brawls.

Colombia's judicial system is unable to cope with the level of crime. A study of crime in Medellín found that of 23,555 crimes committed in 1986, only 30 per cent resulted in a prosecution; 81.5 per cent of the 2,415 murders in the city in 1987 went unpunished. After 1984 a relatively new crime in the city, bank robbery, began to appear. Between 1984 and 1986 the number of bank robberies tripled in the city, from one a month to three a month; by 1987 there were six a month. The city is also notorious for car thefts; in 1986 1,320 cars and 1,065 motor bikes were stolen (*El Mundo* 11 June 1988).

DANE figures published in 1989 found that, in 10 years, the homicide rate had trebled, from 7,013 in 1978 to 21,129 in 1988 (*LAN Andean Report*, 27 July 1989). This rise in murders paralleled the emergence of an industry associated with violence the world over: drug trafficking, in particular the cocaine boom of the 1980s.

The cocaine economy

The drug industry first took root in Colombia with the marijuana boom of the 1970s. Marijuana was first grown in Urabá in the early years of the decade. It was exported in the banana boats with the complicity of the police and customs. But, as the US began to monitor the boats from Turbo more closely, cultivation moved to La Guajira where it flourished between 1974 and 1978. Here it was initially funded by North American drug dealers, while growers were easily found to plant a new and lucrative cash crop. Many of those who did so in the foothills of the Sierra Nevada de Santa Marta were peasant colonisers.

The age of marijuana came to an end in the late 1970s. In 1978 President Turbay, under suspicion himself of links with drug traffickers, acceded to US demands to stamp out the crop. A vast and costly programme was drawn up to militarise La Guajira, and 10,000 troops entered the area. They used a great deal of violence against the peasants, arbitrary arrests and curfews. The government of the department was moved to protest at the behaviour of the army. Although impressive numbers of statistics were produced on the quantities of marijuana destroyed, many concluded that one of the main effects of the exercise was to corrupt the army. So many of the army officers and soldiers became involved in the drug business themselves that the Minister of Defence decided to abandon the campaign and hand over the task of suppressing the drug to the police.

Although the US had pushed for the eradication of the drug in Colombia, it was now increasingly grown, legally or semi-legally, in a number of states in the US itself. By 1980, 40 per cent of the US market was supplied by home-grown marijuana, while Jamaica was allowed to supply the rest. The consequences for the Atlantic coast of Colombia were increased unemployment, crime, insecurity and poverty.

Even worse was the gradual replacement of marijuana with something far more lethal and lucrative — cocaine. The volume of cocaine exported to the US rose from 15 tonnes in 1978 to 270 tonnes in 1988; in 1988 a further 40 tonnes made their way to new European markets (*El Espectador* 4 October 1988). Within Colombia itself, *basuco* or crack (cocaine paste mixed with marijuana and/or tobacco) is smoked by increasing numbers of young people; in 1987, the Health Ministry estimated that over 400,000 Colombians were regular *basuco* smokers (Craig 1987:24).

Colombians had been involved only in the wholesale side of the marijuana market, but came to control an estimated 70-80 per cent of the world cocaine trade, including the most profitable area of distribution. Colombia has become the centre for processing and marketing coca from its Andean neighbours. Although it is not a major coca grower itself, an estimated 16,000-25,000 hectares have been planted with coca, mostly in Caquetá, Guaviare in the eastern *llanos* and in the south-eastern jungles of the so-called National Territories. Peru, on the other hand, has over 100,000 hectares planted and Bolivia between 35,000 and 50,000.

The fortunes made by Colombia's cocaine magnates are legendary. In 1984 they had an estimated annual income of between US$10,000 million and US$12,000 million, which fell to US$4,000 million by 1988. The US market had gradually become saturated and prices had fallen and transport costs risen. The cocaine mafia began penetrating the European market, where prices are much higher. In October 1987 *Fortune* magazine put two leading drug barons, Jorge Luis Ochoa and Pablo Escobar, among the 20 richest men in the world. Twice they have reportedly offered to pay off Colombia's foreign debt.

'Mama Coca'

It is convenient for the US to be able to point the accusing finger at the countries that produce and process cocaine, but as one deeply offended Colombian youth leader asked: 'wasn't it they who turned the coca leaf into a diabolical drug for sale in classy city discotheques?'

The dramatic increase in the production of the coca plant in Bolivia and Peru and its conversion to cocaine in Colombia is due to increased demand in the developed world. This situation led Peruvian President Alan García to state that 'drug trafficking is the only successful transnational in Latin America'. An article in *Fortune* magazine described it this way: 'the Colombian drug barons finance Andean peasants to cultivate coca in Peru and Bolivia and under their careful supervision, the coca "base" is transported to clandestine airports in the Colombian jungle for refining and purification.'

What accounts for the huge profits associated with cocaine is quite simply its illegal nature. It is one of those products where the final price bears little relation to production costs. The distribution chain which converts US$1 million worth of raw material into a US$5,000 million profit, makes drug trafficking the most lucrative business in the world. Or in other words: 'at the present moment, a kilogram of cocaine paste, the basic raw material, may cost about US$800. Once it has been purified and refined, the value goes up to US$4,000. Unloaded in one of the consumer countries, we can talk about US$12 to 15,000. Finally, once it has been sold in small doses for personal consumption, the original kilo of paste now has a value of approximately US$50,000'. (*Semana* 25 April 1989)

Despite this astronomical rate of return, only US$1,000 million out of the estimated US$4,000 million, is ploughed back into the country by the drug traffickers each year. The economy simply cannot absorb any more. The impact of drug money in the Colombian economy is something in the neighbourhood of 3 per cent of the national wealth.

The drug traffickers have purchased land and set up cattle ranches; they have created a spiderweb of limited companies with influence in the financial sector, sports clubs, mass communication media, the arts, and the cooperative sector; they have penetrated the export sector of the economy; and they have made large investments in urban land-holdings and real estate.

Pablo Escobar Gaviria, the Ochoa Clan, and Gonzalo Rodríguez Gacha, alias 'el Mexicano' representing the Medellín cartel, accumulated immense fortunes after becoming familiar with the possibilities of the US market. Due to their violent and bloodthirsty way of dealing with opposition, they soon made their presence felt, both within the country and on the international scene. The Cali cartel, on the other hand, under the leadership of Rodríguez Orejuela, is much more sophisticated and has more easily penetrated the social and political structures of the country. The bloody war being waged between the two cartels is due to the fight over markets; on the one hand for control of the New York market and on the other, the European. The fall of cocaine prices in the US has sent the Colombian drug barons further and further afield. Europe is the main target. But even far-away Japan has not been excluded from their prospecting.

In a few years a handful of drug barons had built up criminal empires in Colombia's main cities, particularly in Cali and, more notoriously, Medellín. Medellín had been the centre of a former drug mafia which had operated in the 1950s with links to Havana-based dealers. But it was a new Antioqueño mafia which emerged in the late 1960s and early 1970s and, after the transfer of marijuana from Urabá to La Guajira, which decided to specialise in cocaine, for which there was a growing demand from its US contacts.

The rise of the cocaine mafia has had profound social and political consequences, as well as economic ones. Indeed, the former might turn out to be more significant than the latter. Calculations on the impact of cocaine on the Colombian economy vary greatly. The most serious are on the conservative side, discounting claims that cocaine alone accounts for Colombia's economic successes in the 1980s while other Latin American countries floundered, although its role has by no means been insignificant.

An estimate in 1988 by two economists from the Colombian think-tank, FEDESARROLLO in *El Espectador* (4 October 1988), suggests that in that year about US$800 million to US$1,000 million (4 per cent of GDP) found its way back into Colombia. This may have been higher in earlier years when income as a whole from cocaine was higher, but there is not much in Colombia for the drug barons to buy, and large parts of their profits are deposited in US and European banks.

In Colombia the mafia has invested in conspicuous consumption -in paintings, racehorses, football teams, car imports, hotels, entertainment and luxury homes. The Federation of Real Estate Agents estimates that US$5,500,000 million was invested in real estate between 1979 and 1988 (*El Espectador* 25 November 1988). The mafia has also bought huge tracts of fertile land, one million hectares according to *Semana* (29 November 1988). It also has interests in banking and industry, in buying up shares in bankrupt companies. Many in the business elite have resisted being taken over by the drug barons.

Money from drugs came into Colombia 'officially' when the *ventanilla siniestra*, (side window), was opened in the Central Bank in the mid-1970s to take in some of the black-market dollars which were undermining the policy of creeping devaluations and adversely affecting manufacturing and agricultural exports. Over the years many other 'unofficial' ways have been found of laundering money. The impact of this foreign exchange has helped finance the external trade balance and has reduced the need for the draconian adjustment policies introduced elsewhere in Latin America in the 1980s, but cocaine is only one factor in this. Coffee earnings fared better than other commodities in the 1980s and experienced a bonanza in 1986. Although energy prices remained low until the late 1980s, oil and coal production still contributed to reducing the external energy deficit. This, combined with Colombia's history of flexible and pragmatic economic management, has helped the economy through the difficulties of the 1980s more than cocaine dollars.

Cocaine has had other economic spin-offs, notably in employment. Some estimates put the number of people directly or indirectly employed by the drug mafia at over half a million, which equals the numbers employed in manufacturing industry. Chauffeurs, bodyguards, assassins and servants of all kinds are on the mafia payroll, as well as those involved in the processing of the coca itself. When the industrial recession hit Medellín's textile industry in the early 1980s, the mafia could provide alternative employment and at much higher rates of pay than legal jobs.

By the late 1980s the cocaine bosses had become what could be described as a 'narco-bourgeoisie', anxious to legitimise themselves as businessmen and to ally themselves with the ruling elite in defending its class interests. That elite, however, has been reluctant to open up its exclusive social clubs to these 'nouveaux riches'.

A study of 20 middle- and top-ranking drug traffickers from Antioquia in 1988 (*Semana* 26 September 1988) reveals their humble origins — 70 per cent were of peasant origin (40 per cent from the rural middle and lower classes) and 30 per cent from the urban lower class; 55 per cent had only primary education, 35 per cent secondary and 10 per cent had been to university. Pablo Escobar himself was a child of the Medellín slums and one-time car thief. Since becoming a mafia boss, he has become renowned for his 'social work' in the poor areas of his home town, building houses and football grounds.

Colombia's cocaine economy has provided livelihoods where the state has failed. But it has also brought unprecedented violence and corruption, which have affected every institution of the state. The alliance of drug dealers, landowners and the army in the 1980s has cost the lives of thousands of popular leaders and activists. It is a reflection of the character of Colombia's ruling elite that it prefers such an alliance to introducing reforms that could create an equitable and democratic country.

The failure to reform

The Colombia of macro-economic statistics is a success story, particularly compared to the severe economic crises facing even its most industrialised Latin American neighbours. Only Chile, where military dictatorship has controlled political pressures from below, offered anything comparable in the Latin America of the 1980s.

But Colombia seen through the eyes of the majority of its population is another story. The rapidity of the social changes of the 1960s and 1970s, accelerated by the population movements created by *La Violencia*, far exceeded the capacity of the state. This pace of change would have created problems for any underdeveloped country, but in Colombia, apart from the brief interlude of López Pumarejo's 'Revolution on the March', social intervention has not been seen as a significant function of the state. The state's role has been primarily to provide the conditions for private sector-led growth.

The relationship of the state to the people is therefore one of neglect and, in many areas, abandonment. The modernisation and expansion of one sector of the economy has taken place regardless of the rights and needs of the majority of the population. The battle between cattle ranchers and peasant colonisers for the agricultural frontier is reminiscent of the Wild West. Unhindered by social responsibility, the private sector has pushed ahead, swallowing up the fertile land and resources to the benefit of the elite and middle-class professionals who have grown up to service it.

Rural poverty: La Mojana's lament

Two hours from Sincelejo, along a terrible road, is Magangué, a port on the river Magdalena and the main commercial centre of the area. From there, by river, you reach the six villages around La Mojana on the borders of the departments of Sucre and Bolívar, with their population of 71,700 people, 80 per cent of whom live in the rural zones.

Although it is Bolívar's second town, in Magangué you already have the impression of a region which has been forgotten and where the state is absent. The river exudes a concentrated odour of decay: it has ceased to be the lung of the region, but is a sewer which collects all kinds of industrial waste and organic residues along its one thousand kilometres or more.

The inhabitants of such a poor region must pay excessive transport costs. The cost of the river boat is double the cost of a road journey taking a similar time. The people have no alternative because there is no other way to reach these villages other than the Magdalena and Cauca rivers or the deep channels which feed into them such as La Mojana and Panseuita.

We leave early in the morning for Sucre in order not to lose a day in Magangué, as there are not many river boats during the day. After nearly two hours up river we arrive at a small village, distinguished by its tall and beautiful church, two main streets, the office of the Agrarian Fund and the police station. We are now in Sucre, some 190 kilometres from Sincelejo with 19,681 inhabitants of which only 3,400 live in this, the municipal capital. It is market day. The peasants are trying to sell their goods (coconuts, avocados, apricots). The middlemen wander freely among them, offering low prices . . .

After midday, along with a peasant from the *parcelas* (the name given to the small plots of land in San Rafael and El Socorro won by peasant struggle), we take the road to our destination, the village of Travesía, two and a half hours away on horseback. The prolonged summer has made the road passable, but a few days later, after a short but intense cloudburst over the area, the road was virtually buried in mud and in the lower parts, water came up to the horses' bellies.

Almost half the urban houses of the La Mojana region have no piped water and what there is doesn't reach minimal health standards. There is virtually no sewerage system. In the rural area, less than one per cent of the population has access to piped water. Electricity reaches under half the houses in the municipal capitals and only just under one-fifth of rural houses, despite what the Treasury calls a surplus of electricity supply. Almost half the population is illiterate; only 15 out of every 100 children finish primary school, fewer than two of every 100 finish secondary education and only 2 out of every 1,000 gain access to higher education. The school of El Socorro, for example, had to be built by the peasants themselves, and the teacher's salary has to partly paid by them. The teacher has to teach all five levels of primary education to over 48 children in two shifts. In Sucre, there are 3.6 doctors and 27 beds for every 10,000 inhabitants, one hospital and two health posts. At the time of our visit, the workers at the hospital were on strike against sackings, the lack of budget, and the clientelist politics used to appoint personnel . . .

The *parceleros* of El Socorro and San Rafael, told me the history of almost fourteen years of struggle against exploitation in the region. It began when 40 families decided to invade a piece of land of 800 hectares owned by the landowner, Remberto Vitar. While many families were dying of hunger for want of land to work, the landowner kept this land idle. Then, and for the next eleven years, the peasant families were attacked,arrested, harassed and taken to court. Thirty-eight peasants were arrested and taken to Sincelejo by a police patrol. A police station was set up in El Socorro; the peasants were accused of being subversives and Travesía was declared a 'red zone'. Often the peasants were stopped on the roads and forced to march with the police patrol; sometimes under the excuse of a State of Siege, the police forced the families to stay in their houses.

Eventually, the peasants were able to win some land, and the repressive action had eased off over the last three years. but now they faced other, more subtle, pressures. The staff of INCORA and the Agrarian Fund wouldn't give them credit or other state services, because they are *parceleros* and not private landowners. The credit goes to the landowners and the intermediaries. The latter use money which should go into expanding agricultural production to travel the rural areas paying derisory sums for the peasants' produce, mostly rice and maize. The state contributes to this, as the areas of production are virtually isolated from the centres of consumption. Rather than run the risks of the transport costs and the uncertain prices which they are paid in Magangué, the peasants prefer to sell to these intermediaries, who artificially raise the price for the consumers with no benefit to the producers . . .
(Prieto 1987)

In these circumstances people have sought a means of survival outside the orbit of the state, which often means outside the law. Paths to quick enrichment, such as drugs, are rapidly seized upon. If there is a culture of violence in Colombia that exceeds that of other poor areas of Latin America, it is historically as well as socially rooted. It is through violence that the ruling class has settled its differences in bloody civil wars. When they finally settled their political differences, members of the ruling elite reasserted their dominance over the political order, as they had done over the economic one. But they constructed a political order that was unable to adapt to the process of economic modernisation and was incapable of reform.

Chronology

1958   National Front government creates *Acción Comunal* (Community Action) Committees throughout the country

1964   Pro-Communist Party Confederation of Colombian Workers, CSTC, established

1970-74   ANUC leads widespread mobilisations and land recoveries in the countryside

1971   CRIC is established in Toribio

1977   First national civic strike in September

1977-78   Peasant movement declines and the multiple division of ANUC takes place

1979   New trade union confederation, the CGT, set up, linked to international Christian Democrat organisation, the CLAT

1981   Independent trade unionists unite to form the Committee of Trade Union Unity, (CUSI) Second national civic strike takes place amid unprecedented repression

1982   National Organisation of the Indigenous People of Colombia, ONIC, is brought together during its First Congress National Movement for the Human Rights of the Black Communities of Colombia, CIMARRON, is launched in Benaventura

1983   The National Coordinating Committee of the Civic Movement, CNMC, established in October

1985   Third national civic strike

1986   United Workers Central, (CUT), is formed with a clear majority of the unionised labour force.

2.2 The Popular Response

Historically, Colombia's two traditional parties have enjoyed a virtual monopoly on political life. The peasant and workers' movements of the 1920s and 1930s and the broader social mobilisation of the 1940s were short-lived. Party violence destroyed what was left of them and, by the end of the 1950s, only organisations loyal to the traditional parties existed among the people. By the 1960s the trade union movement had split into the pro-Liberal CTC, the pro-Conservative UTC, and the pro-Communist Union Confederation of Colombian Workers (CSTC). The peasantry had no organisation apart from the small Conservative Party-affiliated National Agrarian Federation (FANAL) and was isolated and traumatised after the years of violent conflict. The weakness of the popular movement contrasted with the ruling class's strength and unity around the National Front. It was not until the 1970s and 1980s that popular movements once more emerged to assert their independence from the traditional parties and to challenge the dominant classes.

Efforts to build an effective popular movement in the 1970s were fraught with difficulties. The traditional party machines still intervened to manipulate and divide. Opposition organisations replicated much of the paternalism of the traditional parties whose patronage politics encouraged people to make their support conditional on receiving a favour. Attempts by the MRL and later ANAPO to provide channels of discontent were thwarted by the traditional elites who, by the time of the 1974 election, had squashed any electoral or political alternatives. Elitism and sectarianism characterised the left; its inability to make inroads into the political system generated frustration and impatience. It had to learn to root itself in the people and to respect the uneven pace of grassroots politicisation.

The movement grew in the 1970s with great geographical and political diversity. It contained Indians demanding their territorial and cultural rights in the south, banana workers waging a bloody battle for basic union recognition in the north, peasants fighting for land and colonisers for basic services in the east, and black people organising for the first time in Colombia's most backward department of Chocó in the west. In the smaller towns multi-class civic protests over lack of services became widespread, while in the larger cities urban workers sought to break free from the shackles of traditional party control.

The peasant movement was at the forefront of the people's response in the first half of the 1970s. After breaking from state sponsorship, it grew into the most militant popular organisation in the country's history, only to face gradual defeat, division and demoralisation after 1974. Its position at the forefront of popular struggles was then taken up by the urban civic movements. Between 1974 and 1978, 61 per cent of the civic strikes of the decade took place, culminating in the national civic strike of 1977. Meanwhile urban labour also became more militant, with public-sector workers leading the strike activity of the 1970s.

Between 1979 and 1981, popular mobilisation declined under the impact of repressive state legislation. The popular movement adapted to the repression and began to construct nationally-coordinated movements. The indigenous movement set up the National Organisation of Indigenous People of Colombia (ONIC) and factions of ANUC, which refused to capitulate to the government, began the process of reunification and of rebuilding the organisation. Important unification and coordination work was begun among the trade unions and civic movements. Rejection of the traditional parties was at the heart of all these initiatives.

By the 1980s Colombia's popular movement already had a history rich with experience. But it had been deeply fragmented by the political influences competing for its support. Other factors reinforced this fragmentation: uneven regional development, the weakness of the urban working class, isolation and lack of coordination. All these factors held back the emergence of a strong and unified popular opposition to Colombia's ruling order. But by the 1980s, many lessons had been learnt. The movement grew in numbers, militancy and level of organisation, but amid unprecedented brutality as the ruling elite found its time-honoured means of social mediation — the traditional political parties — no longer able to play that role.

The peasant movement
Militancy and mobilisation (1970-4)

The peasantry began to respond to the encroachment of commercial agriculture and to the expansion of cattle ranches in the 1960s, but these were mostly spontaneous responses. The dynamic movement of the 1930s had lost much of its former vigour. The Ministry of Labour estimates that out of 567 registered peasant leagues and syndicates, only 89 were still active in 1965, and most of these were on the Atlantic coast (Zamosc 1986:37). This area was less touched by *La Violencia* that had devastated peasant organisation elsewhere, but conflicts with cattle ranchers were acute. The Communist Party retained some influence, and in the 1960s the Conservative Party had set up its rural branch of the UTC, FANAL, but it gained support in only a very few areas.

ANUC was the first national peasant organisation. It was set up by President Lleras Restrepo in 1967 to encourage peasants to participate in the provision of services and to press for agrarian reform. The organisation was to be outside the control of the political parties, but not autonomous. It would provide a direct link between the peasants and the state; behind it lay an attempt by the ruling class to build an alliance between the peasants and the reformers in the ruling class.

The state's financial and organisational resources created a huge and sophisticated organisation which, by its first congress in July 1970, represented just under one million peasants. But, while encouragement by the state gave it legitimacy, it came into being as a grassroots body, based on representational principles.

The initial organisational drive centred on the areas of highest land concentration. Promotors were trained by radical Brazilian, Argentinian and Chilean social scientists, as well as Colombians, who talked, in the words of a national peasant leader, Froilán Rivera, 'about the agrarian problem and land concentration . . . the promotors came with anti-oligarchic ideas and transmitted notions of independence to the peasantry' (*ibid*:225-6).

Between 1970 and 1971 the movement gradually moved away from its government sponsors. Demonstrations, occupations of INCORA offices and land invasions grew. February 1971 saw the most widespread popular mobilisations in the history of the country. An estimated 15,000 families participated in occupations of some 350 estates in 13 departments.

The movement was particularly strong on the Atlantic coast, a region of traditional *latifundia* where landlessness was already an important source of conflict. At least 51 per cent of the 1971 land invasions took place there, 21 per cent among the *minifundia* of the Andean regions, another 19 per cent in the inner valleys where commercial agriculture was transforming rural life, 6 per cent in the cattle region of the eastern *llanos* and 1.5 per cent in areas of colonisation.

ANUC was faced with the challenge of how to create a national organisation out of very disparate situations. Debates raged around the organisation's platform, as the agrarian problem came to be defined in political terms. A number of political groups had attempted to influence the movement. The Communist Party lost its influence early on when, in 1971, the organisation voted to abstain in the forthcoming elections — a rebuttal of its position at the time. Trotskyists, various intellectuals, and students in socialist groupings became the organisation's early advisers and it was under their influence that ANUC adopted the slogan, 'land without masters', which called upon the peasants to carry out the agrarian reform themselves, not to wait upon the state or abide by its legal processes. But they did little grassroots work among the peasants, believing that the working class, not the peasants, were the revolutionary force.

The Maoists gained a more lasting influence. There were three main splinters from the Communist Party after the Sino-Soviet split of the mid-1960s. The Independent Revolutionary Workers' Movement (MOIR) adopted a legalist path of electoral participation and urban trade-union work. But the Marxist-Leninist League (*Liga M-L*) and the more important Communist Party-Marxist Leninist (PC-ML), which also had an armed wing, the Popular Liberation Army (EPL), that operated in the Upper Sinú region, sent their cadres, mostly students, into the countryside in late 1971. They believed that conditions were ripe for a 'popular democratic revolution on the road to socialism' and saw, in the emergence of ANUC, the opportunity to develop the peasantry's revolutionary consciousness and praxis. They established strong bases of support in Córdoba, Sucre and Bolívar. Their slogan, 'land for the tiller', which expressed the peasants' wish for a plot of their own, won overwhelming approval at ANUC's Second National Congress in 1973.

Meanwhile, the rural *gremios* had gone on the offensive. In a joint memorandum to the government in 1971, they demanded 'an immediate end to the impending threat to the institutions and the social peace of the nation'. Together with representatives of the two traditional parties and the government (now under the Conservative, Misael Pastrana), they met in the town of Chicoral in January 1972. The resulting Pact of Chicoral has been described as the 'formal declaration of agrarian counter-reform'. New legislation in 1973 gave important concessions to landowners and the government agreed to give financial incentives to large-scale mechanised agriculture.

Two weapons were now used against the organised peasants — division and repression. ANUC members who remained loyal to the traditional parties were manipulated by the government into splitting and forming a parallel organisation, know as the ANUC-Armenia, named after the town where its first congress took place. The former ANUC, now without government support, held its Second National Congress in Sincelejo in 1973, which was inaugurated by a demonstration of 10,000 peasants from Sucre. ANUC-Sincelejo found that the army was now brought in to deal with land invasions and peasants were arrested and ill-treated. Some landowners reorganised the *pájaros* (assassination squads).

It was against this background that the last large peasant mobilisation took place in 1974. Weaker than previously and concentrated in fewer regions, the movement was torn by a number of conflicts. The left had played an important role in encouraging militancy when ANUC might easily have fallen into the manipulative hands of the traditional parties. But it, too, had manipulated the movement. Believing that the countryside was ripe for insurrection, the Maoists sought to turn land invasions into armed conflict. In 1973 they argued that the revolutionary situation along the entire Atlantic coast was such that it was possible to make 'a direct call for the general insurrection of the masses'. Their extremism and their attempts to control the peasants' daily lives created serious disagreements.

Those opposing them entrenched themselves in ANUC's political committee, but it's leadership was degenerating into factions and secret caucuses, with left-wing intellectuals rather than peasant leaders guiding the movement's ideological development. In the absence of strong organisation among the urban working class, these intellectuals acted as substitute allies for the peasants, but were unable to break the isolation of the peasant struggles. National leaders rallied to the independent line they advocated in opposition to the Maoists. They controlled the funds flowing from foreign aid agencies and from the bureaucratic apparatus and, at the Third National Congress in 1974, launched a successful offensive against the Maoists.

Division and defeat (1974-81)

A sectarian and manipulative leadership took over ANUC as the PC-ML split and began to lose its hold on the peasantry. The grassroots membership was confused and demoralised and the peasant movement lost its momentum.

It had, however, made some gains in its years of combativity. Three times as many families benefited from land redistribution between 1970 and 1979 than between 1962 and 1969, reaching a peak at the time of ANUC's greatest activity. Although the numbers affected were relatively low, in certain areas militancy declined as a result. ANUC had to face the problem of what to do once the peasants had won their access to land. There were cases, too, of peasants giving up their occupied lands, sometimes in exchange for money. In others, however, peasants were forcibly evicted as courts decided in favour of landowners. INCORA — the supposed vehicle for land reform — was itself now operating under the conditions of the counter-reform.

Interview with leaders of ANUC

Gabriel Salazar: 'Land invasions began in about 1971; they initially had a very defined aim corresponding to the immediate needs of the peasants. From 1971-72, the struggle shifted as sectors of the left began to win influence among the peasants, talking of the struggle against the large landowners. Thereafter it was no longer just a question of winning a piece of land, but of defeating the landowners. That's what happened in the departments of Sucre, Bolívar, Córdoba and Guajira, against those with over 2,000 hectares, much of which was unproductive. Sometimes the land invasions were carried out by as few as 25 or 30 people.

The situation has changed over the years, in terms of repression. Today a land invasion has much less chance of success, especially when landowners with more economic and political power are hit. In Sucre, for example, there is a family called the Guerra-Tulena. When their land has been invaded, the army and the police have been sent in. The names of the peasant invaders are put on a list, and the government has legislation that says that those who invade land are attacking private property. So the land invasions of today take place in very different circumstances to those between 1971 and 1981. I remember in 1973 over 450 families were expelled from their land near the Venezuelan border. We sent a commission there and all the peasants gathered on a farm, called Aguadulce, on the highway from Santa Marta to Riohacha. The lands were owned by Martín Ceballos, and we won the fight for those lands, although it was valuable land by the sea. Our sheer numbers helped us win the land invasion.

That land was then acquired by INCORA, who gave it as compensation to those peasants who had been expelled from the Venezuelan frontier, in lots of up to 25 hectares a person. INCORA gave them titles and credit to create an *empresa comunitaria* (a community enterprise, a semi-collective farm which combines individual and community farming in different proportions according to the type of settlement). This was a kind of success, but there were negative aspects which we are still trying to overcome. We have a problem of how to maintain the economic and political conditions and the discipline which enable the organisation to survive. Land invasions have to have an element of conscientisation of the peasants; our experience in Guajira, for instance, was that four years after the invasion, the very same landowner began to give economic help to the peasants to grow marijuana. The peasants then began to fight between themselves. Then they themselves named a commission to sell the land they had worked back to the landowner.

In Sucre, Bolívar and in many other parts, the peasants have often not held onto the land, but have had to sell it. Sometimes this is because of debt; when they receive credit it is at high interest rates and there is no security in the harvest. And in some parts of the coast, transport costs more than growing the crop. The peasant is asphyxiated by the debt, and then has to sell his last resource, the land. That's why, today the organisation is putting a lot of emphasis on production. But also, where INCORA has given credit, people often pay more attention to it than to us, the peasants' organisation. We think that the peasants must look to their own organisations to solve their problems. Otherwise, we support the struggle to win the land, but INCORA wins the influence among the peasants. The peasant movement has often lacked a policy with respect to these problems. Some people say even, that it is the bourgeoisie which has benefited from all our struggles

Often we have failed to talk at a level most people understand; we start from a belief that everyone has a certain level, but this isn't always the case. We are organising education and literacy programmes and seminars to raise awareness amongst the peasants. We are trying to give our struggle continuity, and we think it important that the peasant links up with other popular sectors.'

Angel Tolosa: 'I want to give an example of one of the more recent land invasions . . . the case of Yacaranda. The great majority of land invasions have been spontaneous and we have often organised the peasants after they have taken the initiative to invade the land. The case of Yacaranda, in the municipality of Barrancabermeja, is important; it was a spontaneous invasion which took place at the beginning of 1980. On 29 August, in the early morning, the landowner, Harold Rodríguez, managed to dislodge the peasants, about 30 families who were occupying about 1,200 hecatres. That seems a lot of land, but it was very poor quality, acid, with only one good part by the River Sogamoso. The peasants were thrown off the land onto the highway which runs between Barrranca and Bucaramanga; their houses were burnt. They reached Barranca by foot, and sought help from the oil workers union, USO, because ANUC which had been very important in the area in the 1970s had practically disappeared. The USO called the *compañeros* who were trying to relaunch the organisation (ANUC). The expulsion had been illegal, because the peasants had occupied the land for eight months. But the landowner had told the authorities that the M-19 guerrillas were there, and because of this both the army and the police had come to dislodge them and beat them.

The first thing we needed to do was to bring what had happened to the attention of the public and denounce it. The peasants were in the USO offices for two days, but we decided then to occupy the Barranca Cathedral. That's what we did on 2 September at 6pm. The peasants went to the mass, but when it ended, a peasant began to speak and said that from that moment the church was in the hands of the peasants. Worshippers, and more peasants and children came in with their pans and mats, and we closed the door. At the time, the message of Puebla in Mexico (the Bishops' Conference of 1979) had a considerable impact, and immediately there was a battle between the two currents in the church. The traditional wing said we should be expelled, that it was sacrilegious, because the peasants had to do all their necessities in the church as there were no bathrooms, and they had to wash dishes in the baptismal fount. That was an affront to God, for them. But the other wing said it was important that the peasants came to the house of God, and that they shouldn't be expelled. At the same time, the workers began a campaign of solidarity and linked up with the student movement, creating quite a serious problem of public order. The Bishop tried to get the security forces to intervene more than once. The Security Statute was in operation, and eleven of the peasants had been arrested. The government then said it would return the land to us, but we wanted the peasants to be freed as well. We stayed in the Cathedral for 43 days until the *compañeros* were freed, although they had been sentenced to 60 days in prison. The same judge who had authorised the expulsion from the land had to take the peasants back again, and he was then sanctioned for having ordered it in the first place.

But what was also important was the community life in the church. We didn't have enough resources for three meals a day. Delegations went out every day in search of solidarity. The people of Barranca supported us and brought us a television. When we returned to the land, we had a big party and solidarity continued to arrive. People lived and worked together while they rebuilt their houses. But then the land was divided up again, and I think that the political work was insufficient, because then INCORA went in and gave people titles to the land and people began to work on their own again. But the experience in the church had taught us a lot. We began to think of new tactics after that. A meeting in the north-east approved what we call "new tactics for land invasions". We agreed that the invasions should be planned in advance, that beforehand an invasion committee should be organised as well as a committee of landless peasants. And that this committee should carry out political work and a technical survey should be carried out on the productive capacity of the land, its size, the availability of water, that it should belong by preference to the largest landowners. Three forms of operation were proposed: that people be granted the land but prohibited from selling it for a certain period; secondly, to give out small plots of land around a communally owned piece; and thirdly to farm the land communally. This last form would be very difficult to implement unless the peasants were politicised. We wanted to avoid the vicious circle of taking the land, and then seeing it privatised and returned to the landowner, already cultivated. That's why the struggle for the land takes place within a political and ideological framework. So that when a landowners says we are invading his land, we say that we are recovering what belongs to us, what belonged to our ancestors. The landowners also often say, "well, it's alright, the peasants struggle against us for the land for four years, but every four years they vote for us as their representatives". We believe we have to change that, that the peasant should recognise that the landowner isn't just an enemy because he has the land, but also because he represents another class. Today, there are land invasions which approximate to what I have described, especially in the south of Cesar, where land is invaded and farmed communally.'

Pastrana's successor, López Michelsen, was equally committed to the Pact of Chicoral and was prepared to halt land invasions with repression (ANUC reported over 40 peasant deaths and hundreds of arrests during

1975), but he also offered certain concessions to better-off peasants through his Integrated Rural Development (DRI) programme which aimed to increase productivity in the peasant sector.

The areas of greatest land conflict were also those where traditional relations of production were disintegrating before the advance of capitalist agriculture. Both Pastrana and López Michelsen gave incentives which encouraged a massive expansion of commercial agriculture in the 1970s. This created many new job opportunities in some of the most conflict-ridden regions, such as Sucre and Bolívar, and agricultural wages improved in these years. Seasonal migration to Venezuela was another source of work. By the late 1970s some 1.5 million Colombians, many from the Atlantic coast, were crossing the border to work in the sugar-cane and cotton fields. Yet another source of income for peasants from the region was marijuana. By the 1970s there were an estimated 6,000 producers in the Sierra Nevada alone, employing 13,000 rural labourers. One study suggests that 30,000 families depended totally or partially on marijuana, one in seven of the rural homes on the Atlantic coast.

ANUC turned its attentions to rural workers, but this was a highly heterogeneous sector. Permanent workers in the big processing plants of the oil-palm and seed industries, and in the cotton gins and sugar plantations, were already organised. Elsewhere organisation was difficult; the cattle estates employed relatively few workers, while the large numbers of temporary workers on the coffee and cotton estates saw themselves as peasants as much as workers and, despite their low wages and poor conditions, did not take readily to the idea of trade unions and collective action.

The government had gone on the offensive in other ways. More controllable *Acción Comunal* (Community Action) Committees were used in areas of strongest peasant activity to revive loyalty to the state and local party bosses. Their numbers doubled from 1966-79, but they increased five- to six-fold on the Atlantic coast, in the eastern *llanos* and in the colonisation areas. In the light of ANUC's failure on the trade-union front, many peasants turned to local bosses to resolve their problems. ANUC-Armenia was reactivated with government encouragement and began to address some of the peasants' immediate problems and to negotiate solutions with the appropriate government institutions.

Despite a burst of activity in 1977-8 ANUC-Sincelejo was in decline and the counter-reform process victorious. By the end of 1977 INCORA has been rendered virtually powerless to redistribute land. In that year regulations favouring landowners were passed to deal with disputes involving clarification of the ownership of public lands. Within ANUC, events took an extraordinary turn. The left-wing intellectuals who had influenced it formed a peasant party and fought the 1978 elections, claiming that ANUC's historical role had been a 'bourgeois democratic' (not a 'democratic-revolutionary') one and advocating a rapprochement with the traditional parties and alliances with the new bourgeois groups that had emerged with the export boom of the 1970s. The rank-and-file base that remained now left ANUC, while the leaders made a deal with the Turbay government and moved to reunite with ANUC-Armenia. Amid a good deal of manoeuvring this took place under government auspices in 1981.

The peasants had been defeated in the space of a decade. While the causes for this are numerous, one important one was the influence of the left, which brought its doctrinaire politics and internal divisions into the peasant union, neglecting the trade-union function of the peasant organisation and treating the peasants as a political instrument in a wider struggle. In the absence of a strong workers' movement in the cities, the peasants were isolated and susceptible to political manipulation of all sorts. At the same time, the government's counter-offensive proved very effective.

Rebuilding ANUC-Sincelejo

In many rural areas tension remained high. The expansion of commercial agriculture had expelled peasants from their land, but the labour power freed could not be absorbed in either the countryside or the city. Pressure on the land increased as the agricultural frontier began to close and the traditional option of colonisation, which an estimated 10 per cent of the rural population had taken, gradually disappeared. Colonisers meanwhile remained under permanent pressure from ranchers seeking to expand their grazing land.

The inadequacy of agrarian reform was resounding, and poverty in the rural areas remained endemic. In 1984 even the Ministry of Agriculture admitted that, in terms of quality of life, the peasant population was 15 years behind the urban one. Government policy remained firmly in favour of capitalist agriculture.

Peasant activists, including a new generation of peasant leaders, began to rebuild the movement. Those who had refused to accept the reunification of ANUC-Armenia and the old leaders of ANUC-Sincelejo were divided into five groups (one of which later split). A sixth, independent sector, had also emerged, which wanted to reassert ANUC's trade-union character and allow a plurality of parties within the organisation. It emphasised work with the rank and file and one of its early disagreements with the other groups was over its assertion that unity should not be achieved through leaders presenting an agreement to the rank and file, but the other way round.

Between 1981 and 1985 three meetings were held to discuss the creation of a unified ANUC, independent of the state and with a class-based programme. A number of other organisations (some local, some regional) also worked with the peasants, while, apart from the government-recognised ANUC-Armenia with its offices in the Ministry of Agriculture, the Communist Party and each of the traditional parties had its own peasant organisation. Over the same period numerous, mostly spontaneous, isolated and uncoordinated land invasions occurred. An estimated 12,500 families took part in invasions in 68 municipalities in 16 departments. Over 40 peasants were killed, over 500 wounded and about 1,000 arrested.

The groups seeking to rebuild the peasant movement entered into the debates on the left over whether or not to support President Belisario Betancur's national dialogue. But when it became clear that no serious agrarian reform was being proposed and the national dialogue collapsed, moves towards working unity, if not political unity, gathered pace. The reconstruction of ANUC-Sincelejo finally took place in August 1987.

The independents won the majority's support for their position that the organisation was a trade union, not a political body, and that emphasis should be given to the needs of the peasant sector (men and women), not just for land, but also for health, education and culture. But while unity had finally been achieved, in the end it had been worked out by leaders rather than by the peasant movement's base.

The process of unity remained problematic. The movement was divided over issues such as whether or not to use parliament to press for agrarian reform. Some believed that ANUC should sponsor its own project through congressmen on the left, while others maintained that, considering 80 per cent of the congressmen were landowners, such an exercise was futile and that the peasants should carry out their own land reform. Another issue concerned the unity of the peasant movement as a whole, not just of ANUC. Should attempts be made to unite with ANUC-Armenia? One organisation within ANUC, the National Association of Agricultural Workers (ANTA), left because it believed ANUC-Armenia should be brought in. It joined the National United Agricultural Federation (FENSUAGRO), a peasant organisation affiliated to the new workers central, the Unitary Confederation of Workers (CUT). The CUT wanted to create one coordinating body for the whole peasant movement, but ANUC claimed that while it was an organisation of small and medium peasants, FENSUAGRO mostly represented agricultural workers and the two should remain separate.

Three competing options emerged for the peasant movement — the CUT via FENSUAGRO, ANUC-Sincelejo, and ANUC-Armenia. Each represented a different perspective on the role of popular organisation.

ANUC-Armenia, which was close to the government, was committed to the 1988 agrarian reform proposal, which every other organisation rejected. The dominant political perspective within the CUT was to open up political spaces (including electoral ones) and to work within them. This carried a danger that the popular movement's demands would be subordinated to that objective. ANUC-Sincelejo, the largest of the organisations, advocated the most radical option. It looked back to the positive experiences in ANUC's early history when the movement generated mass participation and peasant leaders emerged from its base, but tried also to learn the lessons of its defeat. The repression of the late 1980s would fall heavily on ANUC-Sincelejo in the midst of its efforts to rebuild and consolidate the peasant movement.

The indigenous movement

Today there are no more than half a million Indians in Colombia, or just under 2 per cent of the population. These are made up of about 150 different (considerably dispersed) ethnic groups, with the highest concentrations in the Cauca (some 200,000), La Guajira (about 100,000) and Nariño (about 60,000). In addition, there are a few dispersed groups of lowland forest dwellers in the Amazon and Pacific coastal regions, the plain dwellers of the eastern *llanos*, the desert Indians of La Guajira and the highland Indians of the Colombian Andes, from Nariño in the south to the Sierra Nevada de Santa Marta in the north.

The CRIC: early history

The Páez, Coconucos and Guambianos of the Cauca are by far the most organised of these Indian groups. The Indians in this region fiercely resisted the Spanish conquest and subsequent attempts to encroach on their reservations (*resguardos*), which the Spaniards had initially granted them. Many *resguardos* were broken up and the Indians forced to pay a land-rent (*terraje*) for use of the land. The Indian councils (*cabildos*), which exercised political and administrative authority over the resguardos, either collapsed or came under the control of traditional politicians, government-appointed mayors or the church. Although originally set up by the Spaniards, over the centuries the Indians had come to regard their *cabildos* as the guarantor of their identity and independence. Losing both them and their lands was thus a double blow to the indigenous population. Both were theoretically protected by law, in particular Law 89 of 1890, which the government has often tried to change and the Indians to implement.

As a result of the seizure of Indian lands, the department of Cauca is dominated by *latifundia* — devoted mainly to traditional large-scale ranching in which the landowners leave vast tracts of land unused. The mostly Indian peasants live by settled agriculture, growing subsistence food on plots that can scarcely maintain a family. There is very little industry or employment outside agriculture in the department, which is backward both economically and in terms of social provision.

The historical legacy of dispossession and subjugation did not lead to a deep-rooted indigenous movement until the 1970s. Encouraged to organise by the establishment of ANUC and by the influence of committed anthropologists, in February 1971 some 2,000 Indians met in Toribio to set up the Regional Indigenous Council of the Cauca (CRIC). The seven-point programme agreed on at its second meeting in 1971 has remained its platform, namely:

1. To recover the reservation lands
2. To increase the size of the reservations
3. To strengthen the Indian councils
4. To stop paying the land rents
5. To make known the laws concerning Indians and to insist on their proper application
6. To defend the history, language and customs of the Indians
7. To train Indian teachers to teach in the indigenous languages in ways relevant to the present situation of the people

Early successes helped to create a strong and representative organisation. From the beginning emphasis was on mobilisation of the grassroots and direct action. Five thousand hectares were recovered in the first three years of CRIC's existence. Many of its initial campaigns were directed against the local Liberal Party boss, Víctor Mosquera Chaux, and the Archbishop of Popayán, Mgr Arce Vivas, who together dominated the region politically and culturally. The struggle to wrest the *cabildos* from the control of the traditional party bosses has become one of the most important focuses of the Indian struggle. By 1986 CRIC had breathed life into over 40 *cabildos* and turned them into the legitimate representatives of the Indian people. It had also recovered 30,000 hectares of land.

The CRIC: politics and organisation

CRIC developed certain characteristics which enabled it to avoid many of the pitfalls into which ANUC had fallen and which ensured its growth and consolidation while ANUC disintegrated. Undoubtedly it has been helped by the organisation's social and cultural homogeneity, although the Indians of the Cauca have not been without their own conflicts, particularly between Paeces and Guambianos.

First of all, CRIC sought to express the immediate demands of the indigenous population rather than to turn the movement into a political organisation overnight — although CRIC has never been 'unpolitical'. The same revolutionary groups that took over ANUC tried to take over CRIC, but the Indians struggled hard and successfully to retain their autonomy. CRIC was initially linked to ANUC at the departmental and national levels, but with the growing sectarianism of the latter organisation and its failure to take the Indian question seriously, the two began to go their separate ways, definitively after the 1977 Fourth Congress. Gregorio Palechar, a leader of CRIC, expressed the nature of its disagreement with ANUC as follows:

> We don't have any discrepancies with the peasant class, not even with ANUC. The problem is with ANUC's leaders . . . We have our own specificities and problems as Indians . . . They have accused us of being racists, indigenists, trade unionists. They have defamed our movement and our leaders. They wanted to swallow our organisation in order to lead it to political goals . . . We see the Indians . . . as an exploited class, in a process of conscientisation. The idea is to keep working until the people understand what has to be done. The political stage will come, but first we have to consolidate. Each organisation should develop the consciousness of its class: ANUC with the peasants, the trade unions with the workers, etc., in order finally to reach a political level in which we can all come together. (Zamosc 1984:249)

Criticisms of ANUC (in a CRIC document presented to the Third ANUC Congress of 1973) reveal crucial differences in the approaches of the theoreticians advising the two organisations, not over the need for radical political change, but over how to bring this about and, in particular, over the role of the grassroots of the movement:

> According to our conception, the fundamental efforts of ANUC should be dedicated to grassroots work which allows a real and solid strengthening of the organisation, and its increasing credibility as the struggles themselves allow the masses, and not just the leaders, to move beyond merely trade-union objectives. The politicisation of the movement and its cadres is indispensable if we are to fulfil our role in the liberation of our country, but politicisation must come as a result of a

Joe Fish

Indian reading indigenous group's newspaper waiting for a human rights demonstration to begin, Cauca.

process in which you cannot jump stages and in which patient and serious work must be the fundamental norm.

These ideas were put into practice in a number of ways. Emphasis was put on mobilising around the Indians' concrete and immediate demands, while keeping up the level of combativity even when some had won their land and retaken control of their *cabildos*. Grassroots political education was important for maintaining awareness of the indigenous population's role in the country's wider struggles, as well as for direct participation in those struggles. CRIC advised local ANUC groups, as well as the shanty-town dwellers and urban workers in Cauca's capital, Popayán.

CRIC also trained its members in administration, set up bilingual schools and ran cultural activities, health programmes, legal assistance and its own newsletter. Within the recovered *resguardos*, CRIC has encouraged community enterprises (*empresas comunitarias*) or semi-collective farms. The *cabildos*, which traditionally distributed land individually, have been at the forefront of the struggle to recover land and distribute it communally. They also form the basis of CRIC's own organisation. The *cabildos* are elected by their communities every year by secret vote. Battles continue in some areas to regain popular control of the *cabildo*. Elsewhere they are under the Indians' own control and operate as a virtual parallel power to the state.

The landowners and government have reacted repressively to this movement. Large landowners who had failed to modernise saw their influence in the region weakened by the rise of commercial estates and the combativity of the indigenous population. This probably contributed to the Indians' success in winning back land, but the landowners had organised their own revenge which, by 1986, had claimed 150 Indian lives. Many of the murders have been carried out by hired killers, or *pájaros*, although the police have often been involved. As well as the murders, hundreds of Indians involved in land invasions have suffered arrest and torture. Some regions, such as Toribio, have been under military control for long periods. In 1979 the army arrested and tortured CRIC's leaders, accusing them of being members of the April 19 Movement (M-19).

In fact CRIC's relationship with the guerrilla movements has been tense. They had virtually no presence in the Cauca until the late 1970s, but since then CRIC has fought against being controlled by the guerrillas and twenty of its members have been killed in conflicts with the FARC. Indians have, however, seen the importance of armed defence and an Indian group, Quintín Lame, emerged in the early 1980s to fulfil that role.

Toward a national Indian organisation

The indigenous movement as a whole remains small and fragmented. While CRIC is by far the most advanced organisationally and politically, other organisations have emerged over the years, including the Regional Council of the Indigenous of the South of Tolima (CRIT), set up shortly after CRIC. Other smaller groups exist among the Indians in Nariño, in the Sierra Nevada, in the Chocó, in Antioquia, in the *llanos* of Meta and Vichada, and in Vaupés.

The strongest groups are in the Andean highlands. The dispersed groups of the Amazon and Orinoco are not only difficult to organise, but many have come under the cultural and religious influence of missionary ventures, such as the Summer Institute of Linguistics. Others, such as those in the Sierra Nevada and La Guajira, were caught up in the marijuana boom of the late 1970s. Whereas the struggle of the Indians of the highlands is primarily the same as that of other peasants of the region, i.e. against the large landowners, that of the lowland Indians, particularly in the Orinoco, is often against peasant colonisers as well as the larger landowners, both of whom push the Indians off their lands as they move the agricultural frontier forward. In the 1980s cocaine added a new dimension of corruption, violence and consumerism in the Amazonian and Orinoco regions, greatly damaging the Indian communities' traditional cultures.

Nevertheless, in 1982 ONIC was set up, bringing twenty groups together under the banner of 'unity, land, culture and autonomy'. This followed in the wake of President Turbay Ayala's attempts to introduce an 'indigenous statute', which would have changed the 1890 law and given the state greater control over indigenous peoples. The repression that accompanied the resistance to (and the eventual defeat of) the statute encouraged various indigenous groups to coordinate their efforts and laid the foundations for the emergence of ONIC. But the groups from which it is composed are very different and this has created a number of difficulties in consolidating the organisation.

Indian organisation is invariably a dynamic process, but CRIC's methodology and practice established it as one of Colombia's most effective and representative popular organisations. As such, it has also had to face increasing repression during the second half of the 1980s. After the earthquake in Popayán in 1983, it increased its activities to defend the interests of the many peasants and Indians who had been made homeless. It also began, in 1986, to recover land in the fertile sugar region of the Valle del Cauca, where the economically and politically powerful agrarian bourgeoisie defends its property even more resolutely than the traditional *latifundistas*.

The Cauca has become another of Colombia's many battlegrounds, but it is one in which the state confronts a powerful, well-rooted opposition with its own concept of people's power. The problem for CRIC, as for many of Colombia's strong regional movements, is how to progress politically when other regions are far behind in organisational and political terms. CRIC might be described in the Cauca as a kind of counter-power to the state, but its role in the broader process of social transformation is more complex.

Trade unions

The labour market and unionisation

Colombia's trade union movement has always been weak — numerically, politically and as an instrument of workers' struggles for economic and social rights. Hostile labour legislation, repression and party political manipulation have acted as historic constraints to union activity.

At the beginning of this century, production of the most important export crop — coffee — developed in the hands of individual peasant farmers rather than those of a strategic group of workers. The strongest and most combative workers, such as those on the Magdalena river in the

1920s and the oil workers of Barrancabermeja, have formed regional and local movements, not national ones. Politically, the traditional parties prevented the emergence of independent working-class or even middle-class parties. The Communist Party, which was established in the 1930s, was smaller than the PSR had been in the 1920s and was allied to the Liberal Party for almost a decade. The struggle to create a national labour movement and one with a leadership independent of the traditional parties, has been a long one. Only in the 1980s, with the emergence of the first independent trade union confederation, CUT, was a significant step made in that direction.

Colombian employers have shown a great deal of antipathy and resistance to unionisation. Few recognise the role of unions in negotiating labour conditions. Perhaps one of the most revealing indications of the weakness of unions is the inspection of 12,452 firms carried out by the Ministry of Labour between 1982 and 1985. It found that only 8.4 per cent met the requirements of labour legislation, while 91.6 per cent violated an average of 3.85 regulations (Londoño *et al* 1987,2:159). Wages are low. According to a regional study of 1980, the minimum wage covered the cost of only one third of a basket of basic goods for a family, whereas in Peru it covered 63 per cent, in Venezuela 78 per cent and in Brazil 64 per cent (Romero Vidal 1986:118).

The level of unionisation among the workforce as a whole is low; it reached an all time high of 16 per cent in 1980, but fell to 10 per cent during the 1986 recession. But the level of unionisation among workers in waged employment as opposed to the workforce as a whole is more respectable. In 1980, 29 per cent of the waged labour force was in unions. Predictably, it is in the waged sector of the 'formal' economy that unions have established themselves most strongly, particularly among government employees and workers in large-scale industry. About half the unionised workers (who are a minority of the waged labour force) are in these sectors.

At least 46 per cent of industrial employment is in firms of fewer than ten workers — 25 workers are legally required to form a union. Most waged urban workers are thus isolated in small firms; many are on temporary contracts. In commerce (which employs a lot of unskilled, young, female labour) and construction (where 56 per cent of the workers are in the informal sector and employed on short-term contracts and rarely for one boss for long) unionisation is very low.

In the rural areas, half the agricultural workforce is seasonally employed for the cotton, coffee and sugar harvest and is very difficult to organise. The more permanent workers employed to cultivate flowers for export, or on the sugar-cane, African palm or banana plantations, have an uneven experience of unionisation. Over 90 per cent of the banana

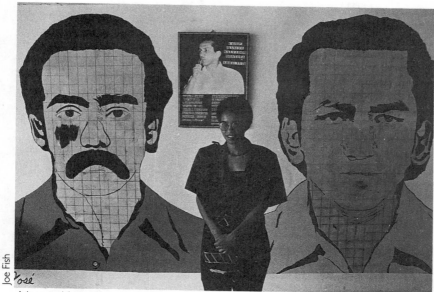

Joe Fish

A human rights worker stands before a mural of two assassinated trade unionists.

workers were unionised by 1985; the African palm workers of the Cesar and Santander regions, with their tradition of struggle, also have a high level of unionisation.

Trade unions and political parties

The structure of the labour force, with its powerful informal sector, has weakened the union movement, but the unions' own trajectory and the large confederations' subservience to the traditional parties have also divided them and restricted their impact. Labour legislation has encouraged unionisation on a factory, or firm, basis rather than across industries and unions are then linked vertically through affiliation to regional and national federations and the two main confederations. Together, the CTC and the UTC had 70-75 per cent of all union affiliates in 1967, although this was still a small minority of the labour force.

The CTC, which is closely linked to the Liberal Party, is particularly influential among state-sector workers, but was weakened by the repression of the 1940s. The UTC became the single most important labour confederation, particularly in industry and the private sector, and has remained closely tied to the Conservative Party and the Catholic Church. While the CTC has used political pressure on the state to win benefits, the UTC has encouraged negotiations between unions and employers in each firm, without state mediation. Both organisations have derived their strength, not from mobilising their membership, but from negotiating with individual state officials and employers. Power within the unions has been concentrated in the leadership, with its privileged access to the employer or relevant state institution, resulting in very little grassroots participation.

The traditional parties viewed the two confederations as vehicles for legitimising the National Front pact, for maintaining labour discipline and for institutionalising the conflict between worker and employer. The Communist Party's influence within the CTC was purged shortly after the pact and the party set up its own confederation, the CSTC, in 1964.

But the National Front's bid to depoliticise the country also weakened the traditional parties' ties with labour. In 1965 inflation and falling real wages led the confederations to threaten a general strike, which was averted only with the intervention by the private sector's associations and an agreement to amend the labour legislation. In the next years the government moved to restrict labour rights, prohibiting strikes within any public-service activity, such as transport, public utilities and banks. The president could suspend a strike and impose binding arbitration whenever the interests of the national economy were deemed to be at stake.

During the 1970s the ability of the two confederations to maintain the workers' allegiance was seriously weakened. The quarter or so of the labour force in the 'modern' sector of the economy most represented by the confederations had won considerable benefits over the mass of workers. The government's policy in the 1970s was to let wages in large industries fall and to raise the minimum wage. At the same time new unions were trying to establish a labour movement that was independent of the traditional parties. These unions first appeared in the early 1960s in Cali, Medellín and Bogotá, and among the oil workers of Barrancabermeja, and, until the CSTC was formed, worked with the Communist Party unions. Various socialist groups had influence in these unions, which never joined a confederation. As with the peasant movement, sectarian divisions were reproduced within the unions, creating schisms and factions. The debates were mostly between union leaders and political cadres of the various unions; rarely was the mass membership brought in. On the positive side, however, as with ANUC, the left did help to establish a radical alternative to the traditional submission of the workers to the interests of government and employers.

Strikes and the growth of the independent unions

Strike activity grew in the 1970s, although never reaching the levels of Peru or Chile before 1973. Public-sector unions flourished; over half the state bureaucracy was unionised by the mid-1970s, at all levels from the ministries to the decentralised agencies and municipal administration. Increasingly they formed independent labour federations. These workers were in the forefront of strike activity despite strikes being technically illegal. Between 1974 and 1980 there were 258 strikes in this sector. Almost half were carried out by schoolteachers affiliated to the Colombian Federation of Teachers (FECODE), who had been highly influenced by the Marxist ideas circulating in the 1960s. They had challenged the traditional party leadership of their union and used their numerical strength and national presence to build a militant and increasingly politicised movement. Grievances were widespread among teachers. Not only were wages low, but there were often long delays in paying salaries. Teachers were hired in large numbers by local departments that could not afford to pay them, often at election times when jobs and votes were both in demand.

The Coca-Cola workers of the Atlantic coast

Coca-Cola is produced under franchise in factories in Cali, Medellín, Bogotá, Barranquilla and Cartagena, employing about 8,000 workers. There are four factories on the Atlantic coast. The struggle to unionise in the coastal factories began in the 1960s. The first unions were often paternalistic 'bosses' ' unions, but gradually in the 1980s, the rank-and-file began to pressure its corrupted leadership for a new direction. Between 1981 and 1982, 80 workers were sacked for their union activity and a further 120 workers had been sacked by 1987. Intimidation of all sorts was used to destroy the workers' movement and by the mid-1980s, workers were receiving death threats from paramilitary groups, such as *Muerte a Sindicalistas* (death to trade unionists). In 1985 a new manager, a US citizen, who had successfully destroyed the union in other plants, set about doing the same for the coastal factories. But the protest movement at the sackings grew, and on 11 April 1987, the workers went on a strike which lasted 67 days, with the main aim of winning job security. The workers occupied the area outside the factory. It was the first big strike on the coast for many years.

The strike had a profoundly politicising affect on the workers, and almost the entire union leadership changed afterwards, as those who had been most active during the strike and proved their commitment replaced the former leadership. This is how they described the experience and lessons of the strike in an interview in February 1988:

'I am a worker of the Coca-Cola multinational, Barranquilla plant. I was head of propaganda during the strike. It was a difficult task. Every day we would go to the radio station to try and get them to broadcast what the Coca-Cola workers were striking for. The company was issuing all kinds of false information. The company had lots of economic power and was using it to prevent the news programmes showing the rest of the country what was happening on the coast; we were filmed protesting in Bogotá, but the film was never shown. It reached the point where unless we said what the radio programme wanted, we wouldn't be broadcast. But we weren't going to be manipulated. We knew what we were experiencing with our own flesh, what the truth was. We had to find other ways of telling people. So we began to produce leaflets, and we explained the struggle to people in them. And then we sent them to workers in other plants, so that our case could be spread nationally. We went on marches with our wives and children, and this was something very new and gave us lots of encouragement. Our women had always been kept out of things, but thanks to them, we were able to progress. Another thing was the meetings in the regional labour office. This office was supposed to defend the workers, but never did. They passed resolutions that they were going to remove us, but we said they could only do so with blood, and neither the police nor the army could get us out.

Then there was the solidarity of the people of Barranquilla. We had some tins and we'd get on the buses and explain the problem of the company, and when the people understood, they would support us. They came to recognise us quickly, because we had arm bands which said Coca-Cola and they would give us encouragement. Once we were on the streets with the tins at a tyre factory. Our company bought from them. When the wife of the owner saw us she turned on us and said, "it's your fault that Coca-Cola are on strike", "No, madam", I said, "You don't know why we are on strike. The company doesn't want to give anyone job security. In the last two years, since the new manager, Mr Staton, a North American, has been in charge, he has got rid of 58 workers. He has an evil lawyer, who works against all the workers of Barranquilla, backing the companies. We workers of Coca-Cola say, either all in the bed together or all on the ground. We also want better wages, but what are we to do, if two months after they've raised the wages, they sack us. Some workers have worked for 9 years in the company and they have dismissed them unfairly. They say they don't want workers with more than ten years. So job security is the most important thing for us." The woman then understood that we were right and supported us; she hadn't known that before because of the company propaganda over the radio.' (Victor)

'I would say that the strike was a school in which all the workers came together as never before. Because there had never been even assemblies here. Our strike was helped by a number of external things. For example the CUT was being formed, and people from it gave us a lot of advice, especially, the *subdirectivo* of Atlántico. I don't know what would have happened if we had been affiliated to the bosses' confederations, we would all be beaten today. Something else that helped us was that the people here on the coast came to understand that our struggle was against a world monopoly, the US multinational Coca-Cola. There was pressure from the government, from Bogotá, to defeat us, and there were other factors which helped. For instance the company began to sabotage our movement by bringing drink in from the interior of the country. But someone put a bomb in some lorries which were used to carry the stuff. We think the CUT is very important for the workers. It is our great hope. You learn through speaking to your father how often we workers have been deceived. The CUT has opened many doors for our Coca-Cola workers' union. We who are now in the union leadership, tell the others that we are not indispensable, that we must be replaced, and as we get better educated we will advance more. We think education is very important and that we mustn't forget what we learned from the strike. We are going to celebrate the first anniversary and invite our families and other unions who supported us. The date must be remembered for all the workers of the coast. It shows that when the workers unite and begin to understand and organise, we can confront any problem.' (Ascario)

Other strong unions existed in the state oil company, ECOPETROL, which organised large strikes in 1963 and 1977 among port and railway workers and among medical workers in the social-security system. Of the strikes that took place between 1974 and 1980, 64 per cent were organised by independent unions and the CSTC. By 1974 the UTC and CTC contained only 65 per cent of the total union affiliates.

With their dwindling memberships and under pressure for action, in September 1977 the UTC and CTC joined the CSTC in the country's first *paro cívico nacional* (national civic strike) against President López Michelsen's policies. The ruling elite's extreme nervousness at this turn of events was seen in the fact that the government itself acknowledged that the security forces had killed 48 people during the strike.

The independent sector continued to grow. Ministry of Labour figures show that, by 1984, 51 per cent of the unionised labour force was in the independent sector; 55 per cent of strikes between 1981 and 1984 and 85 per cent of the workers who participated in them were organised by that sector. State-sector workers still accounted for a larger part of these statistics, however, for the recession hit the industrial workers and unemployment rose.

Towards unity

Colombia's trade union movement was breaking away from the control of the two traditional parties. At the same time, the radical left was taking

Health worker demonstrates outside the Ministry of Health.

a new look at how to work with unions. Sectarianism had resulted in each political group competing for support and influence among union memberships. They still controlled union activity from above and divided the movement in a way that made little sense to most workers. Pressure for unity mounted; the onset of the recession was threatening many workers with dismissal and they sought a common response from their organisations. An acceptance of political pluralism was beginning to take root in the union movement, as well as in the peasant movement. This meant that not only members of other Marxist parties would be made welcome in the same union, but even Conservatives or Liberals, who could be effective in fighting for their immediate needs even if they remained politically loyal to the traditional parties. This awareness brought dissident members of the traditional federations and the independent unions into discussion.

Three unity processes got underway — within the independent sector itself, between the independents and the Communist Party, and between these and the dissidents of the traditional union confederations. In 1981, the independents themselves united to form the Committee for Trade Union Unity (CUS).

In October 1981, amid unprecedented moves by the government to stop it, a second national civic strike took place. The UTC, the CTC and the General Confederation of Labour (CGT) — a new confederation formed in 1979 from a split in the UTC and affiliated to the Christian Democrat union international, the CLAT — were persuaded by the government to withdraw. The rest of the union movement faced the repression; about 50 trade unionists were arrested days before the strike took place and many other arrests took place later. The universities were closed, unions had their legal status revoked for a year and teachers who participated were dismissed.

But in organising the strike another step was taken towards uniting the independent and Communist-led unions. Although the three traditional confederations formed their own Democratic Union Front in 1984 as a counterweight to the parallel process of unity, schisms were opening up within the traditional sector. Aware that the CTC was losing its role of negotiator between workers and management, a group responsible for 'reform' was organised within the union. But the leadership and bureaucratic apparatus remained in the hands of those faithful to the traditional party system and, with backing from the state and from US labour institutions, they had considerable resources at their disposal. Corruption and mismanagement of foreign funds became a source of dispute within the confederation.

A social-democratic current had emerged within the UTC. This was led by Jorge Carrillo, who became Belisario Betancur's Minister of Labour. He proved receptive to the CSTC and independents' unity proposals.

Preparations for another *paro cívico nacional* in 1985 encouraged the movement towards unity. The CSTC and most of CUS reached an agreement in the first half of 1986 and, in July, the UTC and CTC each divided, with 17 federations from the former and three from the latter moving towards unity. Jorge Carrillo assumed a key role in leading the dissidents of the traditional confederations and, together with the CSTC and a 'democratic left' wing of the independents, formed a majority bloc.

The minority of independents criticised them for reproducing the old anti-democratic and hierarchical methods of the earlier union confederations and for rushing the process of unity without consultation at the base. They were more interested in direct action and in mobilising the base than they were in reaching agreements with the government. These differences remained, but did not prevent the formation of the CUT on 19 August 1986. The minority's acceptance of the majority's position was a new departure for the left, which in the past would have simply created its own separate organisation. It remained despite the changes in the rules for electing the CUT's leadership which left it holding only five seats, as opposed to the majority's 25.

The CUT acquired legal status in 1987. It came to encompass a clear majority of the unionised labour force, including the key sectors of the economy in production, distribution and services. But while it represented a historic step, it was none the less surrounded by problems. It had essentially arisen out of agreements between leaders of well-established federations and unions, influenced by a variety of political currents. The mass of unionised workers had been little involved. Issues such as representation and democracy were only just beginning to be addressed, but would be important if the CUT was to reflect the mood and needs of organised labour and mobilise it at given moments.

Though the Colombian left had shifted sufficiently far to allow the unity process to take place, the unions' relationship to politics was still fraught. Nevertheless, the CUT remained a meeting ground for many currents — from the Communist-oriented CSTC, to the Liberals and Conservatives of the traditional federations, from the independent unions with their radical-left leadership, to a newer 'democratic-left' current, with its strong influence in the teachers' union.

Two broad blocs have emerged at the executive level of the CUT which, unlike the sectarian disagreements of the past, do reflect a very real debate about political options. The majority position is more labourist, concerned with strengthening the trade-union movement as a pressure group. It is prepared to enter into a dialogue with the government and give the trade-union movement a voice in the national political debate. This view tends to correspond to the politics of the social-democratic current, who believe in the importance of opening up democratic spaces in the country. The minority position favours class confrontation and seeks a radical transformation of society. These political views are translated into very different forms of trade union praxis, the one encouraging caution and pragmatism, the other militancy and grassroots mobilisation.

Interview with a CUT member from the Atlantic coast

'My name is Gonzalo Rubio González. I work in the water and sewerage departmental corporation of Atlántico. I am a member of the union of the department and also of the executive of the CUT. I have been a union leader for seventeen years. Until we disaffiliated from it, I was a member of the Executive Committee of the CGT.

The emergence of the CUT, nationally as well as in the Atlántico was a hard struggle, because there were many obstacles, especially parallel unions and government interference. The UTC was always affiliated to the Conservative Party, and counter-posed to it was the CTC, affiliated to the Liberals. Later the CSTC emerged, oriented towards the Communist Party and more recently, the CGT, to the Christian Democrats. Both at the union and rank-and-file level these orientations prevented a centralised workers' struggle since one union central was set against another and there was never a united policy against the government. That's why the most important demand for a long time has been for workers' unity in Colombia.

Apart from these four union centrals, there was also a large group of organisations and political currents which were called 'independent'. Little by little, this revolutionary and independent sector began to penetrate the four centrals. This led to an internal rupture within the UTC and brought some people closer to the CSTC. We formed a force to create a unified and democratic central whose main aim was the defence of the workers and which wasn't affiliated to any international movement or political power. In Barranquilla we formed a *sub-directivo* of the CUT in March 1987. My union was part of the independent bloc, and we have fought continuously for the unification of the workers of Barranquilla. Sometimes we would discuss unity amongst the federations, although nationally they were affiliated to the traditional confederations. But that never happened. Now, with the consolidation of the CUT, it has awakened the interest of other union organisations affiliated to the UTC and the CTC and now there are about ten unions in the process of disaffiliating in order to join us.

The level of unionisation here in Barranquilla, is low for many reasons. One is because the previous leadership has never responded to the expectations of the workers. The other is the strong pressure of the bosses not to let their workers organise unions. It is common practice here, as in the rest of Colombia, that when a boss realises that his workers are organising, he dismisses the leaders and other workers. Recently, the workers from a mechanical plant in the free-trade zone went on strike spontaneously although they had no union, because two workers had been sacked. They saw the need for a union, but it took so long to get legal status, that they affiliated to an industry-wide union that already had it. The following week, the boss dismissed 450 workers, of which 250 had affiliated to the industry-wide union, SINTRAIME. In the metropolitan hospital of Barranquilla, where nearly all workers joined ANTOC, a union of hospital and clinic workers, the response of the boss, Manuel Acosta, a member of one of the traditional parties and of a public corporation of Barranquilla, was to sack 250 workers.

We are trying to build industry-based unions as the best way to respond to the government and bosses, this is a major aim of the CUT. Recently, the Coca-Cola workers went on strike throughout the Atlantic Coast. Unions based in one factory only confront their own boss, but there are other factories which produce the same goods and can continue to produce them. The workers of the electrical energy sector have organised SINTRACOSONAL, for instance.

The coast is like another country in relation to the centre of Colombia. Although many historical struggles have happened here, such as the banana workers who were massacred in 1928, the river workers of the Magdalena and the railworkers, the workers' movement is weak here. This is reflected, too, in the level of repression. This has not been very high here compared with elsewhere because the level of struggle has not worried the government. It was not usual for workers to be harassed during negotiations. Now, as soon as a union, whatever its political orientation, presents its demands, the security forces begin to single out the leaders with visits to their houses and threatening telephone calls. At the beginning, these were just threats. But now, in the last fortnight (February 1988), three *compañeros*, members of the *Junta Directiva* and of the negotiating commission of the Public Municipal Corporation of Barranquilla were imprisoned just for defending the workers' interests. They are still in prison, although the CUT organised a big demonstration in front of the prison. They've been accused of being members of a guerrilla group. Another member of the *Junta Directiva* of the Barranquilla municipal telephone corporation was kidnapped and later tortured. His name is Libardo Sánchez. He was taken by some assassins at 10pm on Tuesday as he came out of the union offices. They were in a big ranger car and it was in the centre of Barranquilla with many people about; we think they were members of the police. He was found by his friends on the Wednesday night at midnight; he was very punctual and turned up at all meetings and they had missed him. His kidnappers had burned his testicles, the soles off his feet, the palms of his hands, raped him, given him electric shocks, and put a revolver in his mouth to make him say he was a member of the ELN and that his friends on the *Junta* were also members. They said he should stop being a union activist and think of his children, and if not they would have him killed and they were sending the same message back to his friends on the *Junta*.

These are new events in this region. But the workers of this corporation had just ended talks with their boss over a series of demands. The union leaders had stood out not just for defending the interests of the workers, but also those of the community. They had publicly denounced some of the corrupt deals of the politicians who control the municipal corporations, the theft, the fictitious contracts. We don't call them politicians, but *politiqueros* (political wheeler-dealers) because they've syphoned public money to favour their own groups. This has destroyed many corporations, such as the Public Health Corporation of Atlántico, and the *Empresa Licorera*[1], has been milked of its resources, so that now these cannot respond to the minimal needs of their workers or the public. It is common to hear the politicians on the radio insulting each other, one accusing the other of theft, the other of fraudulently taking money from the municipal coffers. Nothing happens. The municipal telephone workers denounced all this, and we think that has got a lot to do with the torture of Libardo Sánchez. I've just spoken to one of the *compañeros* from the corporation, and he thinks they should stop work immediately in response to attacks like this. Because the message the police sent back with Libardo, was that he was only the first and there would be others until they ceased causing trouble.

There are differences within the CUT; basically two blocs exist. The majority is composed of the *compañeros* of the Communist Party, those independents who supported the politics of the PC-ML and the *Unidad y Democracia* (Unity and Democracy) sector of Jorge Carrillo. The minority, of which I am part, comes from the independent sector who rejected the peace process of Belisario Betancur, as we believed it was a manoeuvre. We formed our own political movement, *A Luchar*. We have a strong position here on the coast. We have a position independent of the state, the traditional parties and the Church, and we believe that is the only way to really defend the interests of the workers. We believe in direct action of the workers. Let's enter a dialogue with the government and with the bosses, but with the people and workers mobilised, because that's the only dialogue the government understands at this moment. Our political movement has mobilised peasants throughout the north east of Colombia while others give priority to elections rather than mobilisation. They say they agree to a strike, but in practice do nothing to organise it. One example is when the *compañeros* of the public corporations here on the coast voted for a strike. One of those advising the workers in the name of the CUT, told them not to go on strike as this would give more ammunition to the bosses to continue repressing the workers, that if we denounced the corruption of the local corporations, we would make them angrier, and that we shouldn't blame the mayor for

---

1. Each department has its own alcohol industry as a means of generating revenue.

> the imprisonment of the workers because that would make things worse.
> We don't see it like that. We believe we should say things as they are,
> denounce those we know to be responsible for the repression of the
> workers' movement. We believe there has to be some defence, some
> minimum security for the workers who struggle democratically for union
> rights. Dialogue is alright, but the workers must be defended against the
> assassins' bullets.'

But more problematic is the question of how a trade-union movement representing only 10 per cent of the labour force (in 1986) relates to the mass of unorganised workers, particularly the 50 per cent of the labour force in the informal sector. For most of these workers, the fight for better wages and working conditions (with which unions are mostly associated), is inappropriate. Public services, health, education, housing, recreation and transport are of much more immediate concern to the majority of Colombians. These issues affect workers in the formal sector too, but have not been addressed by the trade unions.

During the 1970s civic movements, led by local people in the smaller towns and poor districts of the big cities, took up these issues and in a very different style to the bureaucratic and hierarchical trade unions. The radical left has also had trouble in coming to terms with this phenomenon. These grassroots movements have shifted the perspectives of some in the trade unions and encouraged them to look at their relationship with the broader society. In Colombia, a strategy for change has to incorporate the vast majority of the population who lack regular employment. But the political nature of that change and whether it can be achieved by peaceful means or armed struggle, still divides the popular movement.

Civic movements

The 1970s: the small towns erupt

Over the years the Colombian elites have developed sophisticated mechanisms for co-opting and controlling the population through the mediation of the traditional parties.

In the wake of *La Violencia*, the National Front government attempted to construct its own communication channels with the people. One of the first laws of the 1958 government was to create *Juntas de Acción Comunal* (Community Action Committees) These grew out of community-action programmes launched in the late 1950s to defuse tensions in regions caught up in *La Violencia*. They were intended to encourage community participation and self-help projects to improve local services, uniting communities across class lines. Most did not emerge from the community, but were created by government officials, and they were soon taken over by local politicians who 'arranged' funding and used the *Juntas* to mobilise electoral support. Some 9,000 committees existed by 1966 and these multiplied in the 1970s as a counterweight to ANUC and other radical organisations emerging among the people. By the 1980s there were 32,000 *Juntas*, with an official affiliation of five million people.[2]

Under the impact of rapid urbanisation, regional inequalities and lack of state provision, the *Juntas* began to lose their legitimacy, along with the traditional parties. Particularly in small towns, people began to develop their own mechanisms, organisations and movements through which to protest and demand action from the state to meet their basic needs. To emphasise their broad-based character and their non party-political nature, these movements were called civic, with their main form of protest being the civic strike (*paro cívico*), which involved the paralysis of all administrative, productive and social activity in a town or region. Other activities include marches, roadblocks, refusal to pay bills for services, and symbolic takeovers of government offices.

The number of *paros* increased dramatically in the 1970s. Before that they were sporadic, with only 16 recorded between 1957 and 1970. But between 1971 and 1980 there were an estimated 128 local and regional *paros*, which involved or affected four and a half million people, according to the 1973 population census of the towns in which they occurred. The vast majority took place in small towns in backward regions dominated by a peasant economy. Three regions accounted for 50 per cent of the *paros* and 73 per cent of those who participated: the Atlantic coast (31 per cent), the south, including Nariño, Cauca, Putumayo, Vaupés and Caquetá (25 per cent) and the Santanderes (9 per cent); three *paros* were organised in Barrancabermeja alone.

Between 1958 and 1980, 80 per cent of the *paros* took place in towns of fewer than 50,000 inhabitants and, of these, 50 per cent were in towns of under 20,000 people. Most were restricted to the municipality, 12 per cent involved several municipalities, just 2 per cent covered most of a department, and there were two national *paros* in 1977 and 1981.

A full 60 per cent of the *paros* of the 1970s were related to public services, such as the provision of drinking water, energy (particularly the constant rise in tariffs) and sewerage; 13 per cent were over transport, 8

---

2. Statistics drawn from Santana 1983 and Giraldo and Camargo 1986.

per cent over education and the rest focused on communications, use of natural resources and the location of industry.

The administrative, political and financial incapacity of local government was notorious. The provision of public services was mostly in the hands of the thousand or so poorly-resourced municipal governments. The state controlled the collection of all taxes and the distribution of the investment, leaving local municipal authorities with a weak financial base, which deteriorated over the years. While in 1960 they received 23 per cent of the total tax income, by the beginning of the 1980s this was only 5.3 per cent. Only the large cities had enough industry to form a substantial tax base; the smaller towns had to depend on scarce government subsidies.

What limited resources were available were controlled by local party bosses and used for political purposes. Governors were appointed by central government and mayors by governors. The locally-elected municipal councils and departmental assemblies owed their positions to the local party machine, as did most of the local government employees. The mayors lacked political legitimacy or any clear function, except as intermediaries between central government and the local population. Decentralised agencies had over the years deprived them of many functions in the fields of housing, roads and electricity.

Some *paros* occurred because of state neglect. In Sarare, Arauca, a region of colonisation, ANUC members organised a massive civic strike in the early 1970s, which lasted 13 days and in which 2,000 colonists took over the region's main town, Saravena, demanding the construction of roads, bridges, a central market for the peasants to sell their produce, and the provision of basic services. In Nariño during the 1970s people mobilised to demand that an oil refinery be built in Tumaco to refine the region's oil reserve and to generate desperately needed employment. Others have taken place because of the harmful manner in which the state has intervened. In the east of Antioquia, in Suárez in the Cauca and Santamaría in Boyacá, the people have rallied against the building of hydro-electric dams which cause flooding to peasant lands.

The movements brought together a range of social classes, as all are affected by the lack of services. Students, peasants, workers, street traders, sectors of the church and small and medium businessmen have joined. In the towns of more than 50,000 people, the workers' movement has had more of an influence. In Barrancabermeja there was a particularly close relationship between the neighbourhood organisations and the oil workers, who belonged to the same neighbourhoods and played a leading role in the *paros*.

The movements often began spontaneously, with civic committees being set up subsequently. In some cases, these became permanent bodies; in others they were formed to fight a particular issue and then collapsed. Nearly all the movements held mass assemblies and the decision to organise a *paro* was rarely taken without such an assembly.

The civic movement of Itagüí: interview with an exile

'Itagüí is a municipality of 300,000 people situated in the Valle de Aburra just south of Medellín. It is an industrial town, but lacks basic services such as water and roads.

We got involved in the "civic movement" in 1974, when we tried to prevent an increase in bus fares, which had been declared arbitrarily by the company in our area. The students organised a campaign and all the schools came out to protest. There was a womens' organisation in the town and another organisation which grouped 12-15 trade unions, and together with the students, the Popular Committee of Itagüí was created, whose acronym is COMPITA, also short for "little friend or *compañero*". We were young, and had no idea what a civic movement was; they weren't yet talked about in Colombia as a movement as such, that only came when they existed the length and breadth of the country.

In 1977-8, and also in 1976, I think, the summer was very long, perhaps 80 per cent of the year, with very high temperatures and drought. And Itagüí, although it is an industrial town, with textile, leather, wood, furniture and brewing industries, doesn't have a proper water system. That is despite the considerable contribution to its budget from its industry; but this didn't benefit the inhabitants. Much went into the pockets of the politicians who controlled the town and its bureaucracy. If a textile firm employing 6-7,000 people had to pay a certain sum in taxes, 30 per cent of it would go in transactions "under the table". The municipal councillors took some of this for their personal benefit.

The water pipe (*acueducto*), detonated the growth in civic protest. It was insufficient to provide all the neighbourhoods of Itagüí with water; council workers turned a tap on and off with special tools, giving the water to certain areas at different times of the day. The people in the poor neighbourhoods of the south of the town fared particularly badly, as often the water pressure was too low to reach them, even if they had pipes.

The water was also extremely dangerous. It was so contaminated that many children had died from drinking it. We carried out an investigation into the water through the *Acción Comunal* bodies in the 43 neighbourhoods at the time (today there are more). We took slides of the water source which fed the municipal *acueducto* and of where it was processed. We had to go to different communities on the periphery of the town, where the streams which fed the *acueducto* passed through. One, Doña María, was well known locally for its smell. Because all the factory waste went into it. Some of the most harmful were from the leather factory, which even deposited decomposed organic waste and it was one of the most polluted streams in the Valle del Aburra. There was also a pig farm and poultry factory, which threw all their waste into the water.

We also showed how this filthy water was scarcely processed. It went through tanks where chlorine was put in every so often but not enough to purify all the water, and during the drought we found that there was mud a metre high. We took samples from the water that came out of the domestic pipes. When the water came, which was during the afternoon, the first thing to come out was a cloud of dust, because the mud had dried in the tube and under pressure came out as dust. We found all sorts of creatures and even locks of hair in the water, and it smelled, it smelled of the *quebrada* (brook). When we took our sample to the Public Health School of the University of Antioquia, they said "We don't have to examine this under a microscope, we can see everything with our eyes". All this we illustrated graphically in our leaflets, and we gave talks with the slides, and collected signatures for a petition.

During the drought the only sources of water were the textile company and the brewery. Because they had to have good water, they had their private system. The companies put a pipe onto the street, and we had to queue up for the water, sometimes from 3am in order to be able to go to work later. Afterwards, we had to take the water in hand-made wooden carts which we pulled ourselves, sometimes for over a mile, over terrible roads.

That was another problem, the roads. We were known jokingly as *Itaguecos*, the word for hole is *hueco*, and our roads were full of them. In the summer the clouds of dust were terrible, and in the winter the mud was so bad that the buses sometimes couldn't move. We began a campaign on this and distributed leaflets which said: "Get to know Itagüí before it collapses". When it rained and the holes in the roads filled up with water, people put up notices which said "no fishing". These things made the people laugh and encouraged them to protest.

In 1979 we dissolved COMPITA, to create something broader, including many local *Juntas de Acción Comunal*. Discontent was running high among the people; the petitions had achieved nothing. A new organisation, the Civic Committee of Itagüí was created, whose leaders were elected by popular assemblies of several thousand people. There were eight, and five of them were housewives. It began to prepare for a civic strike. Such a thing was unthinkable in Itagüí. The town is only half an hour away from the second most important town in Colombia, Medellín. And close to the town passes the Autopista Sur, the most important motorway to the south. Still, we set about organising the strike. We saw the need to attract as broad a sector of the population as possible, to link them. We produced a newspaper. Harassment and arrests began in 1981, but in November 1982, we managed to organise our first strike.

People put up barricades to prevent the transport moving, and some people prepared "popular grenades" and bent nails to stop the traffic. The stoppage was total and lasted 48 hours. There were over 2,000 arrests, and the municipal and departmental authorities were forced to negotiate. They promised to meet the people's demands within four months. But this often happens; to demobilise the people, the authorities sign a document, a photograph is taken and is shown on TV, and when people ask for the agreement to be carried out, there's a new mayor, who says that it was signed by his predecessor.

Well, in April 1983, we organised a second civic strike, "for the fulfillment of the agreement of November 1982". This time the leadership was more political, members of the PC-ML had won influence in the Committee. The strike lasted a week, and there were confrontations on the streets. People now knew what the response of the army and police would be, and they fought back against the tanks and guns with stones and homemade weapons. Some guerrillas were present to protect the withdrawal of the people. As a civic movement we opposed that since it could bring reprisals. But we couldn't control everything that happened amongst a crowd of 8,000. One worker, who in fact had nothing to do with the strike, was arrested by the police and died as a result of the beating they gave him. The police went into people's houses, broke the windows and doors. Many housewives were attacked. But support was total, and we forced them to resolve the problem of water and roads.

Many people were politicised through the strikes. Itagüí became known as a "red zone" to the military, meaning that it had Communist and guerrilla influence. Whenever there was any departmental or national strike, the town was completely militarised. This has created a state of tension in the town. Little pieces of paper began to appear saying, "Death to the Civic Leaders". One of the participants in the two strikes, not a public figure but behind the scenes, Rodrigo Penagos, "disappeared" in Itagüí in 1984 and we never heard anything more about him. Sometimes we took over the church to denounce his disappearance. The civic movement became a paramilitary target.

We kept up our campaigns, even though some demands had been met. We had educational campaigns, a campaign to clean up the Doña María *quebrada* for ecological reasons, as now our drinking water came from other healthier sources, and a reforestation programme. Itagüí has grown over the year with no planning. There is an area in the south, which we call the Lung (*pulmón*), which is the only green area left in the town, and they were going to build on it. We stopped this, and the authorities said they would make it a public park. They won't do that, but just leaving the trees there is an advance.

We were divided on participating in elections; most of us didn't believe in them and some wanted to abstain on principle. I was one of those who helped creat a political group in 1986 to fight the municipal elections; we

> were inexperienced and poor and weren't very successful. And then the paramilitary began to threaten us. I was a pre-candidate for mayor in 1988. It was three months before the elections and I was trying to decide whether to stand or not. If they didn't kill you during the campaign, once you were elected you were in danger. And if you managed to survive till 1990 or 1992, you had routine movements which were easy to detect. The moment comes when you step out of the house and you don't know whether you will return or in what state. In the end, I had to leave the country.'

Many people participated in these movements because they objected to the local party machine and the manipulations of the local political bosses. Any party presence in the movements was therefore regarded with suspicion. The left gained influence in some through the influence they had in local popular organisations, but the movements were about finding effective ways of satisfying immediate needs, which were of personal rather than ideological concern. Some people were radicalised by repression from the state, for over the decade 44 per cent of the *paros* were greeted with the imposition of a curfew, direct military intervention and the arrest of leaders. In only 21 per cent did the state make any concessions at all and even these involved it in very little investment, such as lowering the prices of services. In other cases the *paros* were lifted following promises of concessions.

The 1980s: protest grows

In the early 1980s, a period of recession, the civic movement began to take on a new dimension. Between January 1982 and March 1984 there were 78 local and regional civic strikes, involving 152 municipalities and an estimated five million people. The movements also spread geographically; 35 per cent of the *paros* in this period were in Antioquia, but there were indications that in some areas the civic committees were becoming more established and stable. In Nariño the civic movement had become a part of regional life and increasing numbers of *paros* were taking place in the larger towns and cities.

The main focus continued to be on the public services, particularly the rise in energy tariffs, which had been the reason for the existence of nearly half the movements. Domestic electicity rates were forced up in the second half of the 1970s to meet the increasing cost of providing the service, but regardless of the low incomes in much of the country which made it an impossible burden.

Civic movements in the east of Antioquia

'The East of Antioquia includes 26 municipalities and ten *corregimientos* (hamlets) and is situated, as its name suggests to the east of Medellín, the capital of the department. It has a population of about 700,000 people. It stretches from the outskirts of Medellín to the borders of the river Magdalena. It has a range of climates, from the hot climate of the low areas around the river, to the cold temperatures of the highlands. It is a region rich in natural resources, producing marble, silver and gold, and in agriculture its range of climates produces a variety of produce, such as sugar-cane, yucca and vegetables. It provides about 70 per cent of the capital's vegetables and much for the Atlantic coast. It also has important hydro-electric capacity. The most important energy projects of the last years have been developed here, and the region provides about 30 per cent of the country's hydro-electric power.

The region has become the natural frontier of expansion from Medellín, a town which is in a narrow valley, the Valle de Aburra, and which has little more room for urban development.In the last twenty years, industrial development has come to the regions to the immediate east of Medellín as well as a number of public works, such as the highway between Medellín and Bogotá, fifty per cent of which crosses this region, the hydro-electric plants and the international airport. This development has not emerged from any agreement with the community, nor from the felt needs of that community. It has obeyed the interests of the oligarchy and the multinationals. The industrial firms which have come are dependencies, technologically and administratively speaking, of those of Medellín. The same in commerce. And the airport, we have discovered, had military objectives, both for the Pentagon because of the importance of the Gulf of Urabá with the conflicts in Central America, and for our army and airforce. A military base is being built there, and the Israeli Kafir jets will be based at the airport.

This development process has involved a massive expulsion of peasants. First, because of the hydro-electric plants in the municipalities of Peñol, Guatapé, Alejandría, San Rafael and San Carlos. These plants involved flooding the best agricultural and ranching land. The airport and the road expelled other peasants. Some became industrial workers, most went into the informal sector and many squandered their compensation money through bad investments. They live in the land invasions which surround Medellín. The mega-projects, have also brought thousands into the area from other parts of Colombia in search of work, increasing the pressure on land, services and housing and causing many social problems. And with the end of the works, a great depression has fallen on the area.

This region has therefore suffered a series of changes, not just in economic structure, land ownership, and employment, but also in the consciousness and ideological perception of its inhabitants. This is traditionally one of the most Catholic and Conservative regions of the country, which has provided many of its priests.

The first civic movements in the area were in 1962, over the rise in electricity prices. Since then, there have been many protests, some local, others regional, and aimed at the provision, price and quality of public services. A second motive has been the popular response to the public works. After 1982, there were three regional civic strikes which directly or indirectly affected all the people of the East and led to the formation of the Regional Civic Movement of the East of Antioquia and its organisational body, the Regional Coordinator of the East of Antioquia.

This body organised assemblies, marches, debates and the formulation of a series of demands, some of which have been met, others of which are in the process of being met and others which have been openly ignored. Peñol, for example, was the town most affected by the hydro-electric workers. The old town was completely flooded. There were many demonstrations and strikes, and even the World Bank was approached when it came to inspect the works to control the loans it had made to carry them out. A contract was signed in 1969 which gave the community compensation and included the building of a new town (the company in charge of the work had wanted people to go to Medellín or other towns) with corresponding services, but it was only partially carried out. Pressure to fulfil the contract built up when the Civic Movement of the East of Antioquia grew strong, but only in 1988, 19 years after the original contract was signed and 25 years after the works had begun, was a definitive agreement reached over the people's demands.

The civic movement also demanded the same treatment as the municipalities receiving royalties for the wealth of their subsoil in gold or oil. It proposed that the East of Antioquia had such rights as regards its water which was taken to install electric plants whose main beneficiaries were not the region itself, but other regions of the country. In 1981 it was agreed that the hydro-electric companies should pay the municipalities a royalty and also repair roads and other damage done by the works. But no sooner was it approved than the law was a dead letter. We have fought for the implementation of the law, and at last it is happening, and a body has been created to use the royalty for development works in the region, giving priority to rural electrification, and management of the water table through reforestation. Now the region is one of the most electrified in the country. We also fought for lower electricity rates because we were paying 20-30 per cent more than the Valle de Aburra. We now have equal, if not lower, rates.

The civic movement has always been autonomous and independent of the traditional parties, Conservative and Liberal, and from the parties of the left; the latter soon realised the importance of the movements and worked within them, but always accepting that the civic movement was autonomous. The attitude of the traditional parties was to completely abandon the struggle to improve the lives of the people. Usually they supported central government or the hydro-electric companies. Many politicians enriched themselves with deals on the sale of land to the companies. They came to see the civic movements as enemies. These are the roots of the repression and violence against the movement, the persecution and assassination of its leaders. Not just the usual arrests which have always taken place every time there's a strike, but direct attacks against civic leaders.

In some cases, the civic movements have put up their own candidates to the local council, such as in San Carlos, and this has led to particular violence. In San Carlos a local political movement was forced, the Santaritano Broad Movement (*Movimiento Amplio Santaritano, MAS*). That's where repression has been greatest against the civic movement. The first assassination was of the doctor and artist and president of the *Junta Cívica*, Julián Conrado David, who was murdered on a Sunday, near his consultancy, half a block from the police station and the town hall. After him, Guillermo López, Mariano Bedoya, Iván Vélez, Benjamín Arias and Santiago Duque were killed. Others had to leave the region. The most important traders who worked with the civic movement were murdered in the public square of San Carlos. One man, Felipe Norena, who worked in the Department of Antioquia went to live in Cali and opened a small business, where he was assassinated. Jorge Morales, professor at the University of Antioquia and one of the organisers of the civic movement was murdered in the University last year (1988). The list goes on, the leaders of the civic movement were selectively eliminated, and those who weren't killed had to flee the region and even the country, and the civic movement in the town was wrecked.

The civic movement today is in a situation similar to that of the UP. An infinite number of leaders from all the regions of Colombia have been assassinated. They are indiscriminately linked with the armed movements to justify the repression. The state has issued a series of repressive measures in which any expression or demonstration practically constitutes a terrorist act, and leads to searches and arrests. There's an intelligence operation directed by the security forces against any type of popular mobilisation . . . We believe that for the popular movement and, in particular, for the civic movement, it is urgent that legal conditions for work return, because at the moment, open work, popular work, civic work is extremely difficult. This we say now, as we said when the first truce was signed under Belisario Betancur. In the present state of armed confrontation we lose the possibility of developing the union movement, the popular movement, the opposition political movement. We want to put pressure on the government and on the insurgent movement that they at least establish some rules by which the struggle is waged, which allows the community to make their demands known. In that context, the civic movement would have a very good chance of developing a serious alternative to the traditional political parties and the traditional left. The experience of the last elections shows us that a large number of people share the proposals and analysis of the civic movement. There are new generations for whom the ancestral and emotional ties of

> the Liberal and Conservative parties no longer count and who don't find in the traditional parties of the left an appropriate political expression, neither in their language, nor in their proposals nor in their strategy and tactics.
>
> We believe that the civic movement expresses the essence of the Colombian people; it picks up the lost thread from the movement of the *Comuneros* to the movement of Gaitán.
>
> *Source*: Interview with Ramón Emilio Arcila, leader of the Civic Movement of Eastern Antioquia (assassinated 30 December 1989).

This was the cause of the strong civic movement in the eastern region of Antioquia. Water and sewerage provision remained major issues for the civic movements in the larger as well as smaller towns and even in the cities of Barranquilla and Cartagena. In Bogotá most of the protests were over water, energy and domestic fuel tariffs, and public transport. Poor public transport was the main cause of the urban protest in Cali and Medellín. Protests in the big cities, however, have been less frequent than elsewhere.

Building national coordination

The first step towards coordinating the civic movements nationally took place in October 1983 with the participation of eleven movements. A national coordinating committee was formed, and a secretariat set up in Bogotá, to promote coordinated action between regions. For example, in 1984 there were *paros* and mobilisations in Arauca, Nariño, and the south east of Antioquia, which were backed by solidarity action in the main cities.

National coordination is particularly important for movements that are by nature diffuse, local, or, at best, regional in coverage, usually spontaneous in origin and motivated solely by immediate issues. The movements have often been fuelled by purely conjunctural factors (such as a rise in electricity prices or building a dam) and it is not always possible to sustain them beyond the immediate issue. This has led many people to question whether they could ever gain national political importance.

In a number of regions they have become part of regional life because of the local or national government's incapacity to resolve the problems for which they have fought. The government also has been unable to co-opt them through dialogue and the old mechanisms of political control. The movements have remained combative and independent of the traditional parties. Although they unite a spectrum of classes, it is ultimately the poorest who are most affected by the lack of services, transport and housing and, in that sense, they are fundamentally popular movements.

The poor also bear the brunt of the repression. Confrontations with the army and police became increasingly violent in the 1980s, which was a politicising experience for people who sought only to satisfy their everyday needs. At one *paro* in Cartago in October 1983, where the security forces killed four participants and wounded hundreds, the people were so angry that they burnt down some government offices.

In that they are highly participatory and stress the role of the grassroots activists rather than the leaders, many consider that these movements present the most serious challenge yet to the country's traditional political culture. Their future political direction will depend on many factors, but at the moment most of those participating in them do not think in terms of transforming society. Though not overtly anti-capitalist, to different degrees they challenge Colombia's model of capitalist development. They are unlikely themselves to become a radical force of national importance, but they may be a vehicle for radicalisation through the experience of organisation and struggle they offer and the channel of participation to people who would avoid movements they consider overtly political.

Joe Fish

Slum conditions, Bogotá.

Some civic movements have developed their own political organisations, such as the *Frente Amplio* of Magdalena Medio, the *Inconformes* of Nariño, the *Movimiento Firmes* of Caquetá, the *Movimiento Popular Nortecaucano*, and the *Movimiento Amplio Democrático* in Tolima. Sometimes they are led by former activists of the left, who believe that the civic movements are pioneering a new, more democratic form of popular organisation. These movements began to participate in local elections.

How the movements relate to other sectors in the struggle will of course influence how they develop. More solid links were established in July 1986 when 3,000 delegates from 2,500 grassroots organisations and hundreds of unions and cooperatives met in Bogotá, where they decided to establish a new body — the Council of Popular Organisations (*Consejo de Organizaciones Populares*).

Over the years, the civic movement has made a considerable mark on political life. Between 1971 and 1986, when the second congress of civic movements took place, there had been over 300 *paros*, 207 of them between 1978 and 1986. Hundreds of municipalities now had a tradition of activity independent of the state and the traditional parties. But the movement's varying local and regional character limited its ability to become a force of national importance. By the mid-1980s, like many of the country's popular movements, it was increasingly seen as 'subversive' and its leaders began to confront repression as never before.

Colombia's social movements: problems and perspectives

As a peasant union (*gremial*), ANUC functions and takes decisions autonomously, as an organisation it is independent of the state and of the traditional parties, but accepts political pluralism. ('Criterios, guías, programa y plataforma', *Speeches and conclusions of ANUC's Congress of Unity & Reconstruction*, Bogotá, August 1987)

CRIC is an organisation controlled by Indian peasants who were elected at the Assembly. Thus it is independent of the political parties and of the government. ('Nuestras luchas de ayer y de hoy', CRIC Bulletin, no. 1, February 1973

The CUT is an organisation independent of the state, of the religious institutions, of the bosses and of the parties and political movements. As a result, the CUT will define the policies with which it leads the workers struggles autonomously. (*Declaración de principios de la CUT*, Bogotá, November 1986)

We confirm that the popular movement will maintain its independence and autonomy before the state and its institutions. (*Declaración del II Congreso de Movimientos Cívicos y Organizaciones Populares*, Bogotá, July 1986)

By 1986, Colombia's social movements were at a new stage, qualitatively and quantitatively. Very diverse and with many problems, one thing stands out: their rejection of the two traditional parties. People were organising around their real needs and sought no mediation from the parties. Social conditions and economic situations tolerated at the beginning of the 1960s had become intolerable as a result of urban growth and rural dislocation, and a more educated population was less easy to manipulate. Even representatives of the *Juntas de Acción Comunal* attended the 1986 conference, for many had begun to participate in civic protest in the 1970s.

The movements described here by no means cover the whole range of people's activities over the past two decades. A full account might include a myriad of local grassroots and sectoral organisations, ranging

Joe Fish

CRIC demonstration, Corinto, Valle del Cauca, on the second anniversary of the assassination of Alvaro Ulcue.

from cultural groups to youth and women's organisations. Some are shortlived, others have become permanent and have sought to forge wider links.

The black people's organisation is an example of the latter. Colombia's black population, brought to the country in the 16th century to work the gold mines of the Pacific coast, is among the poorest in the country, and the Chocó, where many live, is one of the most disadvantaged of Colombia's departments. Towards the end of the 1970s a movement of middle-class black people emerged, but collapsed after one of its members put himself forward as a presidential candidate for the black people and then ended up giving his votes to the Liberal Party candidate. Then, in 1982, a new movement was launched in Buenaventura — the National Movement for the Human Rights of the Black Communities of Colombia (CIMARRON). It proclaimed its independence from the traditional parties and has grown in influence. It organises around the ethnic and cultural issues that unite the communities, but is also concerned with social and economic problems, particularly the lack of services and economic opportunities in the impoverished Chocó.

Women have also begun to develop their own organisations and to press their case within the popular movement. As elswhere in Latin America, women suffer very particular forms of discrimination and hardship, exacerbated by the traditionalism of the Catholic Church. A report in *El Mundo* (13 August 1984) claims that each year there are 250,000 illegal abortions in the country resulting in the deaths of 1,200 young women and that 114 women die in childbirth for every 1,000 live births. Social and economic change has had a marked effect on the female population. The number of women in the labour force has grown from 2.5 million in 1973 to 4.3 million in 1985; most of these are in the informal sector (Barco 1987). Increasing numbers of women are ending up as single heads of households. In Bogotá and the four main cities, between 10 and 21 per cent of poor families are headed by women. Many women have begun to make their voices and needs heard for the first time, forcing organisations such as ANUC and the CUT to address them, and playing an active role in many civic movements.

These and other movements have brought the people into Colombian political life in an unprecedented way. But there is much debate about their role, about whether they have a broader political part to play and if so what? Are they a force for democratising an elitist society or are they a force for radical social transformation? Politicised by their experiences, many within the organisations seek a more coherent political expression for their activities and various political projects compete for support.

Some make clear distinctions between the traditional class-based organisations (notably the trade unions) and the newer movements, which bring people together on the basis of interests shared by a local community, sector or region, where class interests are less explicit. The fundamental contradiction in society is seen less as that between capital and waged labour, which has won some privileges, than between capital and the excluded (unemployed, underemployed, street traders, etc.) who are denied work and the means to a livelihood. Social movements are seen as a force for change in their own right, building popular power from below, challenging not only the traditional parties but also the orthodox ideologies of the Marxist left and the various strategies of armed struggle. Not concerned with the seizure of state power, social movements are seen as building an alternative society from below.

The orthodox left, especially the Communist Party, sees the task of the social movements as opening up electoral spaces and pressing for greater democratisation. The revolutionary left believes that only by strengthening the people's organisations and providing a revolutionary political leadership can change come about in Colombia. It has been forced to question the elitism of the past and show greater respect for popular organisations and their autonomy. Methods of work, the role of popular education, the role of the mass movement and its relationship to guerrilla struggle, the role of basic union demands and their relationship to revolutionary transformation, the left's weakness in the urban areas - by the mid-1980s these issues were on the agenda as never before.

But by then political spaces were beginning to close for the popular movements and, as they became more radicalised, so the repression fell harder on them. With hardly any time to consolidate, these still relatively young and fragile movements, found themselves working in semi-clandestinity and subjected to the most systematic repression they had ever experienced.

Chronology

1964   Army of National Liberation, (ELN), established its first guerrilla centre in southern Santander

1965   Father Camilo Torres creates the United Front Movement, *Frente Unido*

1966   Camilo Torres killed in military action after joining the ELN

1967   The Popular Liberation Army, (EPL), armed wing of the Communist Party-Marxist Leninist, (PC-ML), formally founded as a reflection of the Sino-Soviet split

1973   Former members of the FARC together with a sector of the ANAPO found the April 19 Movement, M-19
ELN all but wiped out after 33,000 troops move into Antioquia

1970-80 Workers' Self-Defence, (ADO), Quintín Lame Movement, 'MIR-*Patria Libre*' and Revolutionary Workers Party, (PRT), create new guerrilla movements

1974   In first public act, M-19 steals Bolívar's sword

1978-82 Liberal President Turbay Ayala presides over one of Colombia's most repressive governments

1983   First National Meeting of the ELN after its 1973 defeat, takes place

1982-85 Conservative Party President Belisario Betancur initiates a peace process with the guerrilla movement, including unconditional amnesty and a ceasefire

1985   Peace Plan fails and the National Guerrilla Coordination is formed in May. Only the FARC continues the truce
M-19 holds hostages in the Palace of Justice in Bogotá and armed forces attack building Patriotic Union, (UP), formed

2.3 The Political Response

Colombia has a long history of armed struggle, but only since the 1960s have independent guerrilla movements begun to challenge the domination of the traditional parties and propose an alternative structure of power.

The rupture with past struggles was incomplete. At least one guerrilla movement, the FARC, emerged directly out of peasants' experiences in certain regions during *La Violencia*. A handful of legendary guerrillas/bandits participated in the new movements — Fabio Vásquez, a founder of the ELN, was not the only guerrilla leader whose family had been wiped out during *La Violencia*.

But the new movements were primarily children of their times. As elsewhere in Latin America, but perhaps more so in Colombia where guerrilla warfare had been going on for ten years, the Cuban revolution made a big impact on the small group of left-wing students. They were impressed by the way in which, in little over two years, a tiny band of guerrillas had taken power in a small Caribbean island, and the belief that a revolutionary situation existed in Colombia soon took root among the urban radicals. Just under half the population still lived in rural areas and most believed that the revolution would start there.

In the wake of Cuba, a student leader, Antonio Larrota, organised the Workers', Students' and Peasants' Movement (MOEC). He was killed in 1961 while trying to establish a guerrilla centre (*foco*) in the north of the Cauca; a few years later Tulio Bayer, of the MOEC, and a former Liberal guerrilla, Rosendo Colmenares, were also killed leading a similar attempt in Vichada in the eastern *llanos*. By 1964 the MOEC had collapsed into factions.

Fabio Vásquez and a small group of mostly student activists were strongly influenced by Cuba and the MOEC when, after receiving basic military training in Havana, they set up the Army of National Liberation (ELN) in 1964. They established their first *foco* near San Vicente de Chucurí in the south of Santander, a region which, having housed the *Comunero* revolt in 1781, the peasant leagues of the 1920s, and Rafael Rangel's Liberal guerrillas in the 1950s, had a tradition of struggle.

The EPL was the armed wing of the PC-ML, which Pedro Vásquez Rendón and other former members of the Moscow-line Communist Party had set up in 1965 as a result of the Sino-Soviet split. The PC-ML began working among the peasants of Alto Sinú in Córdoba and the Bajo Cauca, a region in which Julio Guerra, the Liberal guerrilla who had helped establish the party in the area, had influence. The EPL was formally founded in 1967.

By the mid-1970s these movements were in deep crisis and faced virtual defeat. Only the FARC, with its very particular origins and character, survived the 1970s with most of its original objectives intact. But in the meantime, a second generation of guerrilla movements began to form and, in 1973, some former members of the FARC got together with a sector of ANAPO to found M-19.

M-19, a radical, nationalist and palpably Colombian phenomenon, attracted a broader base of sympathy and support than any previous group, particularly from the young urban middle class. By 1973, 60 per cent of the population lived in urban areas and M-19 was the first guerrilla group to acknowledge the demographic shift and to work in urban areas. This gave new impetus to the armed struggle, which the repressive government of the late 1970s fuelled rather than checked. Even the FARC went on the offensive.

Other new guerrilla movements appeared in the 1970s and 1980s: Workers' Self-Defence (ADO), Quintín Lame in Cauca, MIR-*Patria Libre* and the Workers' Revolutionary Party (PRT). From the ashes of the old EPL and the pro-Havana National Liberation Army (ELN) emerged movements that had thrown off their Chinese or Cuban ideological straightjackets and were seeking to root themselves more firmly in Colombian reality and among the population.

The resurgence of the guerrilla movements coincided with a deepening crisis in the traditional political parties. Political exclusion had contributed to the rise of armed organisations that refused to form an allegiance with a political order that served only the interests of a profoundly conservative ruling class. Economic developments in the countryside, particularly in regions of colonisation or expanding commercial agriculture, encouraged peasants to turn to an option that offered defence against rapacious landowners and a political project in which they figured as actors and subjects.

In an audacious move, President Belisario Betancur (1982-6), in search of a political rather than a military solution, recognised the reality of the situation and began negotiating with the guerrillas. The failure of these efforts culminated in the drama of the Palace of Justice on 6 and 7 November 1985, when the army stormed the building, which M-19 had taken over, killing 95 people who, apart from the guerrillas present, included twelve of the country's 25 supreme court judges and many members of the Palace staff. Fourteen people 'disappeared', including eight members of the cafeteria staff, three casual visitors to the Palace and three guerrillas. This marked a significant turning point for Colombia. The peace process was over. A period of polarisation began in which the guerrillas gained in strength and support and the army and right-wing elites organised to stop them and all forms of popular organisation and protest.

Guerrilla struggles: the first generation (1964 to mid-1970s)
The FARC and armed colonisation

The FARC was born in the 1960s in the wake of army operations against peasants who had settled land during *La Violencia* and maintained their own armed defence under the leadership of the Communist Party. The party had organised the peasants and their armed defence, but as a party; 'armed struggle' in the rural areas was always subordinate to a broader political strategy, which included electoral participation. When the FARC was founded, the Communist Party was fighting elections with López Michelsen's MRL. Just two months later Gilberto Vieira made it clear that armed struggle was not to be the party's priority:

> Our party . . . nevertheless considers that there is no revolutionary situation in Colombia as yet. It does not consider armed struggle in cities because such a struggle can be little more than a series of isolated events accomplished by little groups . . . The guerrilla struggle is not at present the principal form of battle. (*L'Humanité* 3 June 1966)

After 1966, the FARC's mobile guerrillas were sent into different regions; one group led by Ciro Trujillo was defeated in Quindío with the loss of many men and 70 per cent of the organisation's arms. Although it subsequently expanded its influence, the FARC remained for most of this period a defensive organisation, with roots among peasant colonisers for whom communism was less a political ideology than a strategy for survival. INCORA's initial programmes of rehabilitation in the immediate aftermath of *La Violencia* were abandoned by the mid-1960s and the colonisers left to their own devices in situations of great insecurity. They faced the constant harassment of large cattle ranchers, backed by the army, only too ready to take over land the colonisers were forced to abandon through lack of resources and infrastructure. In these circumstances the FARC offered protection both from the ranchers and from unscrupulous middlemen, and also organised basic services.

This is how the FARC's influence spread between 1965 and 1976 from Caquetá, the Meta and Guaviare to the middle Magdalena valley, Bajo Cauca and Alto Sinú. In a number of areas the FARC took over the role of the negligent or absent state to become the governing authority for large numbers of peasants. Zones of self-defence became guerrilla fronts. In the Magdalena Medio, the FARC became a virtual rural civil guard, supported for a period by landowners as well as peasants as the only force to provide law and order. These roots enabled the FARC to survive the 1970s.

The ELN

The ELN made its first public appearance on 7 January 1965, the sixth anniversary of the founding of the MOEC. Equipped with hunting rifles, 27 men and one woman held the town of Simacota, near San Vicente in Santander, for two hours. The ELN itself looks back to these years with considerable self-criticism. In an interview in the 1980s (Harnecker 1988:33) its leaders describe the problems of this early period: 'A great problem of our practice at that time was the absolutism of the armed struggle . . . we married it and didn't let it go. Whatever we believed didn't accord with that line, we cast it aside; that's why we thought that the union movement and trade union struggles were a deviation.'

The ELN gained a great deal of publicity and sympathy when a radical priest, Camilo Torres, joined it at the end of 1965. Before taking up the armed struggle, Camilo had attempted to build a political movement, uniting all those hostile to the National Front. The 1963-6 period was one of recession and unrest. His programme, entitled 'a platform for a movement of popular unity', caused a great stir when it appeared in March 1965, bringing him into conflict with his religious superiors.

Camilo planned to build a United Front of popular movements to bring people with disparate political and religious beliefs together around a common revolutionary platform. He contacted the ELN in July of that year and began a long series of discussions. The ELN was interested in his work, recognising the need for a mass urban movement that might parallel the work carried out by the Cuban 26 July Movement in Havana.

Camilo's own charisma generated an initial wave of support. The first edition of his movement's journal, *Frente Unido*, cost about twice the price of a normal newspaper but sold 50,000 copies almost immediately. But the more Camilo spelled out his programme, the less unity it generated; too left-wing for some, such as the small Christian Democratic Party, and too liberal for the sectarian left, he abandoned the project at the end of the year. His decision to join the ELN caused a considerable stir, for he had won much respect for his political work, which was in fact more valuable to the ELN than his presence in the mountains. He was killed during his first action on 15 February 1966.

Many sought to follow Camilo's example; the ELN's military capacity grew and it extended its operations to the south of Bolívar. But it remained militaristic and did little organisational or political work among the peasants. Its authoritarian, vertical structure centred around a handful of key leaders. Tensions between them ran high and differences were often resolved through executions. Two basic conflicts emerged between those who began to stress political work in the urban areas, and those who stressed the military aspect and the peasantry. The urban work suffered a major blow in 1968 when the organisation's urban network was destroyed with the loss of many cadres.

By 1973, when the movement began to extend its operations into the north-east of Antioquia, the ELN had 250 armed men in five columns. But the organisation had done no prior political work among the population of peasant colonisers and gold miners, and it was not difficult for the army to detect them. The army mounted its biggest counter-insurgency operation ever, Operation Anorí — 33,000 troops moved into the region and wiped out the ELN column. Only 70 members of the ELN in the countryside survived the operation and this was reduced to 36 by 1978. The urban structures in Bogotá and Medellín were badly hit by an act of betrayal in 1977. The ELN had entered a period of internal crisis from which it would not recover for almost a decade.

The EPL

The EPL was always seen as an instrument of the PC-ML. It established a strong base of peasant support in Alto Sinú and San Jorge, and other areas of the Colombian north-west. It aimed initially to establish a liberated territory in the region, from which the countryside would surround the city in a process of prolonged popular war, according to classic Maoist teaching. This view began to shift, with more emphasis given to work among peasant and worker unions and urban work. Its influence with ANUC's peasant base was to create many problems in that organisation. But it was able to extend its influence, notably among banana workers in Urabá in the early 1970s.

Army operations took their toll, repression fell heavily on its peasant base and the organisation lost many key leaders. But internal divisions were what tore the organisation apart and had nearly destroyed it by the mid-1970s. These began to appear in the late 1960s, but became most serious in 1975, when the movement split into several factions, from which it did not recover until the early 1980s. One tendency, the MIR-*Patria Libre*, eventually established a new guerrilla group, another established an urban terrorist front, while the PC-ML's remaining cadres began to question Maoism, breaking with it formally at its XIth Congress in 1980 and criticising much of the organisation's previous methods of work and orientation.

Guerrilla struggles: the second generation (1974-82)

M-19

The origins of M-19 are very different from those of the first generation of guerrillas. One of its wings came from the experience of ANAPO, the movement founded by Rojas Pinilla in 1964 to spearhead his political comeback. ANAPO established a strong presence in the cities, often dispensing services in the poor neighbourhoods. By the election of 19 April 1970, ANAPO was set to be the first major challenge to the National Front. Rojas with a vote of 38.7 per cent to Pastrana's 40.3 per cent in the biggest turnout since 1958, was widely believed to have been deprived of victory by fraud.

Carlos Toledo Plata, a future founder of M-19, witnessed the events in Bucaramanga, where he expected to be elected to the Chamber of Representatives:

> On 19 April, at night, the people gathered in the houses of ANAPO. They were convinced that they had power . . . The bands arrived. The people danced in the streets. Then, they informed me on the radio that throughout the country the government had suspended the transmission of the ballot which was continuing to give a majority to ANAPO. I spoke on the telephone immediately with Samuel Moreno, the general's son-in-law. He told me that a fraud was being prepared and we should mobilise the people to alert them . . . On 20 April at nine in the morning, the streets were full of people. There were demonstrations throughout the country . . . In Bucaramanga several Anapists took the town hall . . . in the streets the march of people continued, they already wanted to begin breaking windows, loot the shops . . . the people were turning aggressive . . . I spoke with María Eugenia Rojas (the general's daughter) who was in Bogotá, in the house of the general. She told me that the army had them surrounded, that we shouldn't let people carry out violent acts, we should wait and see what happened, that they were talking . . . That night the President spoke on television and announced that in fifteen or twenty minutes, at 8 o'clock,

no more people should be on the streets in Colombia, because the curfew would begin. (Lara 1986:37-8)

After the election, ANAPO went into decline; Rojas Pinilla died in 1975 and his daughter took over the movement. The fraud had left a legacy of frustration. Student radicalism grew in the early 1970s; educational opportunities had expanded and the middle class grown. López Michelsen, whose past leadership of the MRL raised expectations of reform, disappointed many when he took the presidency in 1976 and launched a neo-liberal economic policy. Popular protest increased. In the course of the decade various socialist strategies emerged that rejected the armed struggle. They ranged from Trotskyist groups to a democratic socialist movement of well-known intellectuals which sought to build an electoral force.

None of these had much impact. Armed struggle in the guise of M-19 was reborn and grew in the urban areas of the 1970s. Colombia's political system was closed to (or increasingly irrelevant to) many, for it was unable to deal with the social and political consequences of economic change.

The organisation was founded in 1972, when a sector of ANAPO joined a group expelled from the Communist Party and the FARC, namely Jaime Bateman Cajón, Alvaro Fayad, Iván Marino Ospina and Carlos Pizarro, who had reached the conclusion that armed struggle for the FARC was a struggle for the land, peasant based and anti-*latifundio*, but not a struggle for state power.

M-19 never belonged to any left-wing tradition or Marxist orthodoxy. It is closer to what might be called 'armed populism', in which its folkloric leadership, in particular the coastal-born Bateman, sought to build an anti-oligarchic and anti-imperialist mass movement with an armed wing. As Alvaro Fayad told an interviewer, 'it is impossible to think of a democratic solution in Colombia if there is no mobilisation of the masses and no military triumph' (Alape 1985:322). M-19 was in the tradition of the Nicaraguan Sandinistas, whose victory in 1979 greatly encouraged the organisation. The Leninist vanguard was rejected in favour of broad mass fronts with a multi-class character.

M-19's first public act in 1974 was to steal Bolívar's sword, a symbolic gesture which established both its Colombian character and its nationalist inspiration. It subsequently built up a following in the shanty-towns of Cali and elsewhere, solving everyday problems, giving out food and seizing milk lorries and distributing the milk. It was not until 1979, however, that it really hit the headlines when in January of that year it stole 5,000 weapons from the armed forces' main arsenal at

(from left to right) Ivan Marino Ospina, Gustavo Arias, Jaime Bateman.

Cantón Norte outside Bogotá. Although most of them were later recovered, the army never forgave the guerrillas.

Turbay Ayala became president in 1978, following the first national civic strike in 1977. Strongly influenced by the armed forces, his response was to establish the most repressive government the country had known, beginning with a draconian security statute. Imprisonment and torture, never absent in Colombia, became systematic. M-19 members were soon filling the prisons, being subjected to terrible tortures and emerging as heroes. Audacious acts, such as the seizure of the Dominican Republic embassy in 1980, while twelve ambassadors and the Papal Nuncio were celebrating that country's national day, caused a sensation.

Guerrillas and coca

M-19 began operating in the rural areas, particularly in Caquetá, in 1979. This was a conflict-ridden region, with peasant colonisers protesting against the assaults of ranchers and the neglect of the state; in 1972, 10,000 peasants had occupied the capital, Florencia, for eight days. The FARC's already solid roots were reinforced by army and police repression of the civilian population. In 1978, Turbay Ayala declared the region a 'war zone'. It was not difficult for M-19 to move into the area, though ultimately only the FARC would survive the 'Caquetá war' of 1980-1, when the army launched a brutal counter-insurgency campaign in the region.

An additional factor was now operating in this and other areas of colonisation. By the late 1970s the marijuana boom was at an end — and that of cocaine was beginning. The coca leaf was imported from Peru and Bolivia, but it was possible to grow it in Colombia. For the peasant colonisers this was an undreamed of opportunity to improve their lives and to strengthen the peasant economy, in constant danger of collapse.

The bonanza brought thousands to the region (including the cities' unemployed) and, between 1978 and 1985, there was a renewed advance of colonisation. Anarchy and violence accompanied the spread of coca production, which the guerrilla movements, particularly the FARC, were able to bring under control.

Both the guerrilla movements associated with the coca boom (M-19 and the FARC) took a pragmatic position on coca. The FARC established law and order in its areas of control and, in return, the producers and traders paid a percentage of their earnings to the guerrillas. It also protected the peasants from the traders (it stopped them paying them in *basuco* or crack) and encouraged the growers to grow food crops as well as coca. The FARC was authoritarian and harsh in punishing wrongdoers, but it established rules in a situation where the law of the jungle would otherwise reign. Its law of the mountain, as it was called, gradually won legitimacy and support. Corruption ran high within the army and police, further reducing their authority among a peasantry already deeply hostile after years of abuse at their hands. If the peasants did not pay the guerrillas, they might have to pay the army and it was usually more threatening and arbitrary in its behaviour than the guerrillas.

The armed struggle revitalised

The FARC expanded its influence considerably in the late 1970s. At the end of 1979 it had nine fronts, by the end of 1983 it had 27. At its seventh conference in May 1982 it conceded for the first time that a revolutionary situation existed in the country, and added the letters EP (*Ejército del Pueblo*, People's Army) to its name. It also decided to adopt more offensive military tactics. These significant shifts were an indication that the armed struggle was on the agenda as never before.

Serious political mistakes and abuses of power accompanied the growth of the FARC's fronts, perhaps as a result of rapid recruitment with insufficient politicisation. The tactic of demanding protection money from landowners began to look more like criminal extortion than politics, particularly when it was used against the less prosperous landowners. The FARC's eleventh front, in the Magdalena Medio, gained notoriety in this respect and, by the early 1980s, the region had become a breeding ground for the extreme right.

The revival of the ELN was the most dramatic of all. Although its military structure had been demolished, its political influence had continued, especially in the independent union movement which had grown out of Antioquia. The organisation's dispersed members, with no national coordination and often unaware of each other's work, now concentrated on organisational and political work among the people. In Bogotá 14 separate groups each worked as the ELN. In Arauca, another neglected outpost of peasant colonisers, they worked within the peasant and civic protest movements which mobilised thousands of people during the 1970s. The ELN's Domingo Laín front was formally set up in the region in 1980 as a result of the sympathy generated for a revolutionary political project, but this time only after political work had created the conditions for it, rather than out of the voluntarism of urban radicals.

By April 1982 the ELN had become sufficiently united to establish a national leadership and its first national meeting took place in September 1983, ten years after Operation Anorí. This was the organisation's first democratic forum of this kind and it led to a collective leadership of nine, with a former priest, Manuel Pérez, being given overall political responsibility. Subsequently the ELN was to grow rapidly. It now considered itself a politico-military organisation dedicated to building a revolutionary mass movement and, abandoning the *foquismo* of its past, was open to a broad range of influences from Vietnam to Central America. The ELN did not participate in the dialogue initiated by Belisario Betancur in 1982, which won it support from those disillusioned by its failure three years later.

The armed truce

Turbay Ayala's repressive government brought international opprobrium, horrified rejection from within the country and did nothing to check the advance of the guerrilla movements. For the first time guerrilla movements were articulating the people's real preoccupations. They were nowhere near taking power, nor did the majority of the population actively support armed struggle as such, but there was a good deal of sympathy for them. The greatest threat lay in the possibility of the resurgent popular movement of the 1980s linking with the guerrillas at a time when the traditional political order was in the throes of a serious crisis of legitimacy.

Even Turbay Ayala had been forced in his last year of office to consider a political solution to the guerrilla problem and to set up a short-lived peace commission. All the candidates in the 1982 election campaigned on the issue of peace. Economic recession added to the climate of insecurity and the desire to deal with the guerrilla threat before it drew more support from the growing numbers of unemployed and dispossessed. At the same time the rise of the cocaine mafia was introducing a new and violent force for political and social destabilisation.

The new president, Belisario Betancur, was a member of the Conservative Party who had begun his political career as an activist of the right. Over the years his position shifted and he adopted a highly personal political philosophy, which included a reforming 'Third Worldism'. He criticised the traditional parties for failing to introduce urgent reforms and appealed beyond the parties to all those disaffected by the old party power structures. This won him a resounding majority.

He immediately set up a peace commission composed of a broad range of political tendencies, including the Communist Party. On 19 November 1982 an unconditional amnesty was granted to all political prisoners, except for those who committed atrocities or whose crimes were committed outside combat. Several hundred imprisoned guerrillas, including top leaders of M-19, were freed.

A process began that was full of contradictions and ambiguities. Objectives and motives on all sides were often obscure. Guerrilla movements (notably the FARC and M-19) wanted peace, but they wanted something in return; they were, after all, at the height of their influence. Given the elites' entrenched opposition to reform and the effect of the economic recession on the government's resources, Betancur had few concrete offers to make. The army was hostile to the process from the beginning and most business elites and the majority of traditional politicians came to share its view. Together with right-wing civilians, the army undermined the peace process from early on. Political realities intervened; power and class interests were at stake and many of the ruling elite saw no need to relinquish anything when the guerrillas were not, after all, anywhere near taking power.

The FARC was the first to reach an agreement with the government. At the end of May 1984, it and the government signed a ceasefire agreement at La Uribe in Meta. M-19 criticised a pact in which, after 30 years of armed struggle, the FARC seemed to have won only vague promises. But the FARC was not required to lay down arms and it won something dear to the heart of the Communist Party — a negotiated political space through which to launch an electoral campaign. In an interview at the time (*Semana* 17-23 June 1986), Manuel Marulanda, leader of the FARC, spoke of his desire to return to political life as a local councillor rather than on the national political stage. In November 1985 a broad political movement, the Patriotic Union (UP), was launched, in which former guerrillas at first participated, together with the Communist Party and its sympathisers.

M-19 wished to consolidate a strong position from which to negotiate further concessions. Jaime Bateman initially responded positively to the amnesty and announced the organisation's willingness to become a political force. But M-19 resumed fighting during 1983 and Bateman himself was killed in an air-crash in April, depriving the movement of its most charismatic personality and an important unifying force. After the agreement at Uribe, M-19 occupied the towns of Florencia in Caquetá and Corinto in Cauca in a demonstration of force, but peace talks were renewed.

Days before reaching an agreement a right-wing paramilitary group gunned down Carlos Toledo Plata, who had opted to live legally under the terms of the amnesty. M-19 responded by occupying Yumbo, an industrial suburb of Cali. M-19 was, however, hoping to press its demands for reforms and for a national dialogue and, despite the police having ambushed the vehicles taking Carlos Pizarro to Corinto to sign the peace agreement, and wounding him, M-19 still signed the pact in August 1984. A carnival atmosphere reigned in Corinto. Pizarro, with bloodstained jacket, signed the agreement in front of the television cameras, and guerrillas charged for a photograph with a fighter or commander. The proceedings were a red rag to the army and the right.

ADO, a small group formed in 1974 which subsequently gained notoriety through the assassination of a former government minister, and the EPL also signed agreements. The EPL had grown since the PC-ML had rejected Maoism and the belief that the revolution was imminent, though less than other groups. It remained committed to revolutionary struggle and saw the peace agreement as an opportunity to build political support among the population.

Despite their inherent ambiguity, the agreements had considerable symbolic value. They were essentially a ceasefire in which both sides kept their arms, hence the description 'armed truce'. They were followed up by a national dialogue in which various commissions representing all sectors of the population were to prepare a series of economic and social reforms and a more lasting peace; these commissions began work in January 1984. The guerrillas had won recognition as a political force; M-19 in Corinto even managed to insert in its agreement a formal recognition of its status as a 'popular movement risen in arms'. The army recognised no such thing and, only one month after the truce was signed, the eighth brigade attacked the EPL.

The army objected deeply to the amnesty; it believed that the guerrillas were taking advantage of a political space in which to grow. The peace talks coincided with a rise in killings by paramilitary death squads. The first of these, 'Death to Kidnappers' (MAS), appeared in 1981 after M-19 had kidnapped Marta Nieves, the daughter of Fabio Ochoa, a leading cocaine mafia boss; it hunted down and killed a number of M-19 activists and sympathisers. Subsequently MAS became an infamous agent of summary right-wing justice, based in the Magdalena Medio but with influence in a number of other departments where popular unrest and guerrilla forces threatened the local elites. Between 1983 and 1984 killings took place in the Cauca valley, Antioquia, Urabá and the Magdalena Medio; in the latter region the situation was explosive. When the attorney-general investigated MAS in early 1983, 59 members on active military service were accused of belonging to it. The army command rallied to their defence. In November 1983 the Minister of Defence, General Fernando Landazábal, declared that the amnesty had expired and, along with four other generals, he was forced to resign.

The army found direct talks with the guerrillas even more repugnant than the amnesty. Ranchers, businessmen, the church hierarchy and most of the political elite came to oppose Betancur's initiatives. In an ominous development, ranchers from Huila and Córdoba and other landowners announced publicly, in paid press advertisements, that, faced with the lack of protection from the state, they were willing to assume their own defence. In a letter to the president in September 1983, the SAC

Colombia Solidarity Campaign

'MAS is the army'

branch from the Cauca valley accused him of confusing 'liberty' with 'licentiousness'. In February 1985 the ten main *gremios* publicly announced their opposition to the peace process.

The political climate was tense; between 1983 and 1985 the popular movement was reorganising and rejecting the influence of the traditional parties. At the same time, escalating, often drug-related, criminal violence added to the atmosphere of social crisis. Colombia experienced more kidnappings in 1983 and 1984 than any country in the world. Kidnapping had become the favoured means of criminal extortion at all levels of society and, for some guerrilla organisations, a political tool and means of extracting funds.

Betancur, representing a current of intellectual opinion far in advance of the society's power structures, was increasingly isolated. The Liberal Party controlled Congress and only a few hand-picked party members had joined his Conservative government. The Conservative Party bosses were as antagonistic to most of Betancur's initiatives as the Liberals. Within the government itself, there were conflicting views of the peace process. Jaime Castro, Minister of the Interior from 1984 to 1986, played a particularly ambiguous role. For him, the peace agreements were intended to lead almost immediately to the guerrillas laying down their arms and participating in the political process.

The guerrillas were not going to lay down arms without guarantees for their safety on the open political stage and the implementation of the reforms they had sought. But death squad killings were increasing and fighting was continuing in several regions. The issue of who was breaking the truce was now a subject of intense debate. The media mostly reproduced the army's version of events, which inevitably blamed the guerrillas, but other evidence suggests that the army had never taken the ceasefire seriously. Laura Restrepo, a member of the government peace commission, claimed that the army launched a full-scale attack on the M-19 camp in Yarumales, not far from Cali, in December 1984.

The reform process was getting nowhere. The 'national dialogue' soon languished amid mutual recriminations, with few commissions coming up with concrete proposals. The government's 'rehabilitation plan' for the country's most neglected regions, concerned mostly with road building, barely got under way. A house-building programme was the goverment's most notable achievement. A balance-of-payments' deficit, a fiscal crisis and growing unemployment overshadowed the peace process and prospects of reform. By the end of 1984 the government had launched an austerity plan.

Distrust was growing in all parties. There were signs that Betancur's priorities were shifting towards appeasing the opposition. Betancur was not the man to use the support he had enjoyed on the streets when he won the election against his own party; he was no Gaitán. A new Minister of Agriculture, Hernán Vallejo (president of the powerful ranchers' *gremio*, the Federation of Cattle Breeders (FEDEGAN), and a notorious right-winger) was appointed in 1985. This did not augur well for the agrarian reform which was meant to arise out of the peace process. Landazábal had been replaced as Minister of Defence by General Miguel Vega Uribe, who had played a notorious role in the repression under Turbay. In 1985 the Council of State awarded a young doctor, Olga López, damages for the torture she suffered during her imprisonment at General Vega's brigade headquarters. Despite the scandal in the press, the general remained at his post and was given the title, 'Minister of Peace'.

Meanwhile M-19 was using the space afforded by the ceasefire to build up political support. But this was as threatening to the ruling elites as its military activity. A poll carried out in the five main cities (by the Institute of Liberal Studies) in 1985 found that, should M-19 stand for election, it would win 36.7 per cent of the vote. In March M-19 filled Bogotá's central square, the Plaza Bolívar. In May its leadership narrowly escaped being killed in a grenade attack in Cali.

Its activists, with a combination of revolutionary rhetoric and old-style Latin-American populism, went into the slum districts of the big cities to set up their so-called 'peace camps'. During the first half of 1985 camps were set up in Medellín, Bucaramanga and Barranquilla, as well as Cali where M-19 had a particularly large following. But the repression fell heavily on the slum-dwellers themselves, whom the security forces never forgave for being receptive to M-19's message. Disillusionment was great among the urban poor who saw hope in that message, but whom M-19 left entirely vulnerable when repression came.

What M-19 hoped to achieve by these activities is still a subject of controversy. Was it genuinely seeking to create a political movement, or was it recruiting support to enable it to resume the armed struggle? According to one of its leaders, Antonio Navarro Wolff:

> The objective of the dialogue was to reach an agreement on minimal reforms (agrarian, urban, political) so that it would not be necessary to press for their implementation by the use of arms. We wanted the political space to be opened in reality. I asked the Minister of Communications to allow us to buy a radio station in Bogotá, another in Medellín, another in Cali, another in Barranquilla and another in Bucaramanga. I said that we committed ourselves to abide by the regulations. But the Minister never replied, although we called her over three or four months and sent intermediaries. We didn't want . . . the revolution to be made by decrees. Simply we asked for

> modernisation, the opening of the bourgeois state. We asked
> for the bourgeois revolution. (Lara 1987:236)

There is considerable naivety in the idea that a ruling elite that had moved so rapidly against all independent political expression, from Gaitán to ANAPO, would allow a guerrilla movement still dedicated to changing the power structure to broadcast freely to the country's main cities. M-19, which attracted the middle as well as the lower classes, was a threat with or without arms. Unlike the Communist Party, which refrained from doing anything that might jeopardise its re-entry into the political arena, M-19 had gone on the political offensive.

After the attack on its leaders in Cali, M-19 announced that it considered the truce over. At the end of May 1985 Colombia's guerrilla organisations created a National Guerrilla Coordination (*Coordinadora Nacional Guerrillera*) which included the ELN. A month later, the third national civic strike took place and thousands of peasants marched to demand their right to land and life. Only the FARC continued the truce, signing a new agreement and, amid great opposition from business, the military and the church, prepared to participate in elections within the UP coalition. As the climate of intimidation against the UP mounted, however, the FARC's main leaders held back from active participation and eventually separated organisationally from the UP.

Colombia fell headlong into undeclared war. During 1985 the paramilitary groups became more systematic in their elimination of guerrillas and suspected civilian sympathisers; one by one M-19 leaders were killed, beginning with Iván Marino Ospina in August of that year. They also carried out clean-up campaigns against delinquents and homosexuals and were responsible for 800 killings in Cali alone. The army launched sophisticated counter-insurgency operations and, by the end of the year, had regained control of the slum districts of Cali. In November William Calvo, an EPL leader and member of its negotiating team, was killed.

Betancur's peace process was brought to a tragic and definitive end on 6 November 1985 when M-19 took over the Palace of Justice in Bogotá. The President had refused to answer a telephone call from the President of the Supreme Court of Justice, who was being held hostage in the Palace, and so the military took control of the operation. It decided to storm the palace at a great cost to human life. The military solution to the country's problems had emerged victorious from Betancur's peace process. Whether this was as a result of the logic of events, the President's own ambivalence, or his open support is a matter of much speculation. The ruling elite and the army did not have the political will for peace; ultimately the guerrilla movements' demands for reform could not be met.

The Palace of Justice

A deathly silence hangs over the centre of Bogotá. The few hundred people who have slipped through the police cordon, which blocks off a square mile round Plaza Bolívar, stare at the ruins of the palace of justice.

Inside, soldiers, Red Cross officials and relatives wearing masks because of the stench, pick through the rubble in search of corpses. They could be at it for most of the weekend.

No one is sure how many people died during the 28-hour pitched battle inside the palace between M-19 guerrillas and the army. Estimates go as high as 120.

About 40 guerrillas stormed the building at 11.40 on Wednesday. There was never an opportunity for negotiation. Within an hour the building was surrounded by hundreds of troops and tanks. The Colombian newspaper *El Tiempo* described it as 'the most spectacular and dramatic counter-guerrilla operation'.

People watched scores of repeats of the final army assault on television and compared it to the Second World War.

The fire from the tanks and rocket grenades from both sides began a blaze that raged out of control and destroyed the building. The explosions blew out windows throughout the district.

Thousands of people kept vigil yesterday, pressed against the police cordon. Many had been there almost since the fighting started. They were awed by the scale of the damage and the occasional slow exit of an ambulance carrying a corpse.

Cannon fire had gouged holes out of the front of the building and the metal window frames have been twisted by the flames. The cost of repair has been estimated at £10 million.

Many people were shocked by the scale of the violence. Twelve supreme court judges were killed in the fighting, including the president of the court, Alfonso Reyes, all 41 rebels and at least 17 soldiers.

On Wednesday Dr Reyes had pleaded over the telephone to have the shooting stopped.

Every guerrilla was killed and Colombians are already turning their death into a legend. One version is that they fought to the end refusing to surrender: others say that they committed suicide, leaving explosives taped to their bodies to kill as many soldiers as possible when the troops stormed the palace.

(*Guardian* 9 November 1985)

Chronology

1974	First competitive presidential elections are held after the National Front, but parity in cabinet and civil service retained formally until 1978
1974-86	Abstention rate in presidential and legislative elections between 50-60%
1981	Right-wing anti-kidnapping movement, MAS, appears
1983	Amnesty International denounces 800 extrajudicial killings attributed to members of the army, police and paramilitary groups. Increasing reports of arrests, torture and disappearances of popular leaders
1984	Rodrigo Lara Bonilla, Minister of Justice, assassinated by drug barons
1986	Supreme Court suspends the extradition treaty with the US. Role of armed forces increases after Palace of Justice massacre

2.4 The State's Response

> You were born Conservative or Liberal, as you were born
> Catholic, without the option that the party (almost like
> religion) was a real choice; besides, party affiliation was lived,
> at least among the peasants, like a kind of faith, similar to
> religious belief, the old people, today with certain scepticism,
> let it come through in what they say: '*In 48 we believed in
> politics and the priests*' said an old Conservative, '*the reverse
> of what happens today*'. (Ortiz Sarmiento 1985:38)

The decline of party struggle also meant the decline of party loyalties.
These loyalties had traditionally held society together, rich and poor, rural
and urban. They did not decline overnight. The paternalistic relationship
of *cacique* and peasant survived in many backward rural areas, but in the
towns and cities it was a material arrangement between patron-politician
and client-voter that came to dominate.

The traditional political order failed to modernise along with the
economy. It depended, as it had always done, on capturing the vote of a
population that was essentially excluded from any genuine participation
or influence in political life. Although clientelism was inefficient and
corrupt, the economic elites welcomed the political stability it brought,
an ambiguity that prolonged the inertia of the political system.

Other institutions were influenced by the 'depoliticisation' that
began in 1958. The church, for instance, had made its peace with the
Liberal Party, while urbanisation brought secularisation and reduced the
church's contribution to social cohesion. The army, meanwhile, was also
'depoliticised'. Over the years it became more politically autonomous,
an actor with its own set of priorities, centring on counter-insurgency and
the fight against the subversion of the social order.

Except in the realm of economic management, the army was the
only state institution with the capacity for strong and decisive action.
When material rather than party interests began to challenge the existing
order, it was the repressive capacity of the state that rose to the occasion.
In other respects the state's weakness stands out, its inability to rise above
the interests of the dominant economic groups and introduce social,
economic and political reforms.

Despite party strife, civil war and the early decades of urbanisation
and industrialisation, the traditional order, based on oligarchic power,
family patrimonies and the dominance of the two-party system managed

to survive in Colombia through the 19th to the 20th century. By the 1980s, however, the challenges were greater than ever before, though from politically, socially and geographically diverse quarters. On the one hand, there was pressure for change from popular movements and guerrilla organisations, on the other hand, there was the corruption of institutions by the rise of the cocaine mafia. The crisis of the two-party system was not just from without, it was also from within, from the inertia and decay of the political order itself.

The crisis of the two-party system

Elite politics

The 1958 pact contained the seeds of future crisis. Although the pact lasted formally only until 1974, power sharing arrangements continued. Colombia was governed by *de facto* coalition rule in one way or another until 1986 when, for the first time since bi-partisan government was developed Virgilio Barco's Liberal administration ruled without the participation of the Conservatives.

The constitutional reform of 1968 introduced some modifications in the pact, mostly to enhance the executive's authority. For instance a simple (rather than two-thirds) majority in congress and other representative bodies was introduced to enable the president to get legislation passed without recourse to emergency measures. Parity in departmental and municipal legislatures was eliminated in 1970 (at the national level in 1974) and elections were opened to all parties. The first competitive presidential election was held in 1974, but parity in the cabinet and public employment was retained formally until 1978. From that date article 120 required the majority party to offer 'adequate and equitable' representation in the executive branch to the party with the second highest number of votes.

In offering guarantees of patronage and power to both parties, the bloody conflict of the past was avoided; fear of single-party hegemony was strong and the Conservatives' attempt to assert it in the 1950s was not easily forgotten. The post-*Violencia* political order rested on agreements within the elite, an elite whose self-perpetuation was apparent in the political families, fathers and sons, who dominated the country's political history before and after *La Violencia*. The selection of the president depended upon delicate negotiations between a few party leaders, within each party, and, finally, between parties. Secret deals were struck, a practice that spread to other areas of policy making and to the selection of candidates for public bodies.

The perception that a party could only survive if it had access to government was deeply rooted in the political culture. It meant that neither of the traditional parties would accept a government-opposition formula, which would relegate its influence to Congress. A sample of private-sector, government and party leaders in 1977 and 1978 showed that two-thirds were unequivocal on this issue (Hartlyn 1988). One Liberal politician claimed that opposition movements or party factions could survive only four to five years without access to state resources and bureaucratic posts.

Congress became the locus of factional and clientelist groups. Congressmen fought for legislation that favoured their own regions and for patronage posts. Battles were not over policies but over access to government resources to bolster local party bosses. Government was seen as a prize to be shared by the political class in order to perpetuate its own power and to ensure that the economy served the interests of those who owned it. The *gremios* maintained direct access to government and influence over policy making. The people remained at the margins of political life, to be manipulated by the party bosses and by their henchmen. They were 'electoral capital'.

This situation was hardly conducive to the emergence of a participatory political culture, let alone a sense of loyalty to the polity as such. Any attempt by a politician to make a direct appeal to the masses was quickly suppressed. The growth of third forces, such as the MRL and ANAPO, was dealt with by co-option or fraud. The two parties controlled all the major means of communication and the economics of electoral campaigns made it difficult for opposition parties to compete. This frustrated not only the urban poor, but also the substantial middle class. When people began to organise independently of the traditional forms of control, the political and economic orders found it exceedingly threatening.

The media and politics: family businesses

Politics in Colombia is very much a family business. The journalist and writer Apolinar Díaz Callejo described it as 'hereditary power without monarchy'. The López, the Gómez, the Santos, the Turbay, the Lleras, the Pastrana, the list of political families who have dominated Colombian political life in the 20th century is endless. And all ex-presidents continue to enjoy political influence after they have left office. This domination of society by the political families is reflected in ownership of the press, radio and television.

The press: The major dailies are *El Tiempo* (circulation, 200,000 weekdays,350,000 Sundays) and *El Espectador* (circulation 215,000). Both belong to different factions of the Liberal party. *El Tiempo*, the more conservative of the two, is owned by a great Liberal political family, the Santos. The paper has considerable power; the present editor, Hernando Santos, boasted of the election of Virgilio Barco:

> We didn't make the new president, but *El Tiempo* certainly was an important factor in getting him nominated. At first we were virtually the only ones fighting for him (*Miami Herald* 18 August 1986)

La República (Conservative) is owned by the family of former President, Mariano Ospina Pérez. *El Siglo* (Conservative) is controlled by the infamous political family of Alvaro Gomez Hurtado. *Nueva Frontera* (Liberal) was edited by former President Carlos Lleras Restrepo, *Guión* (Conservative) by former President Misael Pastrana Borrero, *La Prensa* (Conservative) by Pastrana Borrero's son, and the weekly *Semana* by the son of Liberal ex-President Alfonso López Michelsen.

Radio and TV: Over ten million Colombians view TV regularly (compared to eight million newspaper readers) and 17 million listen to radio. Although radio is a state monopoly, most broadcasting licences are granted to private companies. There are two Conservative Party radio networks, *Cadena Radial Colombiana* (Caracol) and *Radio Cadena Nacional*, and one Liberal, *Circuito Todelar*. Together, these three control one-third of the system. Particularly interesting is TV news. All the major news programmes are controlled by the children of ex-Presidents:

Noticiero de la 7 — Felipe López Caballero, son of López Michelsen, grandson of López Pumarejo
Noticiero 24 — Mauricio Gómez, son of Alvaro Gómez Hurtado, grandson of Laureano Gómez
Noticiero Crypton — Diana Turbay Quintero, daughter of Turbay Ayala
Noticiero TV Hoy, — Andrés Pastrana, son of Misael Pastrana Borrero
Tele Noticiero de Mediodía — María de Rosario de Ortiz Santos, from the Santos family of *El Tiempo* and ex-President Eduardo Santos.
Sources: Article 19 1988 and interviews.

The contradiction created by these arrangements was that economic modernisation required a modernised policy. But the very nature of the party pact, its need to guarantee each party and all the local networks a measure of political power and patronage, undermined efforts to introduce rational planning. It was impossible to build an efficient bureaucracy when civil-service jobs depended on the parity agreements of the traditional parties rather than on merit.

Carlos Lleras Restrepo (1966-70) pioneered efforts to introduce rational planning, but many of his attempts were thwarted by the nature of the agreement that had brought peace between the parties and by the traditions of clientelism. Administrative and financial centralisation under Lleras Restrepo did take key areas of policy-making out of the hands of Congress and partisan politics and into those of technocrats. But the private sector maintained its influence over economic policy-making and, after Lleras Restrepo, checked the growth of the public sector. Opposition to state intervention remained strong.

The political system was designed to prevent radical policy shifts, so reform initiatives rarely lasted long. The two-party system, opposition from party bosses, and landowner and business interests in Congress were all barriers to such initiatives. Presidents who nevertheless persisted had either to resort to emergency measures, such as declaring a national economic emergency and bypassing Congress, or end up in prolonged negotiations with the party bosses.

The new clientelism

The *caciques* — often natural leaders with a personal influence over a traditionally servile peasant community — brought out the vote at little cost. Colombia's shift from being a rural to a predominantly urban society brought with it a new form of clientelism which fed on the deprivation, unemployment and powerlessness of the urban poor. Those with power acted as brokers between the population and the source of benefits and services, exchanging these for the only leverage available to the poor, their vote. The personal loyalties of the past became pragmatic loyalties. The parties lost their mystique but retained their influence through material favours. The professional politician replaced the old-style political boss with his 'natural' claim to leadership.

Clientelist relationships shaped the political system from top to bottom — from national, to departmental, to municipal government. For people at the local level, government was personified in the professional political fixer:

> The rule of the (party) machines over public bodies meant that all past, present and future action of the state appeared personified, that is headed by a local political boss. From the installation of electricity, the construction of a bridge, a school or of a health post, to the most everyday things such as medical attention, a job, agricultural credit etc . . . (all) are considered the product of his action or of his benevolence, they are his

works. 'Look at this health centre. The Guerras put it there'
. . . 'the light in this district was given by Martínez Simahán'
. . . 'the sewerage system was put in by Dajer'. (Díaz Uribe
1986:46)

Each political boss, usually a congressman, headed a regional fiefdom
and controlled a political machine. His immediate subordinate controlled
sub-regions through various close associates, mostly public employees
and local municipal leaders who owed him allegiance because promotion
depended on the electoral chances of the boss they had associated with.
Finally there was the local *líder* or political fixer, who did the daily work
of negotiating services and state works in exchange for votes.

The power of the regional boss usually depended on his influence
in national government and in the party directorate, which in turn
depended on the electoral advantage he brought his party. As a
congressman he had an allocation of funds to use as he wished, the
auxilios or pork-barrel funds. Lleras Restrepo tried to reduce the funds
available in the 1968 constitutional reform and encountered huge
opposition.

Even more important than these to the political boss was his ability
to provide jobs in state agencies. In the early years of the National Front,
dismissals were politically impossible and the bureaucracy mushroomed
at all levels. Efforts were made at civil service reform, but with little
success; the 'parity mentality', as it is called, prevailed. The growth in
public employment slowed down in the 1970s, but partly because labour
problems were increasing in the sector as party affiliation became less
important than wages and conditions.

Clientelism and the urban poor: the case of Pereira

The following accounts describe the way in which clientelism — the trading
of favours in return for political loyalty — operated in the 1970s in one
region of Colombia.

'Pereira is the capital of the Department of Risaralda, which consists of 14
municipalities. Political life in the Department is largely dominated by the
struggles between the Liberals and the Conservatives, but it is largely Liberal
in its political persuasions . . . The 14 municipalities in the Department
according to the parity agreements have to be shared equally with seven of
the municipal administrations (*alcadías*) being Liberal and seven Conservative
. . . Because of particular conditions in the development of the Department
of Risaralda it became established that the mayor of Pereira would always
be a Liberal. In order to compensate for this it also became established

practice that the General Manager of the council-controlled Public Services Corporation would always be a Conservative. The rate of turnover of Governors has been particularly rapid in Risaralda — between 1967 and 1975 it had 15 Governors, an average period of office of 6.4 months. Each change of Governor has meant the resignation of the Departmental Government and the 14 municipal administrations and necessitated the reshuffling of the posts in the Departmental Government and municipal administrations to arrive at a new and locally agreed on combination based on the parity agreements . . .

Both the Liberal and Conservative Parties are deeply divided into factions, and the conflicts between these factions are often greater than the conflicts between the parties. Thus in the mid-Seventies the Conservative Party in the city was split into two factions — the Official Conservatives and the Unified Conservatives — and the Liberal Party was split into three factions — the Official Liberals, the Front for Liberal Integration, and the Integrated Liberals . . . their identity is in large measure bound up with the personal rivalries and tactical considerations of local *caciques*. Thus for all intents and purposes the Official Liberals were Camilo Mejía Duque, the Front for Liberal Integration was Oscar Vélez Marulanda, and the Unified Conservatives were Jaime Salazar Robledo.

Although these *caciques*, in the course of developing their power base, have held at one time or another the most important political posts in the municipality and department, they have generally been content to use their positions on the local Party Directorates in order to put their placemen on the factional electoral lists and in the various administrative structures. However in many cases they have also become members of the Senate and House of Representatives. By delivering the vote of their factions to the *caciques* who stand at the head of the national factions they have often been able to gain considerable power at a national level. This in turn has enabled them to channel resources at the national level down to the [housing] settlements supporting them at the local level. Occasionally new factions based on aspiring *caciques* have emerged through the political mobilization of the settlements, and the gaining of seats on the elected bodies, but once established, *caciques* and their factions seem to be remarkably resilient. Thus the political life of the Liberal Party and the city as a whole since the Sixties has been dominated by the factional disputes between the followers of Camilo Mejía Duque (Official Liberal) and Oscar Vélez Marulanda (Front for Liberal Integration), and by the attempts of the latter to overthrow Mejía Duque's long-established control over the local party, the municipal council and the allocation of public posts in the municipal administration and council-controlled agencies . . . In the process of so-doing the Front has not hesitated to use the political opportunities thrown up by the conflicts surrounding the process of land invasions, and the formation of squatter settlements on the periphery of the city. Indeed through his sub-*caciques* (see below) and political lieutenants Vélez Marulanda has sponsored and organized invasion movements in order to pose as a champion of the people, to win the votes of the people thus organized and their friends and relatives, and to force the Mejía Duque administration into repressive actions that expose its anti-popular attitude to the electorate. The period immediately before elections has been the preferred time to carry out these activities.

The basis of the relationship established between the *caciques* and the settlement populations is one involving the exchange of their electoral support in return for access to the resources in the state apparatus controlled by the *caciques*. However it is only very rarely that a *cacique* will deal directly with the settlement populations largely because many of their demands and activities may be illegal or on the borderline of legality (e.g. in invasions of public land), and some of the *cacique's* strategies used to meet them may also be in the grey area of legality (e.g. handling of national *auxilios*). Therefore there usually exists a group of sub-*caciques* dealing with the urban demands being made by the settlements and whose job it is to deliver the vote of the settlements to the *cacique*. Generally speaking they are prominent local politicians who seek advancement through the local party and state apparatus with the good offices of the *cacique*. They can be deputies to the House of Representatives, or acquire positions in the municipal administration, the council *juntas* or the departmental government . . .

Although these sub-*caciques* do make frequent appearances in the settlements, day to day affairs in them are handled by a number of political lieutenants. They are crucial figures in the patron-clientage hierarchy and are directly involved with the identification of settlement demands and the organization of the settlement into the political camp of the *cacique*. They are often rank and file party members in direct receipt of party patronage either through receiving funds from the party or by having secured a job in the lower rungs of the state apparatus through the influence of the party.

However, in most settlements the political lieutenants will operate through a local settlement leader who will not only act as an organizer and informal opinion leader, but also as a political broker who mediates between his followers, higher levels of authority and the broader political system. He . . . will use his connections with the *caciques* and their placemen in the state apparatus as a means of exercising control over the political life of the settlement. In return for the total or partial satisfaction of the demands of the settlement (or more commonly the promise of their satisfaction) a settlement leader will be expected to mobilize the settlement into the *cacique's* political faction. This can take the form of attendance at political meetings and rallies, demonstrations in favour of the mayor or the municipal administration..and the organization and propagation of electoral support for the candidates for public office on the faction party's lists . . . In return for all this he may get privileged access for the settlement to state resources as well as a number of important favours for himself. These can include the unofficial sanctioning of illegal means of acquiring personal wealth such as the fraudulent collecting and handling of community funds, illegal trafficking

> in lots, special fees for service provision and income from properties in the settlement . . .
>
> These patron-client linkages with the political *caciques* are often considered critical for the establishment and the development of a settlement — so much so that low income settlements quite frequently publicly demonstrate their allegiance by naming themselves after the *cacique*. Thus in Pereira there are settlements called *Barrio* Camilo Mejía Duque, *Barrio* El Plumón (Vélez Marulanda's nickname), *Barrio* Salazar Robledo . . .'
> (Burgess 1986)

Although the public administration has become more professional at the national level, appointments for party loyalty remain common. At the departmental and municipal level, party patronage is still the norm. The administration for the department of Sucre in 1983 (*ibid*:92) not only kept a record of each employee's party affiliation, but also knew what fraction of the party he or she belonged to. One employee explained what this meant for his work:

> If for example, I begin a (public) work, this becomes a political flag for my group . . . the others oppose its development. Not to enter into details, a departmental secretary said that this street cannot be finished because it is the work of a certain group, a certain man. How does one relate to a political boss? Promoting the works which serve him politicallly; that is, those that mean votes for him. (*ibid*:47)

It is not surprising that so much failed to get done at the local level and that the civic movements took off with such force in many urban areas, keeping their distance from 'politics'. For many, politics has come to mean 'politicking', associated with administrative corruption and the use of public office for private gain. And, by the late 1970s, cocaine money was oiling the political machines and corrupting them on an unprecedented scale.

The decline of the two-party system

The traditional parties continued to dominate political life. *Caciquismo* and clientelism sustained local party control in many areas, particularly in the countryside. A study of municipal elections (undertaken in 1986) concludes that since 1981, 88 per cent of municipalities have given a majority to the same political party (Pinzón 1986: 9). Pinzón also found that in 1984, 35 per cent of the municipalities were still giving 80 per cent majorities to one party. In only one-third of the municipalities was there anything resembling genuine competition.

But fewer and fewer people actually voted. With high levels of abstention, the bosses only had to mobilise sufficient votes to secure a victory. There was no incentive to develop strong party institutions or accommodate opposition interests.

Abstentions were high at elections even before the National Front. The largest turnouts were in 1942 and 1946 — a period of great polarisation. The National Front's first presidential election attracted nearly 58 per cent of the registered electorate, but thereafter the decline was marked, except when real change seemed likely. The 1970 election, with ANAPO in the ascendent, brought a much larger turnout (52.5 per cent) than the 40.1 per cent in 1966. The 1974 election, the first competitive presidential election which held great expectations for López Michelsen's candidacy, brought a 58.1 per cent turnout. But abstentions were high again in 1978 when only 40.9 per cent voted.

The 1986 presidential election — held during a period of intense political debate and following improvements in the registration process — attracted just over 50 per cent of the vote. It was the third election to attract more than half the registered electorate in the six presidential elections since 1966; only two elections attracted more than half the eligible electorate. Elections to the legislature attracted even lower turnouts, an average of 40.3 per cent from 1958 to 1978, with only 33.4 per cent voting in 1978. Abstentions in the big cities were notorious; in the 1976 legislative elections in Bogotá, 80 per cent abstained.

So long as the parties continued to dominate, overall attachment to them declined. In one study carried out in 1976/7, only 59 per cent of those surveyed in urban areas claimed a party affiliation, compared to 74 per cent in rural areas (Hartlyn 1988: 162). This was particularly marked among the younger and poorer urban sectors. For large numbers of people the traditional parties were no longer seen as relevant mechanisms of mediation with the state. Nor did half the population of voting age consider elections important; many who did participate were simply exchanging their vote for a favour or service more immediately useful to their lives.

Cocaine politics

At a meeting of the mafia in Cali, it was reported that 'we have to finance the campaigns of the politicians and keep them on our side. We can participate in business without causing a scandal, in family businesses so that they get used to dealing with us. In the end, they receive innumerable benefits' (Castillo 1988:224). In the late 1970s and 1980s the economic importance of cocaine money was in many ways outweighed by its usefulness for irrigating and corrupting the political system. The army, the legal system and Congress have all been corrupted by the fortunes to be made from drugs and protecting the traffickers. But many of these institutions were in any case vulnerable to corruption. The archaic judicial system was already notorious for its inefficiency and ineffectiveness; Congress already functioned on the basis of the ambitions of political bosses who had won their seats through vote-buying and rigging; and abuse of power in the army was institutionalised after years of counter-insurgency in which it was never held accountable for arbitrary violence against civilians.

The judicial system failed to operate in relation to the drug mafia; bribery and intimidation persuaded most judges to release any member of the mafia who has been arrested. Some sources suggest that 80 per cent of the Medellín police are on the mafia's payroll. Two ministers of defence have been involved in drug scandals: General Miguel Vega Uribe's daughter is married to a congressman indicted for drug trafficking in the US, and General Luis Camacho Leiva's brother was caught with cocaine aboard a Ministry of Defence plane. In 1983, an elite army corps, using airforce planes, transported an entire cocaine laboratory from the Colombian to the Brazilian jungle. Some middle-ranking officers were punished, but the general who reportedly ordered the operation was promoted.

The names of prominent politicians began to be linked to those of drug traffickers in the 1970s. In 1978 a US television programme, *60 Minutes*, implicated two cabinet ministers in the López administration and a presidential candidate, Turbay Ayala, with drug-trafficking. Since then numerous members of the political elite have been named for their connections with the Medellín-based cocaine cartel, while many local politicians have used cocaine money to buy votes and influence.

The mafia has been particularly concerned to prevent the signing of an extradition treaty with the US, for extradition goes right to the heart of its self-image, which is one of successful businessmen rather than of common criminals. In 1982 several drug barons stood for Congress and Pablo Escobar, a leader of the Medellín cartel, was elected a *suplente* (substitute) to another congressman. This was the year when an extradition treaty with the US was due to come into operation. The mafia campaign against it was backed by numerous congressmen, who called it an abandonment of national sovereignty.

The president at the time, Belisario Betancur, resisted US pressure to sign the treaty for two years, but gave in when Rodrigo Lara, the Minister of Justice, was assassinated in 1984. Lara had been appointed because he was not in the pocket of the drug barons. With Colonel Jaime Ramírez Gómez, the head of the narcotics unit of the national police, he launched an offensive against the cartel. By tracking down the US source of ethyl ether, an essential chemical for processing coca, Ramírez made a major breakthrough. The information led them to Tranquilandia, the largest cocaine-processing laboratory in the world, which they raided and destroyed. Seven weeks later Lara was murdered. When a Bogotá judge found evidence that leading cartel members were behind the killing, he also was murdered, and Colonel Ramírez was murdered in November 1985.

The killing of Lara was an indication of just how far the mafia had penetrated the heart of the political system. It had bugged his phone before his death and sent him recordings of his own conversations. The mafia was flaunting its virtually parallel security system. The traditional political elites were more threatened by the evidence that they were becoming a state within a state than they were by the fact that millions of dollars were being made illegally. The government came down hard on the mafia in the immediate aftermath of Lara's murder. The threat of extradition was revived and the mafia hired 50 high-ranking lawyers to demand the annulment of the treaty before the Supreme Court of Justice. The judges responsible for making the decision all received the following threat:

> We are writing to you to demand favourable positions for our cause. We do not accept resignations, we do not accept sabbaticals, we do not accept fictitious illnesses . . . Any position taken against us we shall take as an acceptance of our declaration of war. From prison, we will order your execution and with blood and lead we will eliminate the dearest members of your family.

Four magistrates connected with the case were killed in November 1985 in the Palace of Justice; another who survived the attack was later killed in July 1986. Before the end of 1986 another ten judges had been murdered. The same year Guillermo Cano, editor of the main Liberal daily, *El Espectador*, was killed after publishing a US report on the mafia. At the end of 1986 the Supreme Court suspended the treaty. While the treaty was in force 18 people were taken to the US for trial on cocaine charges. Only one top mafia boss, Carlos Lehder, was ever extradited and that is believed to be because he had come into conflict with rival mafia bosses.

The mafia constantly hoped to secure some tacit acceptance of its trade and to seek legitimacy and entry into the social and political establishment. Its members were 'cocaine capitalists'; as businessmen they shared the anti-communism of the ruling elite. In 1982 Carlos Lehder even set up his own extreme right-wing political party, the *Movimiento*

Latino Nacional (National Latin Movement). Ideologically they were inclined to join the right in the war against subversion in the belief that this would enhance their status in the eyes of the 'establishment'. In areas of growing social conflict, such as the Magdalena Medio, they have bought up huge tracts of land and become landowners themselves, concerned to pacify the rural areas for economic reasons. Between 1979 and 1988 the mafia is reported to have bought one million hectares in Córdoba, the Magdalena Medio, Urabá, Caquetá, Meta, Sucre and elsewhere, investing huge sums in improving the land (*Semana*, 29 November 1988).

This formed the basis of the 'functional alliance', the so-called 'dirty war', that emerged in the 1980s between the drug barons, sectors of the army, businessmen, landowners and political bosses to eliminate suspected guerrillas and left-wing civilian activists. The appearance of MAS in 1981 is often given as the starting point of that war, but it was quickly followed by a plethora of mostly local death squads.

Private and violent settling of accounts for political and criminal purposes is not new in Colombia. The paid assassin (*sicario*) was present during *La Violencia*, as was paramilitary private justice. Landowners and political bosses made use of both. But the amount of money cocaine has generated has turned the *sicario* into a well-equipped and well-trained

'We don't want MAS, we want peace' — peasant farmers' demonstration.

professional. The number of homicides increased substantially in the late 1970s and 1980s, and private criminal and political justice became a notorious feature of Colombian society.

Although the various death squads to emerge in different parts of the country during the 1980s targeted different sectors, they were all profoundly 'anti-communist'. Some engaged in 'clean-up' operations to eliminate petty criminals, prostitutes and homosexuals; others took on the guerrilla organisations and their sympathisers. Others again specialised in the artists, intellectuals, journalists and lawyers who were thought to be critical of the political order. Many of this group went into exile in the mid-1980s when their names appeared on death lists.

Private paramilitary justice was taken up by landowners, businessmen, army officers and others who believed Betancur's peace initiative favoured guerrilla organisations and the popular movement. In their hands, MAS grew into one of the most powerful paramilitary groups, operating out of Puerto Boyacá in Magdalena Medio. In the mid-1980s the mafia began to invest huge sums into turning MAS and other groups into private right-wing armies which, when not murdering peasant and worker leaders, could help to defend the drug industry.

Political responses

Despite a growing awareness during the 1970s that 'something was wrong', the political class was slow to recognise the need for political reform. President Lleras Restrepo's reforms met intense opposition inside and outside his party and made him lose his party's nomination in 1973. Conservatism was built into political arrangements, which were set up to protect privilege. It was easier for politicians to use the party machines than to challenge them. López Michelsen used Turbay Ayala's machine to support his nomination and won the presidency in 1974.

López Michelsen, however, proposed that institutional reforms, such as strengthening local government and reforming the judiciary, be carried out by a constituent assembly of the two traditional parties. After tortuous negotiations with political leaders, the idea went forward but was declared unconstititional by the Supreme Court. Fierce debates over how to bring about political reform were to become a feature of Colombian politics, with few reforms making the statute book.

The 1978 election, with its poor turnout, represented a low point for the political system. The new president, Turbay Ayala, had engaged in all sorts of political machinations and the election took place amid accusations of fraud and drug-funded campaigns. People were taking their opposition onto the streets for want of any other political channel. Social unrest had grown under Turbay's predecessor and the national civic strike of 1977 led to calls from the army for strong state action.

Turbay responded with the security statute. Unrest was regarded as the result of communist subversion, not the failure of the traditional order — it called for repression not reform.

Article 121 of the constitution gave the president wide powers to introduce a 'state of siege' in cases of 'internal unrest' and, after 1947, Colombia was in an almost permanent state of siege. A series of decrees gradually increased the armed forces' control over public order, with the authorities' ability to protect the public against abuses of civil liberties and human rights correspondingly diminishing over the years. A security statute (*consejos de guerra verbales*) increased both the army's power to arrest and the kinds of crimes that could be tried by a military court. Peasant and worker organisers and suspected guerrillas were arrested, tortured and ill-treated on a large scale. M-19 became active at this time, gathering legitimacy in the face of government abuses.

There was a strong backlash, and antagonism to Turbay's repressive policies eventually split the Liberal Party. 'New Liberalism' (*nuevo liberalismo*), a movement attacking corruption within the party, was led by Luis Carlos Galán. But he only managed to win 10.9 per cent of the vote in the 1982 election when he stood against López Michelsen, the official candidate backed by the powerful regional boss of Tolima, Alberto Santofimio.

Although the Liberals had until then carried an easy majority, Belisario Betancur won the election for the Conservatives because he appealed beyond the party machinery to the people, particularly the urban middle class. He spoke of reform, renovation and building a national movement; he was seen to be making a fresh attempt to create a third force in Colombian politics and a serious effort to deal with the national crisis without recourse to more violence and through pragmatic and political solutions. He seemed to offer leadership and ideas to those who were sickened by violence, not just the political violence, but also the criminal violence in the cities, which had reached epidemic proportions by the early 1980s.

But his electoral rhetoric did not translate well into coherent government policies. He was preoccupied with his domestic peace initiative and with his part in the Contadora Group working for peace in Central America. He paid less attention to political reforms at home and had no substantial economic and social reform programme with which to back up his peace initiatives. There was strong opposition from within his own party and the promised national movement never materialised; a few selected Liberals participated in his government, the rest opposed him from their congressional majority.

Though it had taken years to get through Congress, the critical second passage in December 1985 of the constitutional amendment allowing the direct election of mayors was significant. Other reforms dealt with some overt abuses of the bipartisan system, for instance one member from a third party was to be allowed to join three members of the traditional parties on a new National Electoral Council. But other reforms including attempts to limit and account for campaign funds and to give minority parties more access to legislative posts, failed to get through Congress, and the two parties failed to agree on how to end Article 120 which perpetuated the coalition rule.

The formation of the UP was perhaps Betancur's most lasting political legacy. Though unacceptable, despite having distanced itself from the FARC, to the army and many in the ruling elite, the UP's participation in the 1986 presidential election gave it the biggest vote in the history of the left (4.5 per cent of the total) and 15 UP candidates were elected to Congress. The 'dirty war' was immediately stepped up, and UP politicians began to be murdered.

The country was polarised. Right-wing solutions were being implemented with a vengeance in regions where social conflict had made the local elite insecure. The cocaine mafia was as powerful as ever and funding the dirty war's proliferating death squads and hired assassins. Drug dealers walked free, while leaders of the popular opposition were gunned down. The popular movement was better organised and more

Human rights demonstrators protest against the murders of UP members.

united than it had ever been before and, though M-19 suffered a serious defeat with the events of the Palace of Justice, other guerrilla movements had never been stronger militarily or enjoyed more support.

The church and social change

The National Front had allowed the church and the traditional parties to place too much emphasis on solving old problems instead of facing new ones (Wilde 1980). The 1958 plebiscite called for respect of the Catholic religion as an essential element of social order. In a letter to the cardinal, leading Liberal notables rejected the errors of philosophical liberalism, and the church, in turn, came to terms with its Liberal enemies. It promised to stop intervening in elections on behalf of the Conservative Party and declared its 'neutrality' in conflicts between the parties — it gave its blessing to bipartisan party rule.

The church began to concentrate on its own structures. It set up a permanent secretariat for the bishops' conference in Bogotá, nationally coordinated the growing number of dioceses and developed a strong, centralised, administrative machine. The number of priests, mostly recruited from the middle and upper classes and from the Catholic heartlands of Antioquia and Caldas, increased. Nearly a third of all the bishops appointed between 1930 and 1970 came from Antioquia; two-thirds came from towns of fewer than 10,000 inhabitants from communities with traditional Conservative allegiances and values. (Medhurst 1984:39).

Over the years the church had grown accustomed to its privileged position; it was therefore resistant to change and afraid of new ideas and secular movements. It was the ultimate authority on moral issues and enjoyed a unique status in public life. Every year in the presence of the president, the Colombian republic was rededicated to the Sacred Heart of Christ. The church was geared to a predominantly rural society with low levels of education and isolated from outside influences and intellectual movements.

It was thus difficult for the church to come to terms with social change that so affected its relationship with society and its institutional cohesion. Because the social threats of the 1920s and 1930s were either defeated or (as in the case of the church-sponsored labour confederation, the UTC) co-opted, it had, like other Colombian institutions, been able to delay its confrontation with the modern world.

But rapid urbanisation, the growth of the middle class and of educational opportunities, and the increased participation of women in the labour force since *La Violencia*, have all worked towards secularising society, changing the nature of family life and reducing the church's influence. Despite the establishment's opposition to family planning, at least half the women of child-bearing age are believed to use contraception, even in the peasant regions of Boyacá, Nariño and eastern Antioquia, where the clergy still has considerable social influence (González 1987:28).

Economic growth and modernisation were accompanied by social inequalities and intellectual movements that questioned the status quo. Under these pressures the church's consensus broke down. When Vatican II forced the church internationally to confront the modern world, the Colombian hierarchy was taken by surprise. It had to give superficial approval to declarations it had scarcely had time to absorb. On disseminating the new teachings, the editors of the official church journal, *El Catolicismo*, resigned and suspended publication. Cardinal Luis Concha Córdoba argued that Vatican II's teachings obliged the Colombian church to make liturgical, not social, changes. The hierarchy rejected the working document presented to the Latin American Bishops' Conference in Medellín in 1968 on the grounds that it had been drawn up by the 'left wing' of the Latin American church and did not represent Colombian reality.

Subsequently the church did become more conciliatory and, on a number of occasions, acknowledged the existence of social inequalities; occasionally it even criticised the political system for creating apathy and maintaining a minority in power. It was, however, careful to condemn violence, put the church above all ideology and never fundamentally challenge the social order.

As the church hierarchy was taking cautious steps towards recognising new social realities, a mainly younger group of priests was moving way ahead. Camilo Torres, who had once been destined for high church office but gave up the priesthood to join the guerrillas, had made a considerable impact. The *Golconda* group led by Bishop Gerardo Valencia Cano (named after a farm in Viotá where it first met in 1968) was formed to perpetuate Camilo's ideas, but, lacking any solid organisation and subject to church persecution, it did not last long after the bishop's death. In 1972 a highly Marxist and fiercely anti-church-hierarchy group, 'Priests for Latin America', tried to pick up from where it had left off.

For the church the 1970s was a decade of confrontation between the hierarchy and the radical wing. In 1973 a new Concordat reaffirmed the church's special position in society, including its prominent role in education. The radicals were creating fissures in a traditionally monolithic church, which was used to negotiating with the state as an equal and having its authority unchallenged from within or without. In 1976 the hierarchy called for a plenary at the bishops' conference specifically to discuss the radical priests' religious and lay groups and at which it criticised all attempts to apply Marxist thinking to society and condemned those who had opted for socialism.

Alfonso López Trujillo, the archbishop of Medellín and later a cardinal, became a leading actor in the Latin American bishops' counter-attack against liberation theology. First as secretary-general then as president of the bishops' conference, he worked to ensure that the radical church did not dominate the second Conference of Latin American Bishops at Puebla in 1979, as it had the first in Medellín. Such were his manoeuvres and machinations that some claimed he was working for the CIA as well as for the Vatican.

Despite his efforts, however, after Puebla there was a decisive growth in the number of grassroots Christian communities linking the church and the popular movement. Two coordinating bodies were set up — the Peasant Christian Communities (CCC), for the rural areas, and the Christian Base Communites (CEB), for the urban areas. In 1981 the 37th plenary assembly of Colombian bishops condemned these coordinating bodies, along with the publication, *Solidaridad*, and the Jesuit research centre, CINEP, which had become a focus for radical popular education and publishing.

Though they never disappeared, tensions between the radicals and the hierarchy eased in the early 1980s. The church continued to be conservative, critical of the popular movement and the civic strikes and reticent towards Betancur's peace plans, but it now had less national political importance. Many churchmen believed that the church could only survive by closing its doors and that those who sought to engage it in the social questions of modern times threatened the integrity of the institution. The radicals maintained that unless the church took a stand in support of the poor, it would merely end up as an ally of the status quo with nothing to offer the people it served. The Colombian church had obviously failed to resolve the 'conflicting imperatives of identity and relevance' (Medhurst 1984:212).

The armed forces and political autonomy

'Military coups in Colombia, far from being an ambition of the military to take power, have been a strategy of the political class to prevent themselves losing it'. (Landazábal Reyes 1983:119)

Colombia's reputation as one of Latin America's most stable democracies owes a great deal to the fact that the military has been largely absent from the political stage. The two successful coups of the 20th century, in 1953 and 1957, both had civilian support and encouragement. Political life in Colombia has been dominated by the two parties, with the army remaining subordinate to the political elite. It was the elite's decision to increase the army's power to deal with 'internal disorder'.

The army's role in counter-insurgency and in repressing student, worker and peasant unrest has made it confront the important social questions of the day. Essentially middle-class and loyal to the social and political order, it has asserted its right to defend this order as it has seen fit; its interpretation of what is wrong with the order does not, however, necessarily coincide with that of the ruling elite. The army's growing sense of institutional autonomy and of national rather than party identity has worried the civilian elite. There have been a number of civil-military crises over the past two decades, which have often been accompanied by rumours of a coup.

The first, in 1965, concerned the then Minister of Defence, General Ruiz Novoa, who wanted the military to study economics and development issues (not just technical and military topics) and to invite progressive social scientists to lecture at military colleges. Though Ruiz Novoa never abandoned his trenchant anti-communism, he thought it important during this period of conflict to develop the army's understanding of the social origins of subversion and he himself proposed certain reforms, including agrarian reform. Such independence of thought was unacceptable to the members of the civilian elite, who feared attempts by third parties to break into their bipartisan control of national decision-making; they, after all, were still supported by many high-ranking officers, and so Ruiz Novoa was removed from office.

But the confrontation with social reality continued. The army became more repressive in the mid-1960s under Lleras Restrepo; it was repeatedly sent into the universities to deal with student unrest at a time when the students were joining the ranks of the EPL and ELN. The intellectual leadership of the armed forces now came from a group of officers who had fought in Korea. They disseminated the Pentagon's new strategic thinking (in the wake of the Cuban Revolution) on internal 'subversion', as well as ideas based on their own experience of counter-insurgency warfare. Repression concerned them, but so did the social roots of subversion, which Ruiz Novoa had been so keen to examine.

Like many of its neighbours, the Colombian army tended to equate legitimate social protest with subversion. In a lecture in the late 1960s the outspoken army commander, General Alvaro Valencia Tovar, who as head of the fifth brigade had hunted down Camilo Torres when he took to the jungle, explained how 'the covert war never shows itself; it is a slow process of infiltration, which penetrates society and the state, to the youth, to the university, journalism, the armed forces themselves, the clergy, the structures of political power, the trade unions' (Leal Buitrago 1984:215). But neither Valencia Tovar nor many other high-ranking officers believed that subversion could be dealt with by arms alone. He himself had promoted preventive programmes to undermine guerrilla support. He had also played a large part in awakening distrust of the traditional political elite within the officer corps. He set up the Military University and encouraged the study of liberal professions, such as law and economics. He was retired from the army in 1975 (amid rumours that a coup was being plotted) after supporting a subordinate, whom the government had demoted without consulting him.

Counter-insurgency operations, involving US-funded civic as well as military programmes, had brought the army face to face with social conditions in areas of guerrilla activity. The 1968 Andes Plan, for example, was a global attempt to eradicate subversion, which contained a number of developmental as well as repressive features. The army worked closely with INCORA in regions of potential social conflict. The civilian elite was not always happy about such projects because they gave the army prestige and influence, which could strengthen its autonomy. In 1969, General Guillermo Pinzón Caicedo, one of the officers behind the Andes Plan, was made to retire when he suggested that the army be given greater control over its own finances.

By the 1970s the military already had considerable administrative autonomy from the state and had become less dependent on the traditional parties for its political orientation. But beyond that there was little unity. Fierce rivalries existed between the different branches of the armed forces — the army being far stronger than the airforce or navy — and ideological differences were growing.

There was some progressive and nationalist opinion within the armed forces and one well-organised group, known as *Estrella Dorada* (Gold Star), which published numerous articles calling for sweeping social and economic reforms and condemning the violation of human rights during army operations. It was particularly critical of the intelligence and counter-intelligence battalion, which it accused of setting up a right-wing terrorist group in the 1970s. But these progressive thinkers were slowly purged. General José Joaquín Matallana, a controversial figure with nationalist views who had openly criticised excessive US influence in the country, was forced to retire in 1976.

General Luis Carlos Camacho Leiva was a leading light among the hard-line conservative officers who now rose to prominence. As commander of the armed forces under López Michelsen, he organised much of the repression of the 1977 national civic strike and subsequently (in an unprecedented move) led 33 generals, airforce commanders and admirals to demand the implementation of emergency measures to deal with the problem of internal security. Such measures had already been drawn up, but López Michelsen left it for his successor to implement.

Turbay Ayala had been a close friend of the armed forces since the 1950s when, as a cabinet minister during the military junta, he had acted as an intermediary between them and the political parties. He had often appealed to Congress to increase military salaries. When Camacho Leiva became his minister of defence the security statute was implemented.

The US increased its military support for Colombia and, as the Central American situation became more serious, Turbay's government became noted for its pro-US foreign policy. The military also drew closer to its Latin American counterparts. The 13th conference of commanders of American armies took place in Colombia in 1979, and the armies agreed to coordinate their struggle against communist subversion.

The military had unprecedented political influence during the Turbay government, for this was when M-19, its most serious left-wing adversary yet, moved centre stage. Torture was an essential weapon in its bid to break this guerrilla organisation (as well as the popular movement) as quickly as possible.

The military hardliners were now convinced that subversion was their sphere of expertise and that the civilian authorities should not interfere. They had, after all, been engaged in counter-insurgency warfare since the 1950s, longer than any other Latin American army. They did not aspire to take over the state and, unlike in the Brazilian, Chilean, Uruguayan and Argentinian armed forces, the 'national security' doctrine was less an ideology for government than an ideological support for their war against communism.

General Fernando Landazábal Reyes, a leading exponent and ideologue of Colombian military thinking, was a Korean war veteran who spent many years in counter-insurgency warfare; he rose to commander of the army in 1980 and to Minister of Defence under Betancur, but was forced to resign at the end of 1984. Throughout this period he published his ideas in a series of books, gaining himself a reputation as an influential and controversial figure.

He maintained that the Catholic church, the middle class and the armed forces were the pillars of capitalism and encapsulated the nation's traditional values. But when the church was divided by Vatican II, the middle class weakened by economic difficulties and the military lost the ruling class's political support, the military was the only force able to confront Marxism and subversion with any resolution. This was his and his generation's war and they were not prepared to lose it.

Such attitudes hardened during the crisis of the early 1980s. High-ranking officers blamed the Communist Party's central committee for subversion, denounced the mass media for allowing communist infiltration and, at the beginning of 1982, General Landazábal even accused the education system of promoting subversion.

The army justified all methods of restoring order. The number of political killings carried out by it, the police, the various state security forces and paramilitary groups with which they were associated rose from 105 in 1980 to 653 in 1983, with 200 people 'disappearing' over the same period. In an investigation the Attorney-General found agents of the state security forces responsible for 70 per cent of the disappearances (Acosta and López 1984).

The army was ill-disposed towards accepting the change from Turbay to Betancur, i.e. from a military to a political solution to the problem of social order. When the Attorney-General named the 59 serving officers who had participated in MAS, General Landazábal asked members of the army to donate one day's salary for their defence. Although Landazábal himself was forced to step down at the end of 1983, the army was supported by a powerful body of opinion among the *gremios*, particularly the ranchers' federation, politicians and the mass media.

Strategic thinking in the armed forces had shifted in favour of low-intensity conflict (LIC). This attempted to adapt traditional counter-insurgency thinking to the 1970s and 1980s — when revolutionary movements were no longer the isolated bands of guerrillas they were in the 1960s, but influenced mass-based social and popular movements. It was far more difficult to defeat such movements by conventional means, while short, high-profile campaigns of extermination did not win the public's support.

The US developed LIC as a way of policing the Third World without recourse to direct military intervention, which was so unpopular at home. LIC is a strategy for prolonged and total war using both conventional and unconventional means; it includes political, economic and psychological warfare, programmes to win the hearts and minds of local populations, and various techniques of terror.

Generals and colonels began to disseminate and implement these techniques during the 1980s. In one of their most successful operations, in the Magdalena Medio, the armed forces collaborated closely with MAS and, despite Betancur's peace initiative, but no doubt helped by accusations, counter-accusations and the general confusion surrounding the initiative, managed to continue the war there and in other regions.

Soldiers stop and search a bus, Corinto.

Joe Fish

In the end the army, not the president, won the day by storming the Palace of Justice in a dramatic display of power and impunity. In failing to support political solutions, the traditional elite had left the way clear for the military to implement its own measures. Describing the events at the Palace of Justice, the former Attorney-General, Carlos Jiménez Gómez (quoted in *Informe de la Comisión Internacional de Observación Judicial en Colombia* 1988:36), recognises the armed forces' political autonomy: 'Not one but two constitutions rule in Colombia: the one sold in bookshops and chemists, a basic edition for the general public, and the other, arriving subtly, unheard and silently penetrating into the heart of society and the state, it is not known when or how or by whom, for the private use of the armed forces.'

Democracy without the people

This focus on institutionalism, on the constitutional and legal formulae on the 'paper' Colombia, has a long history. When the traditional parties were not engaged in bloody battle, this was the ground on which they fought out their rivalries and ensured that neither party monopolised the state apparatus. These are the Colombian political system's trappings of modernity — regular elections, two main parties, a legal Communist Party, a parliament, and pressure groups of all sorts. But this is formal Colombia. To call the real Colombia a 'democracy' is to wrest content from that word or to reduce it to a set of institutions.

But neither is Colombia a dictatorship. The military has never seized control of the state and tried to 'end politics', as elsewhere in Latin America. Civilian and electoral traditions do exist and, until recently, the traditional parties commanded loyalty and legitimacy. Political spaces (if not access to power), though rapidly closing by the mid-1980s, did exist for opposition movements. Colombia has variously been described as a 'formal authoritarian democracy', a 'restricted democracy' and a 'constitutional dictatorship'.

The Colombian political system is essentially *sui generis*, worked out over time between an elite divided politically but not economically — the result of an intra-elite negotiation. The state operates at two levels. At one level, democracy exists for the elite, the private sector (through its *gremios*) has direct access to the executive branch of government, the state is responsive to the international funding agencies and to the interests of capital, and is technocratic, centralised and stands above the demands of particular regions and departments. At another level, at the 'political' level of the legislature, the system operates to meet local and regional needs through brokerage and mediation.

Colombia thus presents the outside world with a modern, rational face and with a relatively successful history of economic management. The existence of a large middle class reinforces the image of modernity and economic development. Underneath, however, at the level of civil society, most people's lives are circumscribed by corruption, inefficiency and neglect which, with the people's own strategies for survival, have ensured a functional political stability.

Colombia is a democracy without the people. Marginalised economically and politically, the state has reserved for the majority the 'state of siege' and all the exceptional repressive legislation and procedures that can guarantee order where other mechanisms fail. Even that sector of the middle class that has been included economically, remains on the margins of the existing political system. By 1986 'official' and 'unofficial' repression dominated and the ruling elite was preparing to go on the counter-offensive against the many challenges that now faced the political order.

PART THREE

Counter-Offensive

Chronology

1986   Liberal Party President Virgilio Barco establishes 'party in power and party in opposition' government for the first time

1987   New agrarian reform law is passed under Barco administration
June: Peasant marches in north-east of country
October: Jaime Pardo Leal, leader of UP, assassinated

1988   January: Carlos Mauro Hoyos, the Attorney-General, killed by the 'extraditables'
Barco government introduces the Statute for the Defence of Democracy or 'anti-terrorist law'
February: Massacre of 14 peasants in Meta
March: First popular election of town and city mayors is a major event in Barco's political reform project
20 banana workers assassinated in Urabá
April: Amnesty International publishes condemnation of human rights violations in Colombia
May/June: 80,000 peasants mobilise during the 'May Marches'. Repression is severe
Urabá and later Caquetá come under direct army control
October: Massacre of Llano Caliente
National general strike, October 27, is partially successful in the midst of repression
United Nations team visits Colombia to investigate increasing number of disappearances

1989   Urban Reform Project becomes law
January: Assassination of 12 members of investigative commission, La Rochela
Constitutional Reform bill begins passage through Congress
April: President Barco admits publicly to the existence of paramilitary training schools and anti-communist terrorist organisations. Relationship between paramilitary, drug barons, landowners and armed forces is uncovered during March and April
August: Luis Carlos Galán assassinated. Government renews extradition treaty. Conflict between drug barons and government intensifies
November: M-19 guerrilla group signs peace agreement with government
December: Cocaine baron Gonzalo Rodríguez Gacha killed

3.1 Counter-Offensive

I have said and broadcast that in Colombia people are tortured, killed and made to disappear; this is carried out by people with authority, by state security agents, soldiers and police. I say this as a state employee and not as a conspirator; as someone complying with a sacred duty. Democracy in Colombia is crying out for revision. (from a lecture in Medellín by Carlos Jiménez Gómez, former Attorney-General, 30 August 1986)

By 1986 Colombia's political crisis had become acute. The ruling class was divided over how to deal with it; different factions held different views, which ranged from advocating all-out war on the entire opposition to acknowledging the need to make some concessions and to open up the political system. Power became increasingly fragmented. In some regions right-wing private justice reigned, everywhere the army operated without constraint, the drug mafia had its own fiefdoms, and the guerrillas controlled large areas in some territories and were on the attack in others.

When Virgilio Barco was elected with a large Liberal majority in 1986 he had the examples of his two predecessors to look back on. Turbay's repression had merely served to strengthen the guerrillas' influence. Betancur's political solution had merely alienated the armed forces and business elite, while the guerrillas had continued to gain strength. Neither had met popular aspirations for social justice, reform and political participation.

President Barco had neither Betancur's charisma nor Turbay's skill as a political wheeler-dealer and was initially vilified for failing to offer leadership at a time of crisis. But Barco cautiously began to steer a course midway between his two predecessors, introducing some flexibility into the political system and widening its support amongst the urban middle classes, while increasing the state's power to deal with popular unrest and insurgency.

Agrarian, urban and political reform were high on his government's agenda. The first popular election of mayors (introduced by his predecessor) took place during his administration. Barco wished to bring back the government's legitimacy and to restore faith in its institutions. He aimed to tackle 'objective' causes of 'subversion', such as the state's absence in areas of colonisation, absolute poverty and land hunger. He did not intend to talk to the guerrillas, but to the communities that gave them support; the army would deal with the guerrillas and those who continued to help them. Only in his penultimate year as president did he even consider peace talks.

Many of Barco's reforms were thwarted by economic and administrative constraints, and by the absence of any political will outside the group of modernising technocrats who had designed them. They did, however, obscure the authoritarianism of Barco's government. Increasing numbers of legislative decrees were made under 'state-of-siege' provisions — 61 by the beginning of January 1989 — which were used to introduce a tough anti-terrorist statute, the 'Law for the Defence of Democracy' (in many aspects more drastic than Turbay's security statute) and to create exceptional legal provision for public-order problems.

Barco economics versus Barco social plans

President Barco followed orthodox economic policies during his administration, and economic growth was still healthy at 4.6 per cent for 1988. The international commercial banks showed their confidence in the economy when they made a US$164,000 million 'challenger' loan in 1989. Overshadowing the future was the fall in coffee prices with the collapse of the international coffee agreement and a 20 per cent fall in oil earnings due to guerrilla attacks on the pipeline. Towards the end of 1989, there were projections for slower growth, and some economists were predicting a recession. The cost of the cocaine war and the climate of insecurity for investment had taken their toll.

But the administration pressed ahead with plans to shift the economy towards export-led growth and the necessary trade liberalisation needed to accomplish this. Plans were drawn up for privatisation of state commercial, financial and industrial activities, and foreign capital was guaranteed 100 per cent ownership in most sectors. Foreign consultants were invited to study ways of furthering the restructuring and modernisation of key industries.

Growth in public expenditure exceeded government plans, due in part to the high levels of violence and increases in the defence and security budget. This fuelled inflation which was 28 per cent in 1988 and expected to be only slightly less in 1989. The real value of the minimum wage decreased 8 per cent between October 1986 and 1988, while industrial wage averages fell by 10 per cent.

Social programmes were the victim of the government expenditure cuts which followed, leading the influential economic review of the Comptroller-

General's office, *Economía Colombiana*, to conclude: 'the administration's "flagship programme, the eradication of absolute poverty" is scuppered and with it the illusion which still maintains that an orthodox economic programme is compatible with a better distribution of income and better conditions of life for the great majority of the population excluded from the "benefits of economic development".' (*Economía Colombiana* Jan/Feb 1989:70) The figures illustrated the point:

Shifts in investment by programme (millions of pesos)

January-August	1987	1988	Variation%
Highways, roads and transport	20,042	26,525	32
Public services and health	4,673	2,695	-42.3
Defence and security	3,873	12,912	233.4
Housing and urban development	754	439	-41.8
Debt servicing and financial investments	14,742	20,176	36.9
Industrial, mining and artesanal development and promotion	2,857	3,374	18.1
Agricultural sector	13,856	5,487	-60.4
Educational development	2,877	2,130	-26.0
Electrical infrastructure	3,521	33	-99.1
Regional development	3,526	4,727	34.1
External trade development	38	0	-100.0
Others	599	2,248	275.3

Barco hoped to discourage private justice by enabling the state to take on the task, but, in so doing, gave official sanction to the abuse of power by the state's institutions. Giving the army greater powers, failing to bring army officers to justice for human rights violations and increasing the military budget encouraged the impunity with which it operated. An international commission that visited Colombia in 1988 concluded that, though many Colombians regard the army as a state within a state, the armed forces in fact only 'enjoy a freedom of action implicitly granted by the Chief of the Executive . . . the Executive gave up the exercise of real control because it knew that this control would be rejected and that rejection would compromise the constitutional order' (*Informe de la Comisión Internacional* 1988:36).

Although less visible alongside the atrocities of the paramilitary, the official repression carried out by the army and security forces was just as lethal. Low-intensity warfare aimed to keep the army's operations out of the headlines. The bombing, torture and killing of civilians went unreported (except by human rights organisations) and, so long as the army and police remained under the exclusive jurisdiction of the military courts, they could not be testified against or prosecuted by civilian courts, even for political murder. The new military penal statute, which Barco signed in December 1988, gave anyone accused of torture a suspendable prison term of only one to three years.

Joe Fish

President Barco and his generals.

The military mind

General Rafael Peña Ríos retired from active military service at the end of 1987 at the age of 49. Since he was sixteen he had been fighting guerrillas. He came first of 800 officers from all over the western world in the Chief of Staff's course in Levenworth, North Carolina, US. He was commander of the XII Brigade in Caquetá, and in March 1988 he gave his first and very frank interview to Plinio Apuleyo Mendoza of *El Tiempo*.

Are we at war, General?

We are at war. Just as they created two Vietnams, two Koreas, there could be a Colombia divided into two.

What is happening? Why isn't there an effective military response to armed insurrection?

In order to develop, the guerrilla needs three supports: one political, another social and the third economic. At this moment it has all of them. The political support it was lacking, it obtained through the peace agreements.

Movements arose which weren't aiming to integrate the guerrillas into legal activity, but were simply their political projection, not explicit but camouflaged. Each guerrilla organisation has its political movement, broad in some cases, small in others.

Don't you think that the political groups are one thing and the guerrillas another? The confusion of these two is dangerous. The identification of the UP and the FARC has produced many assassinations.

The violence of the so-called paramilitary groups comes from that transparent relationship between political group and guerrilla group. It wouldn't have arisen if from the beginning the former were made responsible in the agreements for what the second did.

Some years back, General, the army had more initiative, it confronted the guerrilla, it defeated it, it recovered stolen arms. Nothing of that is seen today, What is happening? The army lost its capacity for combat, because it was taken from it. It was taken away at the very moment when military justice was deprived of its function of judging public order crimes . . . at the moment army commanders began to face charges, when their hands were tied. The army lost the protection of the state . . . the basic problem is that the army is not being used as a military force. It is being used a preventive force, as a civic force. Not even as a police force, because the police has more powers. A simple interrogation carried out by a military authority has no legal validity. It is not, as it should be, a force of repression.

Repression is a vetoed word..

The function of the army with respect to subversion is repression. But today you can't shoot before you're shot at. The Statute for Defence of Democracy was left with no backbone when the Supreme Court annulled the right of the armed forces to carry out searches . . . we are not asking for a licence to kill. But just to arrest, search, keep a detainee for eight or ten days and carry out an interrogation . . .

Don't you believe in a political solution to the problem of subversion?

I don't. The aim of these groups is subversive, that is the seizure of power by arms to change a system and a society. It is not insurgency, it is subversion . . . Insurgency corresponds to political, economic and social problems. When those problems disappear, so does insurgency. If new political spaces and reforms are open, insurgency loses its reason for being. Subversion, no. It accepts dialogue from a purely tactical sense, to strengthen itself, but never abandons its objectives . . . Here, there are politicians who say that we must enter into dialogue with the guerrillas. They are people who already accept defeat and who want to win their favour or those of their political groups in certain regions for electoral interests or for protection.

How to defend the country better, General?
We must recognise that there are insufficient troops to protect the thousand municipalities. Besides, civil support to the police is not allowed as it is not legal. That would create armed self-defence or paramilitary groups, it is thought. We are at war, that is forgotten . . .

And how do you defeat the guerrillas militarily? Is it possible within the institutional framework of a democratic system, without recourse to a dictatorship, which the democrats, the immense majority of the country, all reject?
It is possible. But the nation has to take the firm decision to confront subversion as an adversary, an enemy. It must be defeated. And in this struggle, all the institutions must take part, the Supreme Court of Justice must take into account the reason of state, the fact of a country in danger, and not abstract legal considerations. If there is will on the part of the government, will from the parties, will from the Court and the judiciary, will from parliament, the armed forces will have the will to fight and win . . . they don't have it now for lack of support. Many officers say, why should we get ourselves killed for those who judge us without taking into account that we contribute our dead?

General, the country is aware of that. But it won't accept the dirty war. It doesn't want torture, disappearances. The complicity of the army in these activities has been condemned. For a democrat, that is to be rejected.
That dirty war exists, but the army is not linked to it. It is caused by private initiatives, due to the absence and weakness of the state and also to the pain caused by the subversive groups. An energetic state would make the dirty war unnecessary.

What do you call an energetic state?
A state which gives us the instruments to act. It must create legislation which supports our operations. It must create a legislation which protects the army's witnesses. Which makes it possible to take special measures, which restrict freedom at a given moment. I am not speaking of arbitrariness nor of despotism, but rather of the institutional framework adequate for a war situation.

If this doesn't happen what will?
A very serious power vacuum. Nothing will remain as an alternative, neither one of the parties, nor the church, nor, as people have come to think, the armed forces. Only subversion. It is the only organised force with a project.

Evidence mounted during the Barco years of the army's involvement in the paramilitary's unofficial violence. High-profile arrests, which had isolated the Turbay government, gave way to extra-judicial killings and disappearances for which the army could disclaim responsibility. No steps were taken to curb this violence until Barco's last year of government, by which time there were at least 140 death squads (eight organised nationally) and a virtual private right-wing army responsible for thousands of murders.

There was a clear shift in the pattern of repression over the Turbay, Betancur and Barco years. By 1988, the most violent year of the decade, a new phenomenon — the massacre — had appeared. In that year alone 691 people died in 84 massacres (defined as killings of four or more people at a time), of which the vast majority were carried out by right-wing paramilitary groups (WOLA 1989:126-9). Serpa Uribe, the Attorney-General at the time, wrote a letter to ministers (*El Tiempo*, 6 August 1988) in which he said that, 'without a doubt these massacres are part of a plan to intimidate and exterminate, conceived and implemented by a network run by the most perverse of human beings'. He went on to say that, 'I also think that the freedom with which they operate suggests that they have the protection and/or acceptance of influential sectors of the population including the authorities'.

By 1989 the combination of official and unofficial violence had taken its toll on the popular movement. By mid-1988 the repression had made it almost impossible to organise peasant marches. Army bombings and raids forced peasants to flee from areas of guerrilla activity, irrespective of whether or not they were collaborators. The general strike called by the CUT in October that year was met with tanks on the streets. The paramilitary groups and army got rid of some of the popular movement's most experienced activists, either by eliminating them or forcing them underground or into exile where they could no longer work with the movement.

There were, however, many differences between Barco and the organisers of the dirty war. Barco was basically a technocrat whose reforms were meant to nudge the political system into gently accommodating opposition and modernising its institutions and structures. But the economy could not meet the demands of the people without massive structural transformation, so the popular demands and popular organisation were repressed. Trade unionists negotiated under the threat of arrest, peasants were at risk from the landowners' assassins and elections were characterised by fraud and vote-buying.

Choosing between democratic and authoritarian paths to political stability posed a real dilemma. Although the modernisers distanced themselves from the dirty war, their main priority was to restore order and efficient economic management, rather than to bring the organised right to heel for its crimes, which explains why left-wing activists were murdered in their thousands under Barco, but practically nobody brought to justice for the killings.

During 1989 another serious misjudgement by the Barco administration became apparent. Its assumption that the greatest threat to the political order came from the left and the popular movement allowed a much more immediate and real challenge to that order to consolidate its power: the cocaine mafia. The alliance of this mafia with sectors of the army and the traditional elite had enabled it to increase its power and influence.

Now owners of vast tracts of land in some of the most troubled areas of the country, the mafia was in the vanguard of efforts to clear them and other areas of popular organisations, trade unions, opposition politicians and activists as well as guerrillas. The mafia was now allied to the extreme right which by the middle of 1989 had its own political expression in the MORENA party. The Barco administration's aim of strengthening the state looked increasingly threatened as the mafia went on to show its readiness and ability to eliminate the highest level of government official in defence of its interests. The cocaine wars which began in August 1989 demonstrated more clearly than ever the vulnerability of Colombia's weak state.

The limits of reform

In 1987 Barco presented Congress with 20 reform projects, all of which his government considered vital. But, by the end of the year, only one (agrarian reform) had been passed and that amid accusations of irregularities such as the absence of a quorum. When it reached its last stage in the senate, only 22 of the 114 senators were present for the debate and that was not the end of the story. The Liberal majority in Congress guaranteed Barco nothing; the regional bosses operated according to a logic of their own.

Congress and its vices

El Tiempo (29 December 1988) made a list of some of the 'vices' of Congress: absenteeism in both Senate and Chamber of Representatives, the poverty of the debates, especially on the part of the opposition, legislation carried out in subcommissions where the discussions are never known, government pressure on MPs and vice versa, legislative incapacity to regulate MPs' foreign travel, failure to pay telephone bills, the exaggerated presence of bodyguards. President Barco's efforts to push through reforms have become ensnared in these obstacles. Here are some examples from press reports during his administration.

'During the final vote (of the agrarian reform project) there were insults, physical aggression, fights and threats with firearms amongst the MPs.' (*El Tiempo* 12 December 1987). But most revealing about the nature of Congress was the fraud to which the government resorted in order to get the agrarian reform passed: 'The MPs who denounced the fraud made use of their legitimate right and asked to be shown the list to check the number of votes cast against the number of persons who responded to the call to vote. Luis Lorduy Lorduy, secretary of the Chamber of Representatives, refused to hand over the list and, taking advantage of the confusion, got it to the table of César Pérez, president of the corporation (Chamber of Representatives), from where it disappeared . . . The journalists present signed a communiqué in which they asked that the list be given to them to prove the fraud. The delay in handing it over could, they thought, give time for it to be altered. The episode concluded three hours after the vote, when, list in hand, the fraud was proved. The list showed that 115 representatives were present and 117 ballots were deposited in the box.' (*Semana* 22 December 1987)

The discussion on the constitutional reform, on the other hand, passed through in record time in the Chamber:

'The initiative, supposedly the most ambitious reform of the hundred year old Constitution of 1886, didn't merit one comment in the plenary of the lower house . . . what it was thought would be a prolonged debate which would fill the last five days of the Chamber's session was the most rapidly concluded debate of constitutional reform of any Congress. Attendance was high. This was helped by the fact that since Friday, in a record time of three days, the Ministry of the Interior authorised, and the Chamber paid, 77 million pesos in travel allowances which was owed to 60 Congressman . . .' (*El Espectador* 13 December 1988)

El Tiempo's assessment of the legislative activity of 1988 was:

'Within the legislative initiative of the Chamber, there was one aspect in which the work of the representatives was evident: homages and commemorations. A total of 35 laws were approved to "give homage" to some municipality which celebrated its anniversary..or to an institution for its "important contribution to national life" . . . There were only eight projects of a social character. In general, it is these that measure the positive and real reach of the legislature.'

Reforms that were implemented were compromises and widely criticised as inadequate. The progress of even these initiatives illustrating the ruling order's deep conservatism, the fear of change among an elite used to exclusive power and privilege.

Nevertheless, it was significant that the executive initiated this much new legislation and that reforms, however limited, were introduced at all against such a bloody background. The Colombian state remained resource-starved and beleaguered by the lack of political will of its elite sector, which found that repression bought it as much, if not more, time as reform.

The Barco plan

In August 1987 Barco published a socio-economic plan to tackle the roots of violence in the most deprived and neglected regions. He reactivated Betancur's National Rehabilitation Plan (PNR) and extended it to include 297 municipalities with a population of five million people. This was a short-term programme of specific (particularly infrastructural) projects in areas affected by violence. Another more general programme aimed to improve incomes and social conditions for those living in absolute poverty — 43 per cent of the population (13 million people) are classified as unable to satisfy their basic needs and, according to the DANE categories based on the 1985 census, over half of these live in absolute poverty.

Together these programmes were to cost 4 per cent of GDP annually. The plans were ambitious and it was clear that the state had neither the resources nor the administrative capacity to implement them. Government revenues were inadequate for the high level of social expenditure implied. In 1987 public expenditure was only 16.9 per cent of GNP (in many countries of Europe it is as high as 45 per cent). Half was funded by indirect taxes and only a quarter from direct taxes, which fell heavily on the middle class. Barco tried to control tax evasion, but account holders merely withdrew their funds from the banks to avoid investigation. He tried to raise value added tax, already high at 10 per cent, but failed to get this through Congress. The planned bonanza from energy exports never materialised because of low world prices and guerrilla attacks on the country's oil pipeline. By 1987 merely servicing the debt cost 30 per cent of public expenditure, i.e. 4.5 per cent of the GDP.

The PNR was slow to start; some aspects of it were implemented in some regions but, according to El Espectador's journalists who were assessing its progress, these were inadequate. The scheme for buying land in rehabilitation areas so favoured the landowners that INCORA received more offers to sell land than it had resources to buy it.

The ups and downs of the National Rehabilitation Plan

Norte de Santander

'In the Norte de Santander, few know the National Rehabilitation Plan (PNR) and even fewer have faith in it. The Plan began in 12 places and was extended to include 18 of the 37 municipalities in the department, covering more than two-thirds of the region's territory. The state bodies obviously know about the Plan, as do some local leaders. But the mass of the people to whom it is directed, don't: the rural community of colonists, peasants and Indians. Nor do some of the local officials really know what it entails, and most certainly couldn't explain it.

The PNR in this part of the country has advanced much more in theory than in practice . . . The communities of Norte de Santander are principally engaged in growing sorghum, maize, plantain, yucca and rice. As in almost all the regions of the country, many have very little land and a few more than enough. The people remember that INCORA has helped them this year, giving small farms to several families with the largest number of children and living in absolute poverty. INCORA has advanced somewhat in giving land titles, but not much, if you take into account that with the purchase of 9,000 hectares it has handed land to some 500 families, while there are at least 3,000 requests. Some families are thinking of going into ranching and others to agriculture, but they haven't been able to get started because since they were given the land, they haven't received the credits to enable them to start planting the sorghum or rear cattle . . .

Most of the land distributed by INCORA is in Tibu where there have been most peasant marches . . . The mayor says that little of the agreement signed with the peasants in the last *paro*, has been carried out. When he speaks of the works carried out, he smiles with scepticism and says, "the problem is that the budget is so slow in arriving". One of the ANUC representatives complained: "The peasant is demoralised by the lack of credit from the Agrarian Fund; there's no marketing, the electric light promised for Gavarra last May hasn't been installed and this year the people will have no energy; the road Cano-Tomas-P-40 has begun but is going very slowly." With respect to education, the Plan has enabled teachers to be contracted to rural schools but, at the same time the departmental government is removing the teachers in the municipalities, with the aim of putting everyone on temporary contracts, which teachers have already protested against . . .

Sardinata is another municipality included in the PNR, where few even of the presidents of the *juntas de acción communal* know much about it. The criticisms are also of the Agrarian Fund, which is demanding collateral to give out loans which are delayed too long, and the lack of rural roads. 'The hospital doesn't even have any beds and there are no health posts. Some of the 87 hamlets have a health promoter, but there are neither resources nor

infrastructure . . . Aziz Marad Ortega, the elected mayor (Conservative) summed up his opinion of the PNR: 'They promised us the sky and the earth and we came out with nothing'.'
(*El Espectador* 10 July 1988)

The plan to combat absolute poverty, which had even more far-reaching implications, never got off the ground:

> After two and a half years, the real content of the programme has not been made known, nor has its global strategy been explained, nor its concrete objectives . . . the effort against poverty has been reduced to a series of isolated, fragmentary and clearly insufficient efforts . . . The responsibility for its technical formulation was given to a miniscule and obscure group of modern economists and technocrats, who from the beginning worked out of the presidential palace with no formal contacts with ministers, politicians or with the academic world. (Jorge Méndez Munevar, *El Espectador*, 16 April 1989)

The social interventionism of the plan went against the macro-economic policies of the Planning Ministry, which stressed the role of the market and the view that income redistribution would adversly affect economic growth.

The Barco government's economic policies were extremely orthodox, with debt repayments being given clear priority over social programmes. While the government was speaking about tackling absolute poverty, food prices were steadily rising — first meat, then vegetables and rice and, in 1989, milk, which was a basic source of nutrition for the poor. A DANE survey in 1984 found that the poorest 25 per cent of households consumed between 40 and 100 litres a year compared with the recommended minimum consumption of 168 litres.

As so often in the past, the economy remained healthy during the major part of Barco's administration despite the social and political turmoil; as the president of ANDI put it, 'the country goes badly, but the economy goes very well'.

Reform in the countryside

> The population of the rural areas of the country is that which shows the highest levels of these social evils: open malnutrition in children reaches 24.2 per cent; infant mortality

is 80 per thousand; 56.6 per cent of homes do not satisfy normal nutritional needs; 84 per cent lack running water; 60.5 per cent lack treated drinking water; only 21.4 per cent have sewerage or a septic pit and to complete the panorama of the rural areas, 31 per cent of women between 15 and 49 have never been to school. (DANE March 1988)

Over half the 13 million Colombians living in poverty are in the countryside and, of these, over 40 per cent live in absolute poverty, without a regular income, food, housing, drinking water, sanitation or education. In its preamble to the agrarian reform the government acknowledged that land hunger contributed to poverty and that 7 per cent of rural landowners controlled 83 per cent of the land, while 92.3 per cent controlled 17 per cent.

The agrarian reform consisted of buying 470,000 hectares for distribution to 25,000 families, a relatively small number in relation to the need. The reform was novel in that the land was no longer graded according to how productively it was being used which, in theory, meant that all land in Colombia could now be expropriated. While this was a welcome change for the peasants, the landowners were given certain assurances; for example, the land was valued according to its commercial value, rather than the municipal authorities' lower official value. The land was to be bought at a high price and paid for in public bonds (at a rate equivalent to 80 per cent of the consumer price index) over a period of five years. Since uncultivated land would be paid for in the same way as productive land, the reform was enormously costly.

INCORA's management structure was changed and this left the peasants with only two representatives against seven appointed by the government, SAC and FEDEGAN. In mid-1988 INCORA's manager resigned on learning that the new minister of development openly opposed agrarian reform. By the end of the year INCORA had been offered 60,000 hectares by landowners in different parts of the country, but the financial problems had not been resolved.

Reform in the cities

'According to statistics presented by the then Minister of Economic Development to support the need for urban reform, '15,700,000 Colombians live in the 100 main towns; 6,200,000 live in poverty; there is a qualitative and quantitative deficit of 1,200,000 houses' (quoted in Santana 1989)

The process of rapid urbanisation has created huge problems in the cities and towns. The move to the cities was unplanned, and people were forced to solve their own housing problems. Speculators quickly bought up the best city land. Ernesto Samper Pizano, the senator who introduced the urban reform project to Congress stated that 1 per cent of landowners had control of 70 per cent of the best urban land; 42 per cent of housing in the main urban centres was 'informal' or unregulated by the state, this figure reached 64 per cent in Bogotá by 1990 (*El Espectador*, 16 March 1989). In the absence of a popular housing policy, the 'informal' sector has taken over house-building in the cities.

'Informal' housing includes land invasions, sprawling shanty towns (such as Aguablanca in Cali), squats on any available land and 'pirate' settlements (*barrios piratas*) organised illegally by racketeers or during electoral campaigns when plots of land are exchanged for votes. These *barrios* cover 10 per cent of Bogotá, 15 per cent of Medellín, 30 per cent of Cali and 50 per cent of Barranquilla. In addition there are 7.2 million Colombians living in depressing multi-occupancy tenancies (*inquilinatos*). One million people are estimated to be at risk from settling on dangerous areas of land; a mud-slide buried the inhabitants of a Medellín shanty town in 1987 (Santana 1989).

Belisario Betancur built an average of 100,000 houses a year during his administration, and this barely met the new demand. Since 1986 house-building has declined to 77,000 a year. But even the working- and

A local action group digs sewers for the neighbourhood, Bogotá.

Joe Fish

lower-middle-classes have been unable to keep up their payments and the very poor have been excluded altogether. The poorer sectors have to have subsidised housing and, given their large numbers, this would require a huge shift in the government's expenditure priorities.

Housing is only one of the crises faced by the towns and cities; inadequate transport, public services and recreational facilities have also generated civic protest. Ernesto Samper's urban reform project (which became law in 1989) was a direct response to the strength of feeling in the urban areas.

The reform focused on housing problems in municipalities of over 100,000 inhabitants and on the urban land market, rather than on all the related issues of urban life. It paved the way for the legalisation of many spontaneous settlements and sought to make land available for housing. Each municipality could declare areas of land 'of social interest' and, under certain conditions, these could be expropriated and a land bank created.

Funding arrangements were, however, problematic. Taxing middle- and upper-class property required complex and controversial property evaluations and these relied on the will and capacity of local government. The poor were being badly hit by having to pay value-added tax on cement, which constituted a large part of the cost of building their own houses. The inadequacy of financial arrangements for popular-housing programmes was much debated, for the vast majority of the urban poor could only afford minimal rents. There was strong opposition both within the government and from business groups to the idea of creating special credit arrangements for very low-income housing.

Urban reform, like any initiative that forms part of 'paper' Colombia, can only be judged by how it works and, months after its passage through Congress, this was still unclear from the debates raging among politicians and businessmen.

Reconciling people and state: the popular election of mayors

The popular election of mayors was important to the reformers within Colombia's elite because it represented an attempt to decentralise which, it was hoped, would make the Colombian state more effective, give it more legitimacy, and force the traditional parties to become more responsive to the population's needs. These views were not widely shared within the ruling elite; the project had taken some six years to push through Congress and was only successful because of the skill of its architects in handling regional bosses and convincing them that they could gain from the reform.

The municipalities were to be given substantial resources (from value-added taxes) and greater access to credit; they would also take on a much wider range of services. Civic movements (which had become politicised through mobilising against the state) would, it was hoped, direct their complaints locally and identify with the local political system.

It was, however, doubtful that the smaller towns would be able to cope with their new responsiblities. Vivas Reyna (1987a) found that 85.5 per cent of the country's municipalities, housing 43.1 per cent of the population, lacked the resources and technical and administrative capacity to carry out the functions assigned to them and would continue to depend on central government.

The election of mayors was seen as a historic step in strengthening democracy and local participation in Colombia. The mayor would set up a local administrative council (*junta administradora local*, JAL) for each 10,000 inhabitants, which would be delegated functions by the municipal council. It would have seven members, of which one third would be elected by direct vote. One of the architects of the reform, Jaime Castro, believed the election would undermine the *caciques* and establish faith in local administration:

> The new mayor, who will not owe his position to any *cacique* and at times not even to any political group, but to the will of the people, will not be under the threat of removal because he works without bias. He will be an autonomous, independent functionary who will defend the common good and not the needs of one group of people. (Castro 1986:41)

The bosses, however, thought that the reform would allow them to legitimise the spoils system. The elections took place amid almost daily accusations of vote-buying and, from the beginning, were clouded by an unprecedented climate of violence. Laws 78 of 1986 and 49 of 1987 (the last to be passed before the election) specifically referred to the procedures to be followed on the death of a newly-elected mayor.

Votes for Sale

About fifty buses left on Friday night for Bucaramanga (from Bogotá). They carried no fewer than 2,000 employees of the Comptroller-General of the Republic on their way to register their identity card numbers and vote for Emilio Suárez, candidate for Liberal Confederation, a group led by Rodolfo González García, head of the body responsible for the country's public expenditure . . . Six years ago something similar took place, only that time the 'travellers' registered and voted for María Cleofe Martínez de Meja, daughter of Aníbal Martínez Zuleta who at that time headed the Comptroller-General's department.

In 1982 the employees were sent to the villages of the department of Cesar. Today the story is the same, but with other protagonists and another location: the main actor is the Comptroller Rodolfo González García and the scene is Bucaramanga and the support is now for Emilio Suárez.

The staff of the Comptroller's department have undertaken two pilgrimages to keep their posts in the public administration. Even so, those who worked there during the period of Martínez Zuleta still faced dismissal at the hands of the new Comptroller and their dream of a promised job evaporated.

The first pilgrimage in this second chapter has gone smoothly; the registration of the identity cards on Saturday before the deadline enabling the people to vote in the elections of Sunday 13 March. Within a month, a similar pilgrimage will lead them back to the town to deposit their vote. It will be an outing and that's how it's taken; brandy and identity card in hand, the ingredients for the grandiose elections which embody the fine spectacle of democracy.

And when González García finally leaves his office, there will surely be yet another purge. Many of 'these aspiring electors of the Mayor of Bucaramanga' will see how the little job which they needed so much, and for which they agreed to vote without knowing who for, 'evaporates' under the 'next electoral fixer' (*electorero*) to take office. (*El Espectador* 16 February 1988)

In the municipality of Barrancas, out of only 18,756 inhabitants 16,922 people have registered to vote. In the 1986 elections there were only 7,446 votes which would mean that in just two years, the number of voters increased by 9,476. The inhabitants and one of the candidates for mayor complained that fleets of buses had been contracted by political leaders to bring people from other parts, especially Cesar, Aguachica and Valledepur, to register in Barrancas. Their expenses, travel and food were paid for and the agreed sums paid on election day. To corroborate this, they quote the case of Tabaco, a district within the municipality of Barrancas where there are only 10-12 houses and 2,000 people registered.
(*El Tiempo* 20 February 1988)

The death toll mounted as the election campaign got under way. Some traditional politicians were killed in local feuds (as a result of mafia penetration of local power structures) or at the hands of the FARC. But the majority of victims were from the UP, with seven UP candidates for mayor being killed in the two months preceding the election. There were also victims from the civic movements, some of which put up candidates for election. Notorious killings included the president of the UP, Jaime Pardo Leal, and the president of the Human Rights Commission of Antioquia, Héctor Abad Gómez, who was the Liberal nominee for mayor of Medellín. Violence was particularly acute in areas where the UP stood the greatest chance of winning seats, such as Urabá, Guaviare, Caquetá, the Magdalena Medio and the region of Ariari in Meta, where its leadership was liquidated.

The bloodbath continued after the elections — the total death toll for 1988 being seven mayors, 28 candidates for mayor, 75 councillors and 19 candidates for the municipal council. A total of 327 politicians and party activists, half of which were from the UP, were killed (*Cien Días*, March 1989:7).

Despite all the publicity, more than half the electorate abstained. DANE calculated that 16 million Colombians had the right to vote, 11,066,785 were actuallly registered, but only 7,375,406 voted.

The Liberal Party won the majority of mayoralties (446 out of 1009), but lost the two great prizes of Bogotá and Medellín to the Conservatives (now known as the Social Conservative Party). The UP won only 16 but participated in winning coalitions in a number of areas. The most interesting victories came from the civic movements which had created regional political movements to contest the election. The classification of electoral results gave 900,000 votes and 101 mayoralties to 'others' — a range of groups of differing political persuasions which called themselves 'civic'. The civic movement showed particular strength in the marginalised regions of Antioquia, Nariño, Boyacá, Chocó and Santander.

But the election was discouraging for the reformers. The two-party electoral machines were still predominant; candidates had almost all been decided by party leaders with no popular consultation and the population had failed to respond with any real enthusiasm. A year after the election little progress had been made in setting up the JALs and there was still an acute shortage of resources with which to fund services and infrastructure in the municipalities.

The situation in Cúcuta was typical of Colombia's municipalities; people wanted solutions to their everyday problems and only they could create a legitimate political order. Shortly before the election of mayors, the World Bank had cut off funding for a vital water project. It complained of the delays and the inability of the municipal government to contribute the agreed share of funding, largely a result of 'politicking' and dishonest administration:

> This town, whose 200 years of existence has not served to bring it development, continued to hope that with the popular election of mayors it would obtain the implementation of the

structural programmes it so needed; especially the new water system (*acueducto*), considered a priority work. The inadequacy of the present system was because it was built to supply 50,000 inhabitants and the town has over 350,000. (*El Espectador* 2 March 1988)

Political reform: the painful path

Liberals and Conservatives had come to accept the need for some institutional and political reform. A government/opposition formula was the Barco administration's first innovation. Barco offered Conservative politicians places in his cabinet, as stipulated by Article 120 of the constitution, but because he had failed to consult the party leadership, the Conservatives refused to participate in his goverment. The Conservative Party was uncomfortable in the role of opposition and, lacking an alternative programme with which to challenge the government, tended merely to be obstructionist.

Attempts to make political changes created enormous friction, for renovating the political system was just not on the agenda. Widening the cracks a fraction as a means of preserving bi-partisan rule was as far as the politicians could safely go.

Barco raised the issue of constitutional reform in January 1988. He suddenly announced his intention to put his ideas to a plebiscite to take place on the same day as the popular election of mayors. He had bypassed the usual lengthy consultation with ex-presidents, the church, the *gremios* and the party leaders, and the Conservatives promptly rejected the date. Fabio Echeverry Correa, leader of the powerful industrialists' group, ANDI, opposed the plebiscite on principle, arguing that 'any day it could occur to a president to call a plebiscite to nationalise the soft drinks industry' (*Colombia Hoy* March 1988).

Tortuous negotiations followed. The party leaders met and, in what appeared to be a new bipartisan pact, President Barco and Misael Pastrana (Conservative Party leader and ex-president) signed an 'agreement for institutional readjustment', involving a referendum on various reform proposals. This was then declared unconstitutional by the Council of State. A new agreement was then drawn up between Barco, Pastrana and ex-President Turbay, who was now looked upon as the figure most likely to unite the Liberal Party.

One of the most significant features of the draft constitutional reform was the elimination of Article 120, the last overt relic of coalition government. Instead Congress introduced a 'statute of opposition', which stipulated that the Attorney-General would always be from the second party, while the holder of a new post, the *fiscal general de la nación,* would be from the president's party; magistrates would be from both parties equally. The reform was also notable for the way in which it further strengthened the executive over both the judiciary and the legislature, two institutions in serious need of reform.

The parties themselves were still a long way from reform. The Conservatives were split between the supporters of Misael Pastrana and of Alvaro Gómez Hurtado. The Liberals were even more fragmented, particularly as the nomination for the 1990 presidential candidate drew near. Regional bosses feared the ascent of the popular reforming politician, Luis Carlos Galán, who had rejoined the party on the promise of a 'popular consultation' to decide the nomination.

Although by no means a radical social reformer, Galán was the politician most seriously committed to eradicating the corruption and dishonesty within the traditional political system. But even he had been forced to negotiate with former President Turbay Ayala, who personified the vices of that system, in order to gain the party nomination. He had undoubtedly won a considerable following for his crusade among the middle classes, but this was to be cut short as he neared the electoral campaign that would almost certainly have won him the presidency. The painful nature of the path to political reform could not have been brought home more dramatically.

'Official' and 'unofficial' repression

Just before his assassination by the mafia, the Attorney-General, Carlos Mauro Hoyos, had said that 'the great problems of the country cannot be resolved through punitive measures, but need thoroughgoing reforms of Colombian institutions' (*El Siglo* 25 January 1988). But governments have used 'the state of siege' almost continuously for 40 years to deal with social instability and guerrilla organisations. On assuming office President Barco reactivated it once more, but was thwarted in March 1987 when the statute empowering the military courts to try civilians was declared unconstitutional.

The government took steps to establish a truly effective 'state of siege' and, in the meantime, a series of measures were taken to enable the state to deal with its political challenges. On 27 January 1988, following the kidnapping of the mayoral candidate for Bogotá, Andrés Pastrana, and the assassination of Carlo Mauro Hoyos, the president introduced a 'Statute for the Defence of Democracy', known as the anti-terrorist law, officially to deal with the drug mafia. It had the support of the press, the traditional parties and the 14 most important *gremios*. It was opposed by the popular movement, the left opposition and a few independent journalists who understood that the law was directed at them rather than at the mafia.

None of the 78 articles in the statute referred to either drug traffickers or extradition — they dealt mostly with 'political crimes'. The statute defines a 'terrorist' so imprecisely that arrests can be made if an individual is under suspicion, or has participated in an act of civil disobedience which, in the judgement of the police, has provoked terror in the population or endangered lives or property. Radio broadcasts or articles about security problems can be taken as public or private incitement to participate in terrorist acts and penalised with up to ten years in prison.

Anyone suspected of participating in 'terrorist' activities can be arrested without a judge's order by a soldier or policemen and held for ten days before being brought to court — a period during which they are often subjected to torture or ill-treatment. The police, the military and DAS were given the right to search homes and arrest people without a judge's order. Two months later, after a wave of army searches without warrant, the Supreme Court declared it unconstitutional, but the practice continued in many areas.

Habeas corpus provision was modified at the same time as the statute, so that an appeal to release someone detained illegally, which could previously be made before any criminal judge, now had to be made before a high court, of which there are only 178 in the country.

The problem of military trials for civilians was circumvented by creating a court of special jurisdiction for matters of civil order. This came to include all conduct contained in the anti-terrorist law. The court had its own 'civil order judges' with their own 'higher court of civil order'. The judges are civilian, but surrounded by military power. Many of those brought before them have been arrested and interrogated by the army.

The government tried to legitimise the 'state of siege' with new regulations in the draft constitutional reform which would distinguish between different types of disorder, but Congress reduced the substance of the changes. After discussion in the senate, two distinct 'states of exception' were identified (Barco had wanted three) — external war and internal civil commotion. These authorised the suspension and curtailment of civil rights and social guarantees and established a special law (*ley de alta policía*) for disturbances that did not warrant a 'state of siege' or promulgation of an anti-terrorist law. The senate also agreed, 'in cases of external war or general disturbances', to allow the military courts to try crimes that 'threatened the security and stability of the state'.

Table 9. Human rights

(1978-1989)					
Year	Murders	Disapp-earances	Tor-tures	Deten-tions	Threats
1978	96		48	4914	120
1979	105		143	4098	237
1980	92		55	6819	127
1981	269	101	414	2322	32
1982	525	130	407	2400	122
1983	594	109	300	1325	454
1984	542	122	360	1783	118
1985	630	82	544	3409	378
1986	1387	191	325	1106	244
1987	1651	109	223	1912	565
1988	3011	210	*	*	*
1989	2128	1140	*	535	*

* No data available.

From 1986 figures for murders include the following categories: political assassinations, killings presumed to be political, and assassinations as part of 'social clean-up' campaigns. They do not include killings in which the motive was unknown, of which there were 1,952 in 1988 and 3,450 in the first ten months of 1989.

Information for 1989 to mid-November

Sources: Solidaridad, Cien Días, Justicia y Paz

Though the constitutional reform spoke of guaranteeing human rights, it also provided the means for suspending them. A guarantee of the right to strike could be overruled by the government in the interests of 'national security'. Such contradictions were present throughout Barco's years. At the same time as his government was erecting its legal umbrella for repression, it was also creating a presidential council to handle human-rights issues, which organised a number of forums. And, though the Attorney-General showed considerable interest in prosecuting abuses, the government's reluctance to act meant that little headway was made. Despite sentences pronounced by the Attorney-General, the government was unwilling to remove officials implicated in abuses. In Colombia it seemed that 'justice' (summary and extra-judicial) was mostly for the poor and underprivileged.

Geographical distribution of victims 1988

KEY

☐ 1-100
▨ 100-200 Meta and Cundinamarca
▨ 200-300 Cordoba and Valle
▧ 552 Santander
■ 895 Antioquia

Human rights organisations reported repeated abuses by members of the armed forces. Amnesty International denounced what it saw as an organised 'policy of terror':

> There is convincing evidence that the Colombian armed forces have adopted a policy of terror, designed to intimidate and eliminate opponents without recourse to law. This policy has become apparent in the context of renewed guerrilla activity and pressure for political and social reform . . . Whole sectors of society are at risk of being considered 'subversive' and in Colombia that is tantamount to a death sentence. (Amnesty International 1988)

Military operations involved bombings, house searches, destruction of belongings, intimidation, torture, killings and 'disappearances'. A United Nations team visited Colombia in 1988 to investigate the increasing numbers of 'disappearances': 'After weighing up all the material available, the Working Group believes that in the majority of the cases communicated to it, indirect evidence allows the suspicion — and the information available shows — the participation of units of the armed forces or of security services in forced or involuntary disappearances.' (United Nations Consejo Económico y Social 1989:34).

San Vicente de Chuchurí — in the grip of fear

The people had never seen them like that. With their heads shaved and their faces painted black, the soldiers began to come out of the Luciano D'Luyer barracks.

At 6pm on Sunday, 5 February 1989, fear gripped the people of San Vicente de Chuchurí. The week just ended had been one of constant anxiety. Slogans had appeared painted on the walls and notes were put under the doors of people's houses, signed by the paramilitary command, 'Colonel Rogelio Correa Campos', announcing the 'cleansing' of San Vicente of the guerrillas and their collaborators. This had happened at times when the army was patrolling the streets and people were forced to hide in their homes.

Bravely, the mayor and town councillors went to the battalion to ask for explanations from the commander. 'The army has more than ten uniforms; that is one and they are entitled to go out into the streets like that', the commander told them.

Night fell and the people began to hear machinegun fire, bombs and grenades. Filled with panic, the people fled to their homes, the streets were deserted, no-one dared go out. A grenade exploded in a house, killing a four-year-old boy instantly and wounding his grandmother and mother with shrapnel. An old nun saw a bullet hit her bedroom.

During that night of terror, no-one could sleep and many regretted that they had not left with the fifty families who had already gone. The next day, the civil authorities again asked the commander for explanations. 'In the evening, a group of guerrillas tried to take the town, the soldiers went out and followed them and there was a confrontation', he answered.

On 16 March, popular organisations, the council and the mayor organised a Forum for Life and Democracy in order to discuss with the district and national government measures to bring peace to the region. Only some regional senators and politicians turned up; the absence of national and departmental authorities was glaring. After the forum, military operations intensified. Holy Week was literally a week of passion for the peasants of the neighbouring villages. According to the President of the Municipal Council, Adolfo Muñoz, peasants from these regions talked of nearly 40 dead and many wounded who could not be brought to the towns because the army stopped them. More than 500 families have left.

Curiously, says the council representatives, it is in the most productive lands that people are being forced out and then they are repopulated with people close to the paramilitary. The area is rich in farming and ranching land, oil, gas and coal. San Vicente is the third most important municipality in Santander, with 85,000 inhabitants, of which 45,000 live in the urban area and the rest in small hamlets around it. Proudly, the people say that 'it was the zone which mobilised most people during the Civic Strike of the north-east in 1987 and the marches of May. During the strike of 27 October 1988, the stoppage lasted eight hours'. Perhaps that is why the majority of the people are now threatened with death and many are constantly on the move to stop themselves falling into the hands of the paramilitary.

'Isidro Carreño, who has been arrested, accused of promoting the paramilitary groups, and his son, used to travel in army helicopters and had direct relations with the commander of the Vth brigade, based in Bucaramanga,' the councillors stated. The difficulties they face have united councillors and mayor, irrespective of party. They are planning to build the Common Front for Life and Democracy, as agreed by the forum of 16 March. After the event, Rafael Gómez, commander of the D'Luyer battalion, had written to the mayor and asked him for the tapes of the speeches and the list of participants. He hadn't attended the forum 'because I knew that there would only be attacks on the army'.
(*Colombia Hoy* March and April 1989)

Joe Fish

The funeral of Juan Gabriel Cuadros, an assassinated trade unionist, in Medellín.

In August 1988 the Attorney-General declared that of 600 investigations opened by the Public Ministry into cases of 'disappeared' persons, 50 had revealed the involvement of members of the armed forces. In five of these cases disciplinary sanctions were imposed, ranging from fines to suspension from duty for up to three weeks. In February 1989 the 15-day suspension of an army captain attached to the Voltigeros battalion in Urabá was ordered for his participation in the arrest and 'disappearance' of Alvaro Falla on 15 August 1986. But in this and most other cases, the individuals have been acquitted or have had charges dropped when their case has been passed to the military courts. 'Disappearance' is not codified as an offence in the Colombian penal code, and this had made the process of investigation very difficult. An attempt in November 1988 to incorporate it into the code in a draft bill presented to Congress by the Attorney-General and the Minister of Justice immediately drew strong objections from the Ministry of Defence, and the draft bill had not been debated in Congress by the end of 1989.

Official repression of the popular movement and of labour strikes became far more overt. Under the protection of a legal umbrella the army and police were able to clamp down hard on activities which they could classify as dangerous to 'public order'. The military immediately responded to the peasant march of May 1988 (for land and the right to a livelihood) by preventing 80,000 peasants from different parts of the north-east from reaching their destination, Bucaramanga.

Marching for the right to life.

The following are testimonies from witnesses of the massacres of Llano Caliente and La Fortuna during the peasant marches of May 1988.

'We began the march on 23 May. We gathered at one place and set off in some vehicles. When we arrived at the Puerto de la Llana, we found an army roadblock; they made us get out hitting us. They called us "guerrilla sons of bitches". They took away a lorry load of vegetables. They took nine hammocks and some foam mattresses. At every roadblock they shouted at us that we were subversives, and they were going to kill us. Each time a peasant put his head up they cocked their guns and threatened to shoot us . . . On 29 May, we all met to protest because some *compañeros* were missing and we knew they were in the hands of the military. Disorder grew from one moment to another, and they began to shoot. The moment that the army was going to disperse the marchers and take aside a number of people whom they had on a black list, someone from the military group fired at Colonel Rogelio Correa and the officers who were with him. Five members of the armed forces were killed as a result of the criminal action of a provocateur who some think was an infiltrator of the guerrilla . . . but what followed had no justification. For over an hour the armed forces shot at us, a group of defenceless peasants. There were officially 14 dead, but we know there were more than 20.' (Llano Caliente)

'At 4pm there was an armed confrontation in the camp, away from the march, between the army and a group presumably of the FARC; one officer and a soldier were killed. At 4.30 the army brought the two dead to the place where the peasants were gathered, and began to shoot indiscriminately at the population; at the same time, they threw grenades. At 5pm, the peasants gathered again, now totally surrounded by the army and were forced to lie on the ground, while they began to shoot above the heads; then they made more than 20 stand up and forced them near a house, beat them, made one lie on top of the other and then shot at them.

After the massacre, the army let the children and women leave, sending them on buses to Barranca and Bucaramanga. Four hundred of the peasants managed to break the circle and reached the oil workers' union offices in Barranca, where they stayed. The initial death toll was twelve, five wounded, four disappeared and over 200 arrested.'
(La Fortuna) (ANUC 1988:11-12)

The authorities treated the general strike, called by the CUT for 27 October 1988, as an act of 'subversion'. Legislation was introduced under 'state of siege' provision declaring the strike illegal. Decree laws 2201 and 2200 suspended the legal status of unions that promoted illegal stoppages and allowed detentions from 30 to 150 days for those who promoted or participated in illegal strikes. According to Amnesty International:

> Over 800 people, many of whom appeared to be prisoners of conscience, were arrested and tried by administrative and police authorities in summary procedures under which the defendents' rights were not adequately protected. Several trade unionists were arrested on the direct orders of the Commander-in-Chief of the Armed Forces, General Manuel Guerrero Paz, who, two days prior to the planned strike on 27 October, sent the Director General of the National Police a list of ten union leaders who were to be 'captured on receipt of this order'. The legal basis of the Commander-in-Chief's order is unclear. Most detainees were released within two weeks although charges were still pending against others when the measures were suspended by the government in December 1988. (Amnesty International 1989)

On the day of the strike many areas were militarised, not just those already in a virtual 'state of war' (such as Urabá which had been under the authority of a military general since April), but also the centre of Bogotá. Five armoured personnel carriers and two lorries full of soldiers were sent into the working-class neighbourhood of Policarpa, an area covering some ten blocks square.

By justifying all available means of combating 'subversion' (whether through legitimate civilian protest or at the hands of guerrillas), the doctrine of low-intensity warfare provided an ideological link between the 'official' repression carried out by the armed forces (and legally sanctioned by the state) and the 'unofficial' repression of the death squads and paramilitary groups. As they saw it, a non-conventional war called for non-conventional responses. There were precedents in many Latin American countries, from Guatemala and El Salvador in Central America to Argentina in the southern cone, where the term 'dirty war', involving mass 'disappearances', killings and torture by death squads, was first coined.

Though the precise relationship between the army and the many paramilitary groups is unknown and may in some cases be indirect, there is some evidence of close collaboration. Most of the death squads function in areas with a strong military presence and aim at the same targets as the army. Impunity characterises the operations of both the army and the paramilitary groups. Evidence from former assassins suggests that the armed forces are frequently implicated.

Civilian investigations of the massacres of banana workers in Urabá in March of 1988 of the murders among the community of Segovia because of alleged ties with the UP and other killings, have identified members of the armed forces, civilian authorities and drug-traffickers responsible for commissioning the killings.

There is some indication of national coordination behind the more carefully-organised assassinations. While in the past army officers participated in death squads as individuals, their involvement now seems to have become more structured. As a UP leader, José Antequera, put it in an interview a few hours before being shot dead inside Bogotá's main airport — his party's 721st victim since 1985:

> There is no doubt that there is a paramilitary organisation of a national type, well coordinated. Before, let's say in 1987, there were regional waves of crimes, as if the assassins covered the entire country, bringing their first *estela de muerte* [trail of death] to Meta, then Huila, then Magdalena Medio, and so on. Now it is different. Now on the same day, we have deaths in different parts of the country, which suggest that there are several groups of assassins working in coordination. I want to emphasise one thing: the extension of the dirty war to almost all the Atlantic coast, from Córdoba onwards, to Sucre, to Magdalena, to Cesar and the south of Bolívar . . . in reality, I only feel safe in Barranquilla . . . the drug mafia is buying thousands of hectares throughout the country. A good part of these are being bought on the coast. These are the people who are financing this wave of crimes. But they couldn't operate without a high degree of complicity from complete structures of the armed forces. Yes, they are no longer isolated officers who sponsor this. In the regions there are structures of officers and non-commissioned officers who are accomplices in the dirty war. (*Semana* March 1989)

Magdalena Medio and the organised right

In October 1985 Pablo Guarín, a Liberal Party congressman named by the Attorney-General as a member of MAS, told the Fifth Assembly of Boyacá, that:

> The danger is not in the Liberal-Conservative controversy, today it is the enemies of the fatherland who declare war on us, the democrats. Peace is the product of a military and

political victory, to make the conquered sit at the negotiating table and impose conditions on them. That is where true peace is born, not in unfulfilled truces. (*Consideraciones generales* . . . 1989:121)

Much has been made of the connection between the drug mafia and the paramilitary, but even more important is the role of landowners and the armed forces. This relationship of 'official' and 'unofficial' repression is best seen through case studies of two of Colombia's most conflict-ridden regions, the Magdalena Medio and Urabá.

As cattle ranchers, the army and drug barons have allied to regain control of an economically-strategic region threatened by popular organisations and guerrilla movements, there has been much bloodshed in the Magdalena Medio over the years.

This economically important region lies along the valley of the middle section of the Magdalena river between the Andes' central and eastern ranges. In the mid-1980s its population was estimated at 800,000. It is crossed by the river and the railway line connecting the interior with the coastal ports of Barranquilla and Santa Marta. Along the river are a number of ports — Puerto Boyacá, Puerto Berrío, Barrancabermeja, Gamarra and El Banco. It has considerable agricultural and ranching potential, as well as oil, natural gas and coal reserves. Barrancabermeja is the country's most important oil refinery. It is a region that the ruling elite wishes to keep.

Until the 1950s the population clustered around the river ports and their surrounding areas. Enclaves emerged around the oil towns, first Barrancabermeja, later Yono and Puerto Boyacá. Barrancabermeja is the region's epicentre; its oil workers' struggles are famous in the history of the country's popular movement, as the interview with one of its present-day activists illustrates.

Barrancabermeja

Barranca is torn between wealth and scarcity. The rivers of oil which pass through ECOPETROL's production centre contrast with the poverty of the majority of its people. They say that social injustice generates violence, and in Barranca they are convinced of it. (*El Tiempo* 29 July 1988)

In order to make sense of current political events in Barranca, it is necessary to look at the town's history. This goes back to the Spanish invasion, when the region was conquered not with the formal submission of the indigenous people but through their extinction. The Magdalena river, which was the main means of penetration of the country, was constantly attacked by the resistance of the Yariguis communities; the communities disappeared completely, but fighting all the way. The same with the Guane, Chanchon and Guarenta, they all disappeared defending their land and their culture.

More recently, at the turn of the century, when General Uribe Uribe declared himself in opposition to the government, he was hunted down by the Conservatives, and it was here in Barrancabermeja and El Opon that he was able to reform his army and where he found a natural asylum to carry on his revolutionary struggle. He finally made an agreement and was then assassinated.

In 1948, when violence broke out, the Tropical Oil Company was already in operation, and the workers took over the company and the people took over the town of Barranca and nominated a mayor of the people, who later became the guerrilla fighter, Rafael Rangel. According to an anecdote, a cannon was made in the very same oil company. This cannon, which today is at the entrance of the army barracks and which looks like its trophy, was made by the oil workers when Barranca was free land. Another story recounts that despite his military power, the Minister of War at that time had to come here to negotiate with the popular government, and they didn't even let him enter the town. They had to negotiate in the airport and the commission had to leave that very day. As radio communications were severed, the popular government thought the movement was the same everywhere; but it was isolated and the rising was over in other parts of the country, principally Bogotá. They had no other option than to negotiate. They handed over the town and launched a guerrilla war. The Liberal guerrillas of Rafael Rangel managed to dominate all that we know today as the Magdalena Medio. When the amnesty of Rojas Pinilla was decreed, the people believed it, and accepted, and that's how the guerrilla movement of the Magdalena Medio which was indestructible, was demobilised. Hard guerrilla leaders went into politics, and were later murdered, as happened to the courageous fighter, Rafael Rangel. He is hardly remembered today. A curious thing: in Sabana de Torres, Santander, I once saw a notice which said: 'Municipal Public Library Rafael Rangel Rueda'. That's the only part where he is still remembered, apart from the land invasion barrio (neighbourhood) here in Barranca which also carries his name.

In Barranca, the oil workers have been at the vanguard of the workers movement nationally and had a great influence on other struggles, although the bourgeoisie has tried to isolate them. The oil industry is now controlled by a state body, ECOPETROL, but it is thanks to the struggle of the workers that this was created. The country would have prolonged Tropical Oil's concession for another twenty years, but the workers demanded that it be given back to the state and occupied the plant. The nationalist struggle has been strong here. In 1971, the strike was over this, not just about hunger . . . it was because they wanted to hand over the modern equipment installed by ECOPETROL to process petro-chemical derivatives to a foreign company.

Today, some 4,500 workers are employed permanently in the refinery and petro-chemical complex, and about the same number are temporary workers who depend on a contract labour system the company uses to avoid having to pay social provision. This temporary labour has produced much poverty. Many people who have come here for work, have had to invade land to build their houses, with no public services. About 80 per cent of Barranca is made up of land invasions. Gradually they have fought for light and water and roads. The oil workers live in Barranca, and side by side with the peasant, the small trader, the unemployed. There is no bourgeoisie here. Barranca is a workers' town. The workers struggled with the rest of the people in the 1977 national civic strike, in 1979, in 1981 and in 1983. The participation of the people was massive despite the militarisation of the town and attacks on them.

The 1980s have seen a real resurgence of the combativity of the people and direct struggle. When the people have decided to go on strike, to demonstrate, to mount barricades , confront the power of the military, that's when they have won their demands. A new epoch began in Barranca. The oil workers' union was badly affected by the repression after the November 1981 strike when about 30 activists lost their jobs, but it later recovered. An organisation emerged to lead the movements of Barranca, the *Coordinadora Popular* (popular coordinator); although it was first set up round about 1976, in the 1980s it has taken on a new role. It is made up of all the democratic organisations of the left and also of the right, political and trade union bodies, peasants, workers and popular organisations. When Barranca rises, the *Coordinadora* controls events.It has even run the town for short periods. It is with the *Coordinadora* that the state has to negotiate.

In 1987, a new level of struggle developed in the town after attacks against peasant leaders and leaders of the UP. It was no longer just street struggle. There was a general strike and the people took control of the streets. Barricades went up, tyres were burnt. We called for the right to life, and we directly accused the military of being agents of the dirty war. Another new element was the support of the guerrilla organisations for the popular struggle in the town, not just with a few leaflets or banners, but armed militias were seen in Barranca. The movement lasted two complete days. Then when a little girl, Sandra Rendón, who was a witness of the attacks on the *compañeros*, was killed, another three days of struggle began for the right to life with massive demonstrations of about 30,000 people. The guerrillas were present, particularly the ELN, and although there was no military confrontation, their presence gave us strength. The *Coordinadora* felt it had an military arm. This gave it much more power to negotiate with the state.

There were other important moments that year, such as on 1 May 1987 and after the death of Pardo Leal in September. The people of Barranca put up the barricades again and took over the main streets. This is when they began to shoot at the people indiscriminately. We were in the barricade of Haz de Copas, which we had held throughout the night, and at 7am, when we were being interviewed on television, the army, without warning suddenly began shooting at us. We had to save the journalists, run with them, help them with their equipment. We lost the barricade. At midday, about 30 counter-insurgency police began beating the workers, insulting us and shooting into the air which caused panic at first. But then we fought back and won back the barricade. When the army returned the next day, they were surprised to find the militias there; there were four hours of fighting and eventually we won again.

On 15 February 1988 they murdered Manuel Gustavo Chacón, a *compañero* with a long history of struggle, a union leader and member of *A Luchar*. This was a blow to the popular movement. But now in Barranca there are permanent organisations, which don't depend on great leaders. When Chacón was killed, the people went out onto the streets, declared a total strike and put up the barricades. There were five days of fighting. Everyone knew who the assassins were; they were in a a military car and they were serving members of the army. They killed Chacón in the commercial centre of the town and calmly got into their car and drove away. It was even photographed. The murderers were denounced by name and rank. In the end they had to retire them from active duty. The local prosecutor bravely began a case against them, but he had to leave the town soon after. With the murder of Chacón, they struck at the backbone of the popular movement and also at the heart of its culture. He was a singer, a poet. He travelled round the villages with his songs. He was born a peasant in Charala, Santander, where José Antonio Galán was born the leader of the *Comuneros*, and he came to Barranca in search of work.

Source: Interviews with political activist from Barranca, February 1988 and February 1989.

Puerto Boyacá further down the river has a very different history. There, the Texas oil-company workers had a terrible battle establishing a union in the 1930s when working conditions were deplorable. Management did everything it could to intimidate the workforce, which eventually lost control of its union to company stooges. Puerto Boyacá became the bastion of the right in the 1980s, while Barrancabermeja remained a focal point for workers' struggle and left-wing opposition.

The rural areas of Magdalena Medio were populated in various waves of colonisation. In the 1920s and 1930s many came in search of jobs in the oil industry; in the 1950s and 1960s many more came as they fled *La Violencia* elsewhere. The *colono's* existence was still precarious and constantly threatened by the cattle ranchers who eventually occupied 60 per cent of the region's agricultural land. Where the hardship of material conditions failed to push the *colonos* from the land, they were dislodged by force.

Each of the post-National Front opposition movements won support here; allegiances shifted from the MRL, to ANAPO and, finally, to the Communist Party, particularly around Puerto Boyacá. Guerrilla movements also established themselves in the region. The ELN's first front was in the south of Santander around San Vicente de Chuchurí, while the FARC was particuarly active around Puerto Boyacá.

The story of the FARC in the Puerto Boyacá region and the rise of the organised right are closely linked. Initially the FARC played a defensive role, building up support in the rural areas where it was more difficult for the Communist Party to operate. Interviews with peasants, ranchers and the FARC itself, show that it established itself as a rural civil guard rather than a revolutionary army; even some local ranchers tolerated it and gave its members food and money. The FARC describes its early role as follows:

> In the beginning, when the organisation of self-defence was weak and very clandestine, the guerrillas made themselves known to only the most trusted people . . . later, the people began to call on them to sort out problems in the area, such as the stealing of cattle . . . It grew and became stronger from 1977 onwards, the movement had won political influence, people sought out the guerrillas to solve their problems. (*ibid*:49)

The region became the FARC's fourth front and, by the end of the 1970s, when its influence had spread, it had given birth to six or seven more. The Communist Party was now strong enough to win a number of municipal council seats.

Attitudes towards the FARC shifted when the region came under the command of the eleventh front in 1979. Kidnapping and robbing local ranchers became a popular means of financing guerrilla operations. As one local rancher describes it:

> Twenty-three years ago, the guerrillas began asking us for a hat, some boots, some shirts, a hen or a cow . . . then their demands grew, 'voluntary quotas' of 20 or 50,000 pesos which at the beginning we paid so that they would let us work . . . there were times when we brought guerrillas to Bogotá for

medical treatment making it look as if they were our workers.
The reward was the kidnapping of many ranchers. (*ibid*:56)

Some ranchers left the region in the 1970s to become absentee landlords, but by 1980 many more had left taking their cattle with them. The FARC began to harass medium and small farmers and farm managers. These activities, which were not combined with any attempt to organise the peasantry politically, created fertile ground for the growth of the right.

With the change of guerrilla front, the army established a permanent presence in the region and the searches, arrests and torture of suspected Communists increased. Roads were controlled so that peasants were unable to market their produce or buy provisions without a safe-conduct pass from the army. Peasants previously sympathetic to the guerrillas began to lose confidence in them. The eleventh front's tactics created internal divisions within the FARC, and the guerrillas seemed unable to protect the peasants from army abuses. Many peasants began to leave the region.

The situation changed again in 1982 when the Barbulá infantry's third battalion was set up in Puerto Boyacá and, in 1983, when the army's fourteenth brigade was established in Puerto Berrío. The army's tactics changed from crude intimidation and terror to the carefully-planned pacification of low-intensity conflict. For the first time the local army was headed by high-ranking officers, schooled in counter-insurgency doctrines. The fourteenth brigade was headed by General Daniel García Echeverri and General Faruk Yanine Díaz. Speaking at a conference, García Echeverri said that 'what happens to us in this region . . . has to be understood at the level of geopolitics, the world is being fought over by two great ideologies . . . [that] of Moscow, which suppresses freedoms and that of the western world which defends the democratic view' (*ibid*:77).

Aerial bombardments of regions in which guerrillas were active and a well-planned military offensive began in 1983, but at the same time the two generals still planned to win back the hearts and minds of the people. Yanine Díaz, a charismatic figure who understood the peasants, organised civic action programmes. As Luis Alfredo Rubio Rojas, mayor of Puerto Boyacá, said of him:

> I heard Faruk Yanine many times say that whoever had the people would win the war, and he would say, when I leave this region, it will be very hard and difficult for my successor, because I have come to have some 300 adopted children, so that the peasants no longer say general, but *compadre* (lit. godfather) and they feel proud that I am their godfather. (*ibid*:80)

The population was organised into peasant self-defence groups and put in the front line of the war against the guerrillas, a strategy made possible by the disenchantment with the FARC and the low level of politicisation. These self-defence groups were one part of the right-wing counter-offensive; the paramilitary group, MAS, was another.

MAS and the army worked closely in the region; local peasants have reported that army bombardments were coordinated with MAS incursions. In the early 1980s Puerto Boyacá (first chosen as a place for the drug mafia to solve its problems with M-19) became MAS's operational centre. At a meeting in Puerto Boyacá in 1982, attended by the military mayor, Captain Oscar Echandía, representatives of the Texas Petroleum Company, members of the local ranchers' committee, political bosses, army officers, shopkeepers and traders, the ranchers agreed to finance an armed group to work with the army. Initially designed to protect the ranchers against kidnappers, this group soon became a movement against 'subversion' in the widest sense (as spelled out in counter-insurgency manuals). Army thinking gave ideological cohesion to the local ranchers' wish to regain control of the region.

MAS's first targets were the Communist Party, the FARC, and their suspected sympathisers. The wave of killings led to a government investigation which was completed in February 1983. The Attorney-General located Puerto Boyacá as the centre of the operations and identified the involvement of local ranchers and members of the Barbulá battalion.

The Attorney-General gave a report to Congress in 1986, in which he stated:

> MAS was an authentic paramilitary movement. The attempts to deny this truth have failed before public opinion . . . The perverse habit of the military of relying on private citizens to carry out its counter-insurgency activities is spreading. In this way the military could make up for its own limitations . . . What we are talking about purely and simply are officers who break all bounds when presented with the temptation of multiplying their capacity for action and who make use of private citizens whom they initially take as 'guides' and 'informants', collaborators and auxiliaries in general, and end up using them as a hidden arm and who, as contract killers (*sicarios*) can do unofficially what cannot be done officially. (Amnesty International 1989)

The paramilitary group then embarked on a new phase; it acquired a more formal structure and extended its operations throughout the Magdalena Medio and even into other regions. It forged links with other right-wing groups and powerful local political bosses. Pablo Guarín, local Liberal boss and purported to be one of MAS's leaders, had a close relationship with Jaime Castro, Belisario Betancur's Minister of the Interior.

In 1984 a new organisation, the Association of Peasants and Ranchers of the Magdalena Medio (ACDEGAM), was created to give the paramilitary and self-defence groups legal cover in the wake of the Attorney-General's report. It took responsibility for the political and military defence of the region and gave socio-economic assistance to the peasants who supported it. The campaign against 'subversion' reached new heights when ACDEGAM started to eliminate trade unionists (from, for example, the Nare cement works), peasant organisers and even dissidents from the Liberal Party. Belisario Betancur himself visited the region in 1985 (at the invitation of Luis Alfredo Rubio Rojas, Pablo Guarín and the president of ACDEGAM) and highly praised the people of the Magdalena Medio, particularly General Yanine Díaz, for restoring peace.

As ACDEGAM's organisation grew, so too did the need for more funds; in 1985 the drug barons Pablo Escobar, Jorge Luis Ochoa and Gonzalo Rodríguez Gacha (all local landowners) made substantial contributions to ACDEGAM's military groups. A school for training assassins was set up in Puerto Boyacá and the paramilitary groups were given the means with which to operate in a more systematic way. The formation of the UP and the rise of the popular movement and other guerrilla groups meant that the mid-1980s was a period of acute polarisation, which was further fuelled by the assassination of Jaime Pardo Leal in October 1987 (by drug-funded *sicarios*) and of Guarín in November 1987 by the FARC.

In 1989 defectors from the paramilitary gave detailed information to the Attorney-General on ACDEGAM's structure and organisation, on the paramilitary groups' relationship to the army, police and local landowners, on the role of the Puerto Boyacá-trained assassins in the massacres of 1988 and on the involvement of Israeli and British mercenaries in their training. In an interview for *El País* (15 May 1989), Ricuarte Duque Arboleda reported that, 'In Puerto Boyacá, the police and the army collaborate with the organisation. I don't know names. The police don't ask us for documents and if they see our arms they don't say anything, they only ask where we work, and we say "with ACDEGAM".'

Puerto Boyacá had become a kind of independent paramilitary republic. ACDEGAM ran its own schools and clinics, it helped to build and repair roads and even had its own communications centre. It had links with all the region's political representatives, including Congress and, although later going into hiding for being indicted for participating in the Urabá massacres, Luis Alfredo Rubio Rojas was elected mayor in the March 1988 elections. From hiding he managed to give interviews on television and in the press, in which he talked of meetings he had had with army officers since the warrant for his arrest was issued. ACDEGAM was proud of winning back the Magdalena Medio; on entering Puerto Boyacá a poster announced it as the 'anti-subversive capital of Colombia'.

During 1988 the paramilitary groups extended their control over much of Magdalena Medio — including Puerto Berrío, San Juan Bosco de Laverde, and San Rafael de Chucurí. Army activities were also stepped up, with frequent reports of bombardments. Many peasants began to flee the countryside, heading for the municipalities or leaving the region altogether. The problem of internal refugees became increasingly serious. The right-wing offensive began to look like good business, the exodus of peasants enabled others to appropriate their lands. A DAS report to the judicial investigation of the Urabá killings in July 1988, gave detailed information on the structure and functioning of ACDEGAM. It also revealed that among the authorities which collaborated closely with the organisation are the regional procurator in Honda, Tolima department, the commander and sub-commander of the military base at Puerto Calderon, the police commander of La Dorada, Caldas department and the police commander of Puerto Boyacá. The report also revealed the participation of Israeli, German and US nationals in ACDEGAM's training camps.

Armed forces bombings in the Magdalena Medio

In four rooms which used to be the local offices of ANUC in the river port city of Barrancabermeja, mattresses and bedding take up all of the available floorspace. Half the families here arrived between August 1988 and the beginning of 1989. The other half arrived during February after the bombardments started. Mary was not afraid to speak:

'This is a terrible tragedy. On Wednesday last, four helicopters came, firing. I couldn't do more than grab my five kids. I have never seen anything like it. Many peasants have disappeared. My sister, she went to ask for help and never came back. Her fourteen-year-old daughter then went looking for her. Perhaps the paramilitaries took her. They come by with their faces covered with bandannas so we won't recognise them. They and the army say that we are feeding the guerrillas from our crops and that the guerrillas recruit from among us. But this is an enormous lie . . .'

Another woman went on:

'I came here on Sunday. Four helicopters flew over firing with machine guns. A plane dropped bombs. So I left with my three kids. I left with a friend and

> we went to a place called 'Tienda Nueva'. But the army arrived. They asked us for our ID. They took my friend away and for three or four days we had no news. Then they found his body, without the head. They mutilated him. I think it was them who killed him, that's what I think. They had dressed him in olive green clothes. An army commander said . . . you only have yourselves to blame because you're aiding the guerrillas . . . The army and the paramilitaries are operating together.
> (Interview by Neil MacDonald, February 1989)

One of the massacres which drew most attention to the power of the extreme right in the region was the murder on 18 January 1989 of 12 members of a judicial commission of inquiry in La Rochela, in the municipality of Simacota, Santander department. The commission had been sent to investigate a series of political killings and 'disappearances' attributed to paramilitary groups and members of the armed forces in the Magdalena Medio. Subsequent judicial investigation of the killings found that army-linked paramilitary forces in the region were responsible. In April 1989, the sixth public order judge of Bogotá subpoenaed an army lieutenant based in Magdalena Medio to appear in court to answer charges relating to his alleged part in the massacre.

Barrancabermeja was under siege. Two hundred popular leaders and activists were killed during 1988, including a much-loved poet and oil worker, Manuel Chacón. But the town was more difficult to pacify than Puerto Boyacá. In Barrancabermeja the people had their own popular and political organisations, and their own means of countering the influence of the right. A local priest explained the difference between Barrancabermeja and Puerto Boyacá as follows:

> One day I was in Barrancabermeja commenting on the difficult situation in and around the town, and a high-ranking officer said, 'Father, if the same scheme of pacification were applied here as in Puerto Boyacá, this region would be totally different' I said to him, 'Well, and what scheme was applied in Puerto Boyacá? One element is that the politicians and people organised with the support of the army and defeated subversion. This scheme can be applied crudely in Puerto Boyacá, because it is not a politicised town, something which is not true of Barranca. Here, there are political movements and trade union and popular organisations which have created a high degree of politicisation among the people'.
> (*Consideraciones generales* . . . 1989:90)

As the people of Barranca struggled to maintain their organisation, the extreme right of the Magdalena Medio moved onto a new level of activity. In August 1989 far-right militants set up a political party, the Movement of National Restoration, MORENA. Its formation was announced by Ivan Roberto Duque García, general secretary of ACDEGAM. The new party would put forward candidates to elections, both in the Magdalena Medio and other parts of the country, and would support the conservative Liberal politician, Hernando Duran Dussan, for the presidency. Asked his response to accusations that MORENA was a fascist party, Duque García replied:

> Well, if fascism implies defending private property and the family with vigour and energy, defending the state, defending democracy and shaking off the dangerous spectre of communist totalitarianism, then let them call us fascist. (*La Prensa* 9 August 1989)

Class war in Urabá

The struggle against the powerful banana growers to acquire basic trade union rights has turned Urabá into a region of particularly violent conflict in present-day Colombia.

Urabá, with almost 300 kilometres of coast along the Atlantic ocean and a shared frontier with Panama to the north, is situated between the north-west of the department of Antioquia and the north-east of Chocó. Like the Magdalena Medio, it is a region of considerable economic importance, for (after coffee) bananas are the country's second largest export and Colombia is the world's fifth largest banana exporter. Apart from bananas, the area sustains a couple of other agro-industries, such as palm oil, alongside subsistence agriculture and extensive ranching.

Urabá's banana industry is relatively new. It began in 1963 when Frutera de Sevilla (a subsidiary of United Brands), which controlled most of Colombia's banana production, shifted its operations from Santa Marta when its plantations there and in Central America were affected by disease. Urabá had good soil conditions and a cheap (mostly black) labour force. By 1984 Urabá's municipalities of Apartado, Chigorodó and Turbo were producing 92 per cent of the country's banana exports.

To minimise the risks of hurricanes, disease, labour problems and expropriation (which had happened to United Brands in Cuba), Frutera de Sevilla encouraged a number of people from Antioquia and Bogotá to invest in the industry by offering them cheap land and ample credit, made available by displacing peasant colonisers from the flat lands. At the end of their contracts with Frutera de Sevilla in 1965, a group of independent producers decided to form their own *gremio*, the Association of Banana Growers of Urabá (AUGURA) and their own banana-exporting company, the Union of Banana Producers of Urabá (UNIBAN). By 1984 UNIBAN was exporting 55 per cent of Urabá's bananas; BANACOL, another exporting company set up in 1981, exported 23 per cent and United Brands exported the remaining 22 per cent.

People were attracted to the region by the economic opportunities it offered, and the population rose from 32,320 in 1964 to 336,930 in 1986. Half the banana labour force came from Chocó; the other half from the impoverished rural areas of neighbouring departments. New workers, who lived and worked in subhuman conditions, were mostly young, single, male, illiterate and very poor. By the 1980s the banana plantations employed 22,000 workers.

James Parsons (see *Cien Días*, April-June 1988:6) estimates that during the 1960s the growers were making cash profits of between US$700 and US$1,000 per hectare per annum. The producers themselves credit their success to their own pioneering spirit of free enterprise. Neither they nor the state have invested in the region: 79 per cent of the banana workers live in unhygienic crowded camps (mostly without drinking water or electricity). Many workers wash themselves with the same water they use to wash the bananas (García Martínez 1987:2). These conditions have led workers to seek housing in urban centres, often invading land to build a shelter, for Urabá has the highest housing shortage in the country (*El Mundo* 21 November 1986).

Peasants from other areas who have been forced off the land by cattle ranchers have also been attracted to the banana plantations. By 1986, 41 per cent of Urabá's population lived in huge shanty towns on the outskirts of Turbo, Carepa, Apartadó and Chigorodó, where only 37 per cent of the inhabitants have piped water and only 10 per cent sewerage. Apart from the roads that carry bananas to the ports, communications are poor. The humid, tropical climate is exceedingly unhealthy, yielding one of the highest infant mortality rates in the country and high incidences of malaria, diarrhoea, gastro-enteritis and typhoid (García Martínez 1987).

Banana production is controlled by a decreasing number of (often absentee) landowners. According to one study (FAO 1986) 17 per cent of the plantations disappeared between 1977 and 1984 and those that remained increased in size by an average of 68 per cent. By 1987 there were 263 banana estates with an average size of approximately 80 hectares (which is considered optimum). Some groups own several plantations. For example, the Jaime Enrique Gallo group owns thirteen, the Peñaloza group nine, and the Banacosta group eight. Half the area planted with bananas and all the most modern estates are controlled by 22 producers (*Opción* June 1988), who also own businesses, shops, transport systems and cattle ranches. These are the modern banana entrepreneurs.

The workers' long hard struggle for the right to unionise formed the backdrop to the violence in the region, which escalated considerably in 1985. The banana producers saw no need to change the backward, authoritarian pattern of labour relations that United Brands had established on their plantations in Santa Marta, in which there were no labour codes, social provisions or proper wages. A spokesman from the banana union, SINTRABANANO, describes what happened to workers who fell ill in 1971:

> [Some] 25 per cent of the workers contract tuberculosis, and to make matters worse, when the doctor examines them he makes red marks and then the boss gives no more work to the worker in question. When a worker get ill, the boss first of all gives him a pill of any sort. If the case is serious, he's reluctantly sent to the doctor who sends him away with more pills. If it's fatal, he's incapacitated or they send him back to work . . . In these conditions, the workers labour in the sun and rain, and curse the managers and bosses, but don't realise that that is no solution to their misery. (*Opción* June 1988)

Merino (1987) shows that workers put in an average of 67.2 hours a week, with overtime and Sundays paid at the normal rate. The average wage covers only 34 per cent of the minimum needed for a family to survive.

By 1979 only 46 per cent of the estates had any labour agreements at all. Of these only a quarter had resulted from negotiations with the union, the rest having been imposed by the employers. The employers' own *gremio*, AUGURA, which represents the interests of the plantation owners, also dominates the region politically. Jaime Enrique Gallo has been the Liberal senator for Urabá for a number of years.

The establishment of SINTRABANANO in 1964 (a union affiliated to the CSTC and influenced by the Communist Party) represented the first real attempt to unionise the workers. It was followed in 1972 by SINTAGRO, in which the PC-ML gained a following. Once the confidence of the workers from Chocó (who traditionally sought solace from hardship in their families and culture) had been won, the unions really began to grow. The employers responded with violence — they dismissed workers, murdered union leaders and, when the workers went on strike, called in the army. The case described by a Dutch researcher in *Cien Días* (April-June 1988) was typical. In 1979, on receiving a list of demands from the workers on the Revancha Galofre plantation, the owner offered the estate's union leader, Armando Tobón, 50,000 pesos to withdraw the list. Tobón refused and, five days later, was murdered. The workers then went out on strike, whereupon the army moved in and forced them back to work.

In the late 1960s and early 1970s the EPL, which had been active in the mountains of Sinú in Córdoba, moved to Urabá to escape encirclement by the army. The FARC created its fifth front in Urabá in the 1970s and, as worker repression increased, so the guerrilla movements became more popular. The plantation owners and the military were now no longer the only armed forces in the region and they were beginning to lose hold of their power. The plantation owners became even more insecure when the guerrillas began to demand protection money from them and from the ranchers.

Members of AUGURA increased the tension by organising courses and conferences and by proclaiming their 'sovereignty' over Urabá. They seemed incapable of distinguishing between guerrilla activity and the workers' struggle for more humane conditions. One plantation owner claimed that he 'no longer [had] . . . to go to Cuba or Nicaragua to see a communist revolution, because [he had] . . . lived it in Urabá'. Another said that, 'if you see the map, you will realise that Urabá is the prolongation of Central America and we are living through the processes of revolution and counter-revolution that they are living . . . it is a confrontation between democracy and communism' (*Semana* 17 May 1988).

The landowners were deeply opposed to Betancur's peace process, particularly since (by 1984) it had become clear that they were losing the battle against unionisation. Political spaces were opening up in 1983/4 and unions were growing fast. In 1983 SINTAGRO had 150 affiliates. By 1985 it had 4,000 (the first of two bomb attacks on the SINTAGRO offices in Currulao took place that year) and, by 1987, 12,600 on 144 plantations. SINTRABANANO had 4,600 affiliates on 78 plantations (García Martínez 1987). In 1987, by which time 96 per cent of the workforce was unionised, the unions made a major breakthrough by forcing the first industry-wide wage negotiations between AUGURA, SINTAGRO and SINTRABANANO.

According to Amnesty International, however, in 1987 there were also 200 political killings in Urabá and these were mostly of trade union leaders and plantation workers. Despite two local mayors having noticed that 'assassinations of trade unionists and workers decrease after an agreement has been reached with the plantation workers' (*El Mundo* 4 June 1987), by the end of the year most of the founders of the banana trade unions had been assassinated or threatened.

There were huge demonstrations in protest against the killings. A march in February 1987 was attended by 13,000 people and work stoppages, known as 'days of grief', were declared after every murder. Popular support for the left was growing. In 1986 the municipal councils of Apartadó and Mutata had UP majorities and, in the 1988 election, both the UP and the Frente Popular did exceedingly well.

The presence in 1985 of five of the Tenth Brigade's battalions, each with 1,500 soldiers (in addition to the notorious Voltígeros battalion frequently denounced by local workers for its abuses of human rights) considerably strengthened the army's presence in the region. The army worked closely with the landowners (who were rumoured to pay it for protection) patrolling their estates and threatening their workers. Although most of the killings were carried out by various death squads (such as the 'Death to Revolutionaries of Urabá') the heavy military presence and frequent roadblocks made it easy for armed assassins who had the army's support to move around — 699 people, mostly banana workers, were assassinated in the area between 1982 and February 1988. Even worse massacres were to follow.

Shortly after midnight on 4 March 1988 a group of assassins shot 17 workers on the Honduras banana plantation near Currulao, before moving on to the next plantation, La Negra, and shooting three more. They called out the victims' names from a list before killing them. A DAS team sent to investigate the crime established that, before the murders, the Voltígeros battalion had arrested and held several people from the area who had been forced to identify local people with alleged EPL links. Some were even taken to the plantations and made to point people out in person. Later evidence found that they had been accompanied by known assassins from MAS in Puerto Boyacá in Magdalena Medio and that Honduras and La Negra were among the estates they visited. According to witnesses, one of the assassins addressed another as 'corporal'.

By May the DAS had established that the massacre was carried out by hired professional killers who were directly supervised and assisted by the regional military command. Those involved, including the police commander of Puerto Boyacá and officers from the Voltígeros batallion, were subsequently arrested. Further investigations implicated MAS, including the mayor of Puerto Boyacá.

The evidence compiled by a civilian court judge, Martha Lucia Gonzalez, and made public in September 1988, found that an army major, head of the B-2 intelligence unit of the Voltígeros battalion had provided the paramilitary groups with the names of workers considered guerrilla sympathisers. He had paid a hotel bill in Medellín for several members of the death squad which travelled to Urubá from Puerto Boyacá shortly before the killings. An army lieutenant and corporal from the same unit were accused of actual participation in the massacre. Just days after the judge had issued the arrest warrants, she was forced to leave the country following death threats. In May 1989, her father, the ex-governor of the department of Boyacá, was gunned down.

A march of 20,000 banana workers and their families followed the Currulao massacre. A total of 100 people had been killed in the first three months of the year. On 11 April armed men in military fatigues kidnapped 25 peasants from the village of Coquitos near Turbo, where there had been some land conflicts; their bodies were later found in different areas or in the sea, with their hands tied and bullet wounds in their heads. On 14 April the government decided to introduce emergency measures. A general from the Ministry of Defence was put in charge of the region and given authority over the civilian population and the elected mayors.

But the violence continued. The permanent army patrols and the threats to the workers and their local union committees merely increased the already high tensions in the population. In May the unions of Urabá protested against the bombing of San Pedro de Urabá. Three helicopter gunships, four armed personnel carriers and a Mirage fighter were used in the counter-insurgency attack, which destroyed six houses and killed at least five civilians — who were officially referred to as 'guerrilla casualties'. A twelve year-old boy wounded in the attack was taken to hospital under guard because he was suspected of being a 'guerrilla'.

The army tried to make everybody in Urabá carry identity cards, but, despite the climate of terror, the people refused, mainly because they feared the implications of the army having data on all the region's inhabitants. They voiced their objection in October 1988 by holding two civic strikes, which paralysed the region and the proposal was put on ice. Popular protest against the military government's abuses in the region continued into 1989 and increased when the banana unions came together to form one organisation.

A typical incident was the arrest by members of the Voltígeros battalion of 19 banana plantation workers in the municipality of Apartadó in March 1989. They were taken to the battalion headquarters in Carepa and twelve were later released. Four others were released after several days during which they were tortured, and three needed hospital treatment for their injuries. The bodies, or rather remains, of two other workers were found on 4 April. They had been killed by having charges of dynamite attached to their bodies and exploded.

Political violence and social conflict

The media tends to present political violence in Colombia as a multi-faceted phenomenon involving paramilitary groups, drug traffickers and guerrillas. It regards the involvement of the armed forces and police as incidental rather than institutional and locates the origins of the violence in local or regional, rather than global, conflicts.

Guerrillas are often assumed to have links with drug-traffickers and the US ambassador, Lewis Tambs, reinforced this view by coining the term 'narco-guerrilla'. In fact, there is well-documented evidence to suggest that the drug mafia has far closer connections with the right than with the left; the DAS even knows what the mafia has paid to finance the paramilitary groups. The FARC and M-19 are known to have made money out of coca production, but their pragmatic relationship to drugs can hardly be compared with the ideologically motivated alliance of landowners, army officers and drug barons.

The media often implies that violence is carried out by evil men and that no general points can be made about its origins or purpose. Nobody in Colombia would deny the existence of individual acts of violence, but more meaningful explanations can be found by looking at the dynamics of Colombian society, at the process of capitalist modernisation and the conflicts it has generated.

These conflicts only became serious when people began to organise and make their voices heard. The first generation of guerrillas (in the 1960s) put down very few roots, whereas the second generation did find support among excluded and marginalised people; this was also the time when people started organisations of their own to put pressure on the state to change.

The state is part of an anachronistic political order and is incapable of dealing with the situation other than through repression. It has always failed to protect the majority of its population. Its effectiveness has been reserved for the powerful; it protects their interests; is flexible in relation to their requirements; intervenes to help ailing businessmen, but is blind to the needs of the mass of the population.

Modernisers have felt that a way out of the crisis would be to 'strengthen the state', which President Barco made some efforts to do. The problem, however, is the attitude of Colombia's ruling elites who fear that, while a strong state and political opposition may guarantee social stability, they would also erode their power and privileges.

Though today's violence is in many ways (geographically and politically) different from that of the 1950s, there is a thread that links them — the character of Colombia's ruling class. In one epoch it led its people into one of the bloodiest civil wars of the 20th century, three decades later it unleashed a wave of right-wing terror against people who demanded their rights.

In social terms the victims of the present-day political violence are overwhelmingly from the poorer sectors of the population. The majority of those for whom information is available are from the peasantry, with 840 victims in 1988.

Murder and massacre in the gold mines

The people of the gold producing areas of the north-east began to protest about the lack of basic services and infrastructure in the region in 1984, as well as the actions of the local army. Guerrilla movements were by then active and the army began to harass the local population. Throughout 1984 there were peasant marches. In August, 1,000 peasants took over El Bagre and were soon joined by thousands more from all over the region. The government negotiated an agreement, which included the provision of schools and the building of a hospital in El Bagre.

When these agreements were ignored, peasants, miners and the urban poor, now better coordinated and organised, declared a civic strike in February 1985. 18,000 people marched to El Bagre and blocked the main road to Medellín. Four peasants were killed and 22 injured in confrontations with the police, until a new agreement was signed. The Civic Movement '21 February' was set up, and kept the people together, organising two marches to protest at the repression which followed the civic strike. This time some of the agreements were kept, and electricity and a water supply were installed in the region, but many others were not.

On 13 March 1988 the people of the municipalities of Remedios and Segovia (as well as those of Apartadó, Mutata and Yondo to the north in Urabá) elected UP mayors. In Remedios, Elkin de Jesús Martínez, a 39 year old miner, who lived from gold-panning and repairing electrical goods, was elected. Only 1962 people voted in the municipality because of the threats against people voting Communist. The new mayor promised the people that they could participate directly in the municipal administration to solve their problems. Two weeks after the elections, the paramilitary group, Death to Revolutionaries of the North-East (MRN) declared that none of the five UP mayors of Antioquia would be allowed to take office.

At the beginning of May 1988, the people of El Bagre, Zaragoza, Segovia, Remedios and the regions of Bajo Cauca and El Nus, sent a list of demands to the local authorities. They wanted the infrastructure and public services agreed previously but not yet provided, the right to monitor the activities of the gold mining companies for ecological damage and guarantees to the people of their right to participate in mining the gold, and finally the observance of the Geneva convention on the rights of civilians in times of war.

On 16 May 1988, Elkin de Jesús Martínez was killed in the centre of Medellín, where he had fled to escape the assassins. He was the first elected mayor to be assassinated. In Remedios and Segovia, commerce, transport and schools were all stopped in protest.

On 23 May, 20,000 peasants from the region participated in the peasant marches of the coast and north-east. 6,000 arrived in Remedios and 2,000 more in Segovia, denouncing the army roadblocks which tried to prevent them moving. The government promised a commission to investigate, but only one representative turned up and did nothing. On 24 May, the organisers of the movement were shot at in Segovia and six people wounded.

In November 1988, Segovia was the scene of one of the worst massacres of the year. This gold mining town has about 30,000 inhabitants and is situated about 240 kilometres from Medellín. According to DANE figures in 1985, it has over 35 per cent illiteracy and 27.7 per cent of the population lack services of any type.

One month before the massacre, the UP coordinator of the town wrote to the Attorney-General in protest at the harassment of the population by members of the Bombona battalion, based in Puerto Berrío and requested an investigation of the following incidents: he accused them of searches without warrant, insults and physical attacks on the inhabitants, whom they accused with no justification of being guerrillas. A maid in one house, pregnant at the time, was pulled by the hair and dragged to the Police command, although she had done nothing wrong. On 2 October, the mayoress's bodyguard was taken to the police station, abused and threatened. On 3 October, the military shot in the air, wounding a local worker, Héctor Darío Mesa. On the 6th, a local driver was arrested and interrogated by the police commander, who told him that the MRN were on their way. Already, people were noticing the arrival of strangers in the town and a number of civilians in the military base; fifteen assassins were known to be there already, and people were told that others were on their way.

On 26 October, one day before the national strike called by the CUT, the army and police took over Segovia, and people were forced to take refuge in their homes. Only the armed forces were on the streets that night, but in the morning the walls were daubed with threats to the UP and the people of the town, all signed by the MRN. On 30 October, the mayoress organised a children's party in the main square; the Bombona battalion arrived and began shooting in the air. During the fortnight before the massacre, the army were constantly carrying out military exercises in the streets of Segovia, shooting in the air and telling the people they were preparing for a guerrilla attack.

Two days before the massacre, the MRN sent out a communique in which they expressed their unconditional support for the armed forces in their war against subversion. On 11 November, at 6.45 as night was beginning to fall, three vehicles, their lights out, stopped outside a bar where a group of miners were having a drink after the day's work. They began shooting indiscriminately, as Rita Ivonne Tobón, the mayoress reported:

> One of the vehicles left from La Reina street, where they broke down the doors of some houses and murdered their inhabitants, while others were shooting in the main park at the population. We can say there were indiscriminate killings and also some selective ones, as some victims were sought out . . . they also threw grenades at a bus which was full of people at that hour . . . 17 people died on the bus, some from shrapnel, some from bullet wounds. The shooting lasted about an hour and took place mostly outside the police station, without them doing anything. About half an hour after the shooting had ended, telephone communications were cut and the military and police arrived on the scene, when they could no longer do anything.

Forty-three people died in the massacre and 56 people were wounded, among them women, children and old people. But this was not the end of the agony of the people of north-east Antioquia.

In November 1988, a military base was installed in El Bagre. 6,000 well equipped soldiers trained in counter-insurgency arrived from the Rifles and Colombia Battalions of the Xth Brigade. In December, 50 families were forced out of the village of Puerto Colombia, leaving only three left in the village, which was then declared a war-zone. Movement in the area, work and the buying of supplies could only be done with the authorisation of the army. Control of the local markets was starving the people as shops were also closed by order of the army. Indiscriminate bombing began at Las Vegas, Arenales, Las Conchas, El Tunel and Bijagual. The president of the *Acción Comunal* of El Pato was forced to leave the village and her daughter and niece were sought by the army and later disappeared at a military roadblock on 23 January 1989.

The peasants of the area were taken to the mountains and forced to act as guides and carry arms for the soldiers. Some were tortured and forced to denounce other people. The Permanent Human Rights Committee investigated the situation and in February 1989 verified the accusations of indiscriminate bombardments.

Sources: Opción June 1988; Rodríguez Solano and García 1988; Lawyers Collective, report June-December 1988, Report to Attorney-General of visit of Permanent Human Rights Commission to El Bagre, 27 February 1989.

In some places militant workers have been singled out — oil workers, cement workers, teachers and others in the public sector, and workers on the African palm and banana plantations. In 14 months between 1988 and 1989 eleven trade unionists at the Nare Cement works in the Magdalena Medio were killed, including the union's president, vice-president and treasurer; others fled the region. In 1989 workers from ASINTAINDUPALMA, the African palm-oil workers of Cesar, Santander and Norte de Santander, protested against the murders of ten of their members during the previous year; 99 members of the teachers union, FECODE, have been killed in three years (1986-9) and 1,000 are under death threat and have had to leave their jobs and homes. In January 1989 the oil-workers union, USO, broke off its negotiations with ECOPETROL fearing for the lives of its negotiators, two of whom had been arrested and held for two days after a trade union meeting in Barranca.

Chronology of death: the cement workers of Nare

8 December 1986. It was 1pm, and Julio César Uribe, President of the Union of Cement Workers of Nare was on a bus from Medellín to Puerto Boyacá. The assassins stopped the bus, got in and shot him dead.

9 March 1987. At 8am, Jesús Antonio Molina, leader of the Nare Cement Workers Union was shot only 300 metres from the police station in Nare, but no-one saw anything.

Days later, and only 30 metres from the police station, Alfonso Lozano, leader of another local union was assassinated. This time the assassins were in a boat, and although they were pointed out by the local people to the authorities, they were allowed enough time to escape.

30 September 1987. At 1.15pm, Pablo Emilio Córdoba, activist of the Nare Cement Workers Union, was killed by an assassin in a jeep. A few days later a squadron of the army burst into a general assembly of the union and kidnapped two workers who were only freed by the action and denunciations of the workers.

19 January 1988. When several Nare Cement workers were travelling on the river Magdalena, people dressed in military uniform brought the vessel to shore and took away Arturo Salazar and Darío Gómez. Days later their bodies appeared with evident signs of torture.

24 January 1988. Jesús Emilo Monsalve was taken from his house and his tortured body found later.

8 February 1988. Héctor Julio Mejía, Treasurer of the Union of Cement Workers of Nare, was shot while on his way to work. He received wounds in the head and thorax and died on 16 February.

In all, eleven trade unionists from Nare Cement were murdered between 1988 and 1989. On 30 July 1989, Henry Cuenca Vega, President of the National Federation of Cement Workers was shot and killed in Bogotá.

The CUT has stated that during 1988 and the first two months of 1989, over 230 union leaders and activists were victims of politically motivated killings.

Priests and members of religious communities who work with the poor have also been targeted by paramilitary forces. On 17 January 1988, Father Jaime Restrepo López, parish priest of San José del Nus in Antioquia department, was shot dead as he was about to say mass. On 1

June 1989, Father Sergio Restrepo, Jesuit priest of Tierralta in Córdoba was shot dead near his church; he had been working with the Zenu Indian community.

In Meta and Antioquia, attacks have been particularly systematic against left-wing UP politicians. In these and other regions the UP lost over 700 people between 1985 and March 1989. Two other left-wing groups, *A Luchar* and the *Frente Popular* have lost 100 and 50 activists respectively. Dr Horacio Serpa Uribe, the Attorney-General at the time of these killings, said that:

> These are neither errors, acts of vengeance, nor irrational acts on the part of some madmen who joined forces to slaughter Colombians hither and yon. All of these events bear all the characteristics of political crimes, committed to punish those belonging to certain parties or adhering to certain ideologies or to intimidate entire communities, to maintain a certain economic status quo or to prevent the rise of certain forms of popular expression. (*El Tiempo* 6 August 1988)

The Government versus the paramilitary right

Not long after the assassination of José Antequera in March 1989, in which Ernesto Samper, a Liberal senator, was also wounded, the government took some action against the paramilitary forces. By then they were reported to have 2,000 men in arms and to have at least 20,000 part-timers and supporters. They had ceased to be a useful ally against the left; they were now a private army, closely tied to the drug barons who were completely beyond the control of the state.

The President finally admitted what most had known for many years:

> These groups are not simply common criminals, but constitute real terrorist organisations. Criminal actions are shielded in vain behind anti-communism and the struggle against the guerrillas. In reality, the majority of their victims are not guerrillas. They are men, women and even children, who have not taken up arms against institutions. They are peaceful Colombians. (*El Tiempo* 20 April 1989)

The role of DAS in particular, with General Maza Márquez at its head, was crucial in the steps taken. The DAS is the only Colombian security agency responsible directly to the civilian authorities and is thus autonomous from the armed forces. Helped by allies in the armed forces, notably General Nelson Mejía, Maza Márquez began to make moves against the army officers most closely associated with the paramilitary.

Armed with a large volume of evidence, compiled by the DAS over a number of years, the state moved against some paramilitary training schools and camps, such as the 'university of assassins' in Meta. Near this macabre institution in Puerto López, three farms were searched by the police and a number of communal graves uncovered, with the bodies of 100 popular leaders and left-wing activists. Mysteriously, only 17 employees were found on the estates, the others having fled days before. The existence of such 'dumping grounds' had in fact been denounced in October 1988 by the Regional Procurator of Ibagué: '[The] bodies are found with . . . signs of torture . . . We have unfortunately discovered that in some cases undisciplined officers (of the police intelligence F-2 department) were responsible'. (Amnesty International 1989)

About half a dozen training camps were dismantled, and deserters told shocking tales of their activities. Asked by a reporter from *La Prensa* how much he had been paid, one assassin replied: 'it depends; for an important member of the Patriotic Union, I might get a cut of maybe 200,000 pesos (US$500)'. (*The Guardian* 8 May 1989)

Maza Márquez was clearly the President's man, and the steps were taken as part of Barco's counter-attack to restore the authority of the state. There were some successes. Lieutenant-Colonel Luis Bohorquez, an officer from the Barbulá battalion, was retired from the army for his association with the paramilitary, accused by both the DAS and the Attorney-General. He was surrounded by solidarity from his colleagues. An assassination attempt against Maza Márquez in May showed that the government's task would not be easy. Indeed, in a report published in September 1989, Amnesty International remained deeply concerned at the level of impunity with which the army operated:

> Colombian authorities have consistently failed to enforce arrest warrants issued against them. In several cases documented by Amnesty International, members of the armed forces involved in multiple killings and 'disappearances' are still free and apparently in active service months after judges have ordered their arrest . . . Amnesty International is concerned that despite the determination of civilian court judges to seek to arrest members of the armed forces and to hold them criminally liable for human rights violations, military authorities are persistently refusing to comply with

such decisions and arrest warrants generally remain unenforced.

The declarations of Ricardo Gámez Mazuera, who fell into the hands of the DAS, revealed the extent to which extrajudicial killings, torture and disappearance had now become part of the army's everyday practice, and not just the activities of an extremist fringe.

Containing 'subversion'

In August 1989, Ricardo Gámez Mazuera, a Colombian national, gave a detailed testimony to a staff member of the International Secretariat of Amnesty International in which he alleges that between 1978 and 1989 he was employed 'extraofficially' as a civilian intelligence operative, by both army and police intelligence units in Colombia. He described the structure and operational methods of army and policy intelligence units and provided detailed information on human rights violations including arbitrary arrest and the torture and killing of both political prisoners and common criminals.

'The army works in the following way. They detect possible suspects, possible ones, that is, there's nothing definite on them. They are put under surveillance. The decision is made to "pick them up". The moment the person is alone, he is taken, kidnapped. They take him, they throw him onto the floor of the car, put on a blindfold smeared with damp earth so that if he opens his eyes he'll get earth in them, and they take him away, blindfold, to army units or totally isolated places where he is beaten or killed. The few who are seen again, it's because they talked. They work out whether it's worth presenting him so that it looks good for public opinion. And if there's really no need they kil! him and he will either appear dead or he won't appear at all.' (Amnesty International 1989)

Barco also suspended the constitutional right to arm self-defence groups, in a bid to undermine the legal justification given to the paramilitary groups by some politicians and army officers. But the extreme right was soon fighting back, with a demonstration of 5,000 members of the 'self-defence' groups of Puerto Boyacá.

In practice, the self-defence groups and paramilitary often overlap, though the latter are theoretically mobile hit squads in contrast to the community-based self-defence groups. Members of the civilian population have been used in army counter-insurgency operations for many years, particularly in the 1960s and 1970s. In 1969, a manual was issued by the army high command, called the *Reglamento de combate de contraguerrillas* (rules for counter-guerrilla combat), which spelt out how to recruit, train and deploy 'selected civilian personnel from the combat zone as forces which will violently repulse the guerrilla actions in their region'. This manual remains in use despite the removal of the constitutional right to arm self-defence groups.

The self-defence groups themselves are in no doubt as to their legitimacy. In October 1989, they issued an open letter to the Colombian people, signed by their 'chief of staff', representing six regions of the country. The commander of the groups of the Atlántico told the press:

> 'The government cannot have a position against the self-defence groups, because it was their creator . . . the government must explain why it created us, why it has supported us, why it continues to support us.' (*La Prensa* 14 October 1989)

Meanwhile assassinations continued. On 4 July, Antonio Roldan Betancur, the Governor of Antioquia, was killed; on 29 July Maria Díaz Pérez, the judge who had ordered the arrest of Pablo Escobar and others responsible for the Urabá massacres; on 30 July Henry Cuenca Vega, President of the National Federation of Cement Workers, was gunned down in Bogotá. On 4 August an attempt on the life of Luis Carlos Galán was frustrated. On 9 August Daniel Espitia, national treasurer of the ANUC, was killed; on 16 August, Carlos Ernesto Valencia, the magistrate who had called for the drug barons who were responsible for the murder of Guillermo Cano, editor of *El Espectador*, to be put on trial, was killed. On 18 August Colonel Franklin Quintero, Commander of the Antioquia police, was killed and later on that day, the most shocking assassination of all took place, that of Luis Carlos Galán.

Cocaine wars

The murder of Galán was the cocaine barons' message that their power was so great, they could even decide who might or might not be a presidential candidate. Galán was not only the politician most likely to take concerted action against them, he was also committed to cleaning up the political establishment, ridding it of the corruption and manipulation which characterised it and which had facilitated its penetration by the cocaine cartels.

Through bribery and intimidation, the cocaine barons had wormed their way into the very heart of political and economic life. The press revealed the existence of a black list of nine Colombian congressmen who had lost the right of entry into the US because of their connections with drug trafficking. Another list included about 20 journalists in the pay of the cocaine mafia. Candidates for public corporations, for mayoral and departmental as well as congressional elections, were known to have been financed by drug money, and the corruption and threats to the judicial system were notorious.

Cocaine and fascism

Galán's assassination was a political crime in which the armed wing of the drug mafia was involved.

A particular characteristic of the Colombian mafia has been its evolution towards an anti-communist and anti-democratic, fascist position. At the same time, Galán clearly represented the greatest possibility of a government which would fight against the 'narco-dollars' circulating throughout the country's social and administrative networks. Luis Carlos Galán represented the maximum expression of honour and honesty on the national political scene . . .

It is probable that not all the numerous small groups and 'mafias' that account for the complexity of the Colombian narcotraffickers are involved in the fascist political evolution of the land-holding, paramilitary groups operating in the Magdalena Medio, Meta, Urubá, and other Atlantic Coast regions. Nevertheless, it has been proven that the 'narco-fascists' do have connections with traditional capitalists and with government, administrative, military and police personnel. This makes one think that Colombian capitalism which has been pumped full of drug money for the last twenty years is now becoming a fascist-capitalist project. A project which enthusiastically embraces the appearance of its legal, political arm: MORENA . . .

It is interesting to note that the headquarters of the narco-fascist paramilitary groups in the above-mentioned regions have not been touched. It is in these regions where the hired thugs with the help of Israeli instructors . . . have assassinated peasant leaders, judges investigating drug-related crimes, and young Communist and Liberal Party cadres. Their latest victim, Luis Carlos Galán, caused the most grief.

If the round-up of drug dealers is limited only to those who can be extradited, to those that have violated the drug laws of the US and Colombia, the real problem is not being attacked. It would appear, so far, that the offensive is against drug trafficking only — something that concerns the DEA [US Drug Enforcement Agency]. However, the fundamental cause of Colombia's political violence, the narco-fascist paramilitary groups, remains.

Unless we are clear about the nature of the real enemy in this historical moment in Colombia's democratic development — the narco-fascist

> paramilitary project — the total 'war' that has been unleashed will accomplish little. The political strongholds where hired assassins are trained will not be dismantled. An increasing number of political crimes will continue with impunity until home-grown fascism strikes its final blow.
> (Jorge Child, *El Espectador* 26 August 1989)

The army and police force have also been heavily infiltrated by the mafia, raising suspicions about their likely effectiveness in dealing with the problem. In September 1989, a public official spoke out for the first time about the penetration of the armed forces and police by the drug traffickers. Alfonso Gómez Méndez, the Attorney-General, told the press that 84 officers of the military and police had been dismissed for bad conduct since the beginning of 1989 and that:

> It is not for lack of military power that the leading drugs barons had not been captured, since they don't have an undefeatable army, but because they have informers in the police and the army who warn them in advance when there are operations to arrest them. (*La Prensa* 20 September 1989)

The economic power of the mafia was by the end of the 1980s enormous, even though most of it was outside the country. Drug trafficking contributed an estimated four per cent of GDP in 1989. Major banks and financial institutions as well as a number of industries have made use of cocaine dollars, while the mafia or narco-bourgeoisie as they should more accurately be called, own about one million hectares of prime agricultural land. The car industry and construction industry have been particularly boosted by the drug barons' taste in expensive real estate. Leading drug baron, Gonzalo Rodríguez Gacha, may not have been exaggerating too wildly when he stated that 70 per cent of Colombians live directly or indirectly from the business.

It has been hard for the country's traditional elites to resist the temptation of the huge amounts of capital on offer when scarcity reigns. The Cali cartel has reputedly penetrated the regional business and political establishment rather more quietly, without the creation of private armies, than their rivals in Medellín, and perhaps even more thoroughly.

But the rise of the cocaine mafia has nevertheless challenged the business sector's own economic control and taken opportunities from them. The criminal origins of the money is clearly of concern to some. And now, with the establishment of MORENA and the barons' bid to lead an extreme-right political programme, there is a new challenge to the control of the traditional elites.

The conflict between 'old' and 'new' money, between traditional holders of power and those who seek to join them and perhaps replace them, has therefore existed alongside the temptation to make use of the free-flowing dollars. This ambivalence has been reflected in the failure of the government to launch a sustained offensive against the cartels. The government has made periodic crackdowns, but rarely waged all-out war. The complexities of the relationship of the new elite enriched by cocaine dollars, and the old establishment and competition within the new elite itself (ie between the Medellín and Cali cartels, in which the latter are happy to back government action against the former), is the necessary background to the cocaine wars. In addition, there is the Barco government's acknowledgement of the danger to its authority now that the anti-popular private justice of the mafia and its allies is totally out of its control.

Impunity in Colombia

At the root of the crisis of consensus is the social indifference derived from the loss of credibility in the effectiveness of the institutions . . . (The state) is ceasing to be a regulator of social conflict or a dispenser of justice and equality of opportunity. The gigantic stain of impunity has spread to almost all our public activities . . . (Alvaro Tirado Mejía, presidential human rights adviser, declaration to the *Encuentro Nacional, 'la lucha contra la impunidad, avances y dificultades'*, 19 September 1988)

Colombia's judicial system has been unable to cope with its task for many years, although it is a country known for its number of lawyers and super-abundance of legal procedures.

The rising rate of crime has produced huge strains on an under-resourced, over-centralised system. There are now 27 rather than 60 legal districts and the 179 higher judges are all in the departmental capitals. In 1985, only 20 per cent of all crimes were reported in the 11 major towns. Of these, only one per cent resulted in a sentence. (Vázquez Carrizosa 1988: 44 and *El Tiempo* 18 December 1988) By September 1988, there were 1.6 million criminal cases pending, such was the huge backlog that had accumulated. (UN Consejo Económico y Social 1989) A member of the DAS stated that even if the present investigative services were tripled and Colombians became angels for a period it would take years and years to deal with this backlog. The slowness of the legal system itself has encouraged the private settling of accounts.

Corruption and intimidation have further undermined the judiciary. Its members are subjected to what has been called 'the theory of the two metals: silver or lead'. In the past, small bribes and tips dominated, but over the years, particularly with the rise of the cocaine mafia, much more money has been available to buy off the judges. A national poll in October 1987 by the research group, the Instituto SER, found that 68 per cent of respondents believed that judges could be bought, and 81 per cent believed that justice was not administered in an equitable way.

Cocaine has also greatly increased the violence against members of the legal system. Many judges have been threatened and over fifty murdered. Two Ministers of Justice have been targets of the mafia: Rodrigo Lara killed in 1984 and, his successor Enrique Parejo González, who was shot and wounded in Hungary in 1987 where he had subsequently accepted the post of Ambassador. Carlos Mauro Hoyos, the Attorney-General, was kidnapped and murdered in January 1988.

Seven different ministers of justice were appointed under the Barco government, his eighth, appointed in July 1989, was a 32-year old woman. But women are not exempt from the killing. In July 1989, María Elena Días Pérez, a Medellín judge and mother of a two year old girl, was shot dead along with her two bodyguards on her way home for lunch. Días Pérez had been investigating several massacres of peasants by paramilitary groups. Her predecessor, also a woman, had begun the investigation and had been forced to flee abroad after receiving death threats. Her father was murdered while she was away.

In August 1989, thousands of judges resigned in protest against the killings of yet another magistrate. Following the killing of Liberal politician, Galán, the government announced the resumption of the extradition treaty with the US and special measures to protect the judges and courts. The mafia bosses announced that for every one of their members extradited, ten judges would be killed.

In the wake of Galán's murder, a series of tough emergency decrees was issued and the most sweeping attack yet on the property of the mafia was launched. Numerous individuals (an estimated 11,000 in the week after Galán's assassination) associated with cocaine, though at a fairly low level, were arrested and laboratories destroyed. Some 2,000 properties were raided, 900 vehicles and aircraft seized and over 1,200 weapons captured in the first weeks of the offensive.

The US urged the government on and gave financial and military help, though the latter was curiously inappropriate for the anti-narcotics war and more suitable for other forms of combat. Many Colombians felt that the drug problem was, in any case, a social not a military problem, in which the US government's role should focus on curbing the demand at home. The extradition treaty was renewed by presidential decree, but not one of the 12 mafia heads wanted in the US had actually been sent there by the end of 1989. The highest ranking figure extradited was Evaristo Porras Ardila, said to be the administrator of the Medellín cartel's operations in southern Colombia. Another six people were awaiting extradition, but three of them had been released by the end of September.

The issue of extradition was still a controversial one in Colombia. Many who were bitterly opposed to the drug traffickers objected to extradition on grounds of national sovereignty. Differences over the issue was reportedly one of the reasons behind the resignation of Barco's eighth minister of justice in September 1989. A young woman of 32, Monica de Greiff was receiving constant death threats, and lasted only two months in her post. Some of her predecessors had lasted only hours.

Cocaine politics: the extraditables

When former Justice Minister, Rodrigo Lara Bonilla, was assassinated on 30 April 1984, President Belisario Betancur declared war against the drug trafficking mafia. The 1979 Extradition Treaty with the US was dusted off and the first extradition was approved in December of that same year. However, the 'Extraditables' had made their appearance several years before.

In the Pascual Guerreo Sports Stadium in Cali, they had managed to stop a soccer game in December 1981 for a few brief moments. The enthusiastic fans let their eyes wander from the green turf to the blue skies above. A small plane flew slowly overhead. A hatch opened up and thousands of leaflets announcing the creation of the group, 'Death to the Kidnappers' (MAS) floated to the ground. This terrifying group claimed that it had been created to exterminate kidnappers, guerrillas, and Communists.

On 30 December MAS launched its offensive. They chained a young woman to the doors of the Medellín-based daily paper, *El Colombiano,* claiming that she was the wife of the M-19 guerrilla who had kidnapped the daughter of a mafia drug baron, Jorge Luis Ochoa. In the following ten weeks MAS was responsible for more than 100 assassinations. Marta Nieves Ochoa Vásquez appeared unharmed on 17 February.

However, 16 May 1982 was the day that 'Extraditables' became a household name in Colombia. That morning the major dailies carried full-page advertisements announcing the official formation of the group. Carlos Enrique Lehder Rivas, now in jail in the US, assumed public leadership for the group and during the remainder of the year, five more advertisements appeared in Colombian newspapers.

From this moment on, the 'Extraditables' launched a full-blooded campaign. They organised open and public debates and obtained the participation of individuals from all walks of life. Bumper stickers on cars became common: 'Colombia is giving away its sons and daughters. Denounce extradition'.

During 1983 there were few newspaper advertisements from the 'Extraditables'. There was one clear explanation for this. Everything was now being handled in the *Free Quindio* press, owned and operated by Carlos Lehder himself. However, after the assassination of Lara Bonilla and the government response, Ledher was forced into hiding in the Colombian jungle.

But the 'Extraditables' found other ways of communicating after April 1984. They took to street pamphlet distribution and graffiti writing, while the terrifying bands of hired thugs became part of daily life in Colombia. Behind a series of crimes claiming the lives of magistrates, judges, journalists, and political activists, government authorities 'presumed' that the 'Extraditables' had been hard at work.

They applauded from behind the scenes when Supreme Court Magistrate, Hernando Baquero Borda, and newspaper editor, Guillermo Cano, were assassinated in 1986. Any time the 'Extraditables' have felt threatened they have called on their powerful private armies to eliminate obstacles in their way. The assassination of former Attorney-General, Carlos Mauro Hoyos, in 1988 and that of Liberal Party presidential candidate, Luis Carlos Galán in August 1989, underline just how far the Colombian 'Extraditables' are willing to go.

In the meantime, the US was extending its military presence in the country; US military advisers were sent to Colombia in September, and the State Department announced the intention of sending between 50 and 100 in all. Many suspected that the purpose of this intervention would not be restricted to drug-related problems, but would give backing to the army in its wider counter-insurgency war.

The power of the armed forces

The US has played an important role in preparing the Colombian army materially and ideologically for counter-insurgency. Colombia is a much more important country strategically and economically than any Central American republic. The gateway to South America — lying just south of the

Panama Canal - its considerable geo-political importance to the US is enhanced by its mineral and energy wealth.

Close ties were established between the army and the US during the Korean war, and the US played a big role in the counter-insurgency operation against the 'independent republics' in the early 1960s. Between fiscal years 1950-79, 7,907 Colombian military personnel were trained in the US, and during the same period, Colombia received US$253 million in military assistance and other military related economic support programmes. Between 1976 and 1980, over 500 military personnel were trained at the US Army School of the Americas in the Panama Canal Zone, 228 in Internal Security Operations and two in military intelligence. Between 1978 and 1986, the US gave just over US$98 million in military assistance, two thirds of it during the repressive government of Turbay Ayala. (Heinz 1989)

The Colombian army has grown from about 80,000 men in 1978 (40,000 police), to 135,000 in 1988 (72,000 police), according to a letter of General Rafael Samudio Molina to President Barco, published in *El Espectador* on 3 June 1988. Its budget increased steadily for most of this period, but substantially between 1987-8. The army acquired a new range of weapons during this period, particularly from Israel. It bought 13 Kafir planes from that country at a cost of US$200 million in 1987, and Israel rather than West Germany now supplies the majority of its infantry weapons, light machine guns and portable rocket launchers. Many of these purchases were funded through foreign loans.

In 1989 the US increased its military allocation to Colombia to enable it to meet the drug threat, although US spokesmen made clear that this also applied to the guerrillas, as General Charles Brown told the Senate Foreign Relations Committee: 'the greatest increase in arms will be destined for Colombia, where the drugs barons and insurgent groups often work together, threatening the survival of the legal system and the democratic government' (*La Prensa*, 8 May 1989). Such thinking coheres with the view of the second document of the right-wing Santa Fe group, which puts Colombia alongside El Salvador as a threatened focus of regional conflict. In August 1989, US$65 million was granted as part of an emergency military package, double the US$24.5 million agreed for the year, half of which was for the anti-drugs programme. By the end of 1989 some reports suggested that the Colombian military will have received about US$167 million, 25 per cent of their total budget in 1987 (CINEP *Análisis* September 1989).

Revelations emerged too, of the role of foreign mercenaries in Colombia, working for the drug mafia. The DAS had apparently known for some time that British and Israeli mercenaries had been training assassins in ACDEGAM's school in Puerto Boyacá. Eleven British mercenaries were reported to be in the country, initially contracted by the Cali cartel to assassinate Pablo Escobar.

The government's measures against the mafia, while well publicised, were in fact very limited. Most of these arrested in the initial sweep were released, and a lot of confiscated property returned. The mafia made clear their resolve to meet war with war. The country's judges went everywhere under armed guard, still felt to be inadequate protection for a group which was taking the brunt of mafia wrath. Of 4,500 judges, an estimated 1,600 had received death threats during 1989. A bombing campaign in the major cities left six people dead and hundreds wounded by the end of September. The main targets were banks, the headquarters of the traditional parties, commercial centres and schools, and *El Espectador* was also bombed. From waging war on the popular movement, the mafia had turned its attention to its enemies within the establishment. Late in 1989 the war took on even bloodier proportions. On 27 November a bomb destroyed an Avianca jet, killing all 107 people aboard; the explosion was immediately linked to the drug mafia. Then, on 6 December, a huge bomb exploded in a bus outside the DAS headquarters in Bogotá, killing 59 and wounding 500 more. Most victims were innocent bystanders and street vendors, while the intended target, General Maza Márquez, again escaped unscathed.

By the end of 1989, many felt that the Barco government would in the end have no choice but to negotiate with the mafia. Even if there had been some temporary dislocation in the cartel's network, the result would probably be to put up the price of cocaine, and there were signs that this was happpening topwards the end of 1989. Once before in 1984 the mafia had offered to give up the cocaine business (and some claim, to pay off the national debt — US$14,000 million at the time) in return for being allowed to repatriate their fortune and operate legally. In October, *La Prensa* and *Semana* revealed that indirect talks had been taking place before Galán's assassination. One of those engaged in such talks had asked Rodríguez Gacha what guarantee of his good faith he could offer. He responded:

> Proof of good faith, doctor? I don't like to talk of money, but I am going to tell you something: what I would give them, if a just agreement is reached, is worth more than ECOPETROL . . . (*Semana* 16 October 1989)

The killing of Rodríguez Gacha in December 1989 was a propaganda victory for the government, but few believed it signified a major defeat for the cocaine barons.

Legitimacy and authority: the counter-offensive stalls

Election year approached with the modernisers in the ruling elite looking considerably weaker than at the beginning of the Barco administration. The man most likely to replace Galán as Liberal Party candidate, César Gaviria, was a technocrat like Barco. He had been one of his more effective ministers of the interior before he resigned to build up a political base in Risaralda, with an eye to the presidential election. While Gaviria may take up Barco's mantle of strengthening and modernising the state, the crisis facing that state at the beginning of the counter-offensive had in all but one significant respect worsened. A relatively healthy economy for much of the Barco presidency had played an important role in offsetting the political crisis but there were signs of deterioration by the end of 1989 as the price of coffee plummeted. The losses following the collapse of the International Coffee Agreement were estimated at US$270 million from September to December.

Barco's initial successes in introducing some flexibility into the political system began to look rather less impressive. The modernising technocrats had won small victories, but the power of the regional bosses was intact. The constitutional reform was scuppered as congressional efforts to amend it tore it apart so badly that Barco was forced to abandon hope of congressional approval. The social programmes had barely got off the ground and the archaic political customs of the traditional elite still predominated. Not only was the crisis of legitimacy — the state's relationship with the people — unresolved, but the state now had an equally serious crisis of authority, in the political as well as economic challenge of the narco-bourgeoisie and its allies.

3.2 Political Options

The political crisis as Colombia approached elections was acute, with conflict between the US government and the national congress, the army and the judiciary, and within and between the traditional parties. Colombia's healthy economy did much to offset the political crisis, while the Barco government's record was most successful in forcing the popular movement into retrenchment. Repression, both official and unofficial, and far in excess of the real strength of that movement, had taken its toll. The ruling elites had won a breathing space which had cost over 8,000 lives in three years, and despite the limited steps against the paramilitary during the Barco government's last year, the killings were increasing once again at the end of 1989.

The UP had established itself as a small, though not insignificant third opposition force, but at terrible human cost. After considerable reluctance to enter into any dialogue with the guerrillas, peace talks began with a much weakened M-19 while the FARC and the EPL agreed to a truce. The ELN was the only organisation which would negotiate only around specific issues such as the humanisation of the war and the energy question. And though the talks with the M-19 did culminate in an agreement (the M-19 constituted only a couple of hundred members by now), by the end of 1989, even the FARC and the EPL had concluded that there was no serious possibility of negotiations.

What were the options for the majority of Colombia's people as Barco's administration came to a close? How had the 'dirty war' affected the popular movement? Did armed struggle still represent an option for change or had the prospects for greater popular participation and democracy improved?

The popular movement

The years 1985-7 were times of growth for the popular movements. The second congress of civic movements was held in July 1986 and in November of that year the CUT was formed. In May 1987 there were coordinated peasant marches and mobilisations in various parts of the country, with a total of 43 peasant marches during the course of the year. In June a civic strike in the north-east mobilised 200,000 people to march on the municipal capitals. In August ANUC held its national congress and the popular movements became united in their demand for the right to life.

During 1988 the situation began to change. The peasant marches of May 1988 took place at the height of the right-wing counter-offensive and mobilised less than half the numbers of the previous year. It no longer seemed possible to make a national impact. Land invasions and other activities also diminished, though there were some significant local actions. In April 1989, 100 peasants occupied the INCORA offices in Pelaya, Cesar, and 200 did the same in Saravena and Valledupar.

The CUT also faced a variety of problems. It failed to achieve internal coherence and was continually plagued by disagreements over its work methods and ideological direction. Criticism of the leadership's failure to act sufficiently firmly to prevent the repression of its members mounted during 1988. In response to this pressure (and after a plebiscite gave a clear mandate for such action) a general strike was called for 27 October 1988.

Although the CGT agreed to participate, in the end neither the CGT nor all the sectors of the CUT succeeded in mobilising their membership. CUT General-Secretary Carrillo's forces failed to come out and even the left was unable to bring out certain key factories. Nevertheless 250 organisations did participate, but it was still felt that the strike was a show of weakness rather than of strength.

Repression and intimidation before and during the strike evidently influenced participation. The weakness of the labour movement also played a role. The industrial restructuring of the 1980s had strengthened employers, who now employed many of their workers on a temporary basis as a way of discouraging militancy. Political divisions within the CUT had also played a part, but, despite the post-strike recriminations, a serious split was avoided. Carrillo blamed the left for the strike's failure and offered his resignation, but this was refused. His own trade union sector had already affiliated to the US-funded Inter-American Office of Labour (ORIT). During 1989 the CUT gave little support to workers who had been intimidated as a result of the strike or to the victims of the dirty war. Real wages fell as the employers and the government took advantage of the labour movement's weakness.

Civic movements were also under fire and, as a result, the nature and extent of their activities changed. CINEP made the following assessment (*Cien Días* September 1989):

Years (1)	No. of civic strikes	Municipalities affected by strikes	Civic Struggles (2)	Municip. affected by struggles
1982-86	97	163	142	152
1986-87	59	151	125	154
1987-88	36	90	66	73
1988-89	29	57	77	91

(1) 7 August-7 August of following year
(2) Mobilisations, takeovers, plebiscites, not including civic strikes

The number of strikes fell sharply in 1987, but the number of municipalities which took part in civic actions of one sort or another was still significant. The government claimed that the participatory mechanisms introduced at the level of local government were bearing fruit. But not only were those channels not yet set up in many areas, but Decree 700 of April 1987 gave the mayor the right to choose the representatives on the executives of public services. While the measures may have had an effect in some areas, repression is the most likely explanation for the reduction in action. CINEP reported that of the 71 civic strikes which it had documented, 33 met with military action, house searches, arrest, curfews, etc. Faced with this repression, civic action has become more atomised, adapting to the situation which made mass mobilisation in civic strikes particularly vulnerable to army attack. Even so, the number of civic strikes during Barco's three years is 124 compared to 97 under Betancur, and even the lowest number, of 29 registered in 1988-9, is higher than any one year under Betancur.

The civic protests of 1988 still mobilised large numbers of people. In Riohacha in Guajira, for example, on 21 September over 4,000 people came onto the streets to protest against the lack of water — only available in the region when it rained which was infrequently. At election time the politicians offered to build wells for the local Indians in exchange for their vote, but the wells were unhygienic because the Indians used the water for all purposes from cooking to washing. There had also been growing resentment because the people felt they gained nothing from having the huge coal project, El Cerrejón, sited in their region.

Another example occurred in Nariño where (though not a department in which guerrillas were active) repression was severe. In the municipality of Tumaco (a port with a population of 90,000 in the south of the department) 10,000 people gathered in September 1988 to protest about the general neglect of the town and almost a month without electricity. Thirty years previously the people had been promised a road to replace the railway line of the Pacific (which had been closed down) but it had never been built. During the protest, one person was killed,

49 were wounded and about 20 were arrested. A curfew was declared and tanks and reinforcements sent into the town; a member of the civic committee and his two children sought asylum in Ecuador.

In Pasto in the same department 20,000 came out, both in solidarity with the people of Tumaco and to protest against the state of education in the town, including the failure to pay teachers. When the army tried to prevent the demonstration taking place it grew into a strike and 400 people were arrested.

Given the level of repression, it was remarkable that people were prepared to organise and demonstrate at all. The popular movement had clearly been forced to be less visible, to reduce its more overt and challenging activities, but it had not been destroyed.

But it was still a relatively young movement and was being denied the space in which to mature and consolidate itself. Time and opportunities were needed to build movements with strong support at the base, to ensure that new generations of leaders emerged, that moves towards unity were sustained and that national organisations remained representative and responsive to their local activists. The climate of intimidation and outright terror meant that the popular movement had to work under very difficult conditions.

Colombia's guerrilla movements were established before the social and popular movements had had time to consolidate themselves. Though the balance of forces was far from favourable for the guerrillas (they offered no chance of a military victory), their growth inevitably encouraged the militarisation of the state. However, it should be emphasised that even where the guerrillas have no real presence, such as in the major cities, the government has not hesitated to use violence in putting down popular protest. It was therefore difficult for the popular movements to establish a legitimate space in which to work, especially given the traditional elite's historical antipathy to popular protest.

The rapid polarisation of the 1980s presented many problems. For example, social conflicts quickly became politicised, with trade unionists arrested during negotiations, peasants murdered during land invasions, or tanks sent in against civic protesters. The government and the right all too frequently identified popular leaders with the guerrilla movements. Since counter-insurgency doctrine called for the isolation of guerrillas from their social base, 'draining the sea from the fish' as it was known, the government was able to justify the repression of all forms of popular protest. This kind of war bears heavily upon civilian populations — guerrillas are mobile and can more easily escape army operations.

The guerrillas and the popular movements therefore had a somewhat controversial relationship. The guerrillas could provide defence under certain circumstances, but in so doing implicated the popular movements in the armed struggle. The guerrillas supported the banana workers in Urabá and helped them improve their wages and conditions, but at the cost of the region being militarised. As they became more effective though, the popular movements faced repression with or without the guerrillas' presence.

Popular movements were also invariably affected by the various left-wing political debates. While the worst of the 1970s' sectarianism had diminished, there were still substantial divisions and, by the 1980s, these had become quite serious. Should the popular movements seek reforms through existing institutions, or was popular mobilisation with a view to radically transforming Colombian society as a whole the only way forward?

Towards a political front

Political movements had emerged from Betancur's peace initiative with different answers to this question. The left had made two attempts to work within the electoral system. The most important of these being by the UP, which the Communist Party had set up in a bid to establish itself as the country's third political force and main opposition party. Initially this initiative was also meant to provide a way of reintegrating the FARC into the political system. This proved impossible, however, for members of the FARC were the first to be murdered when they put on their civilian clothes.

The second was by the Popular Front (FP), which the PC-ML set up in an effort to widen its political influence. Both the UP and the FP were meant to provide an umbrella to allow broad sectors, rather than just the parties' own members, to participate.

Those who opposed electoral politics and the peace plan gathered together in another movement, called *A Luchar*, in 1984. These included a number of independent workers' collectives, some factory-based groups, the Movement for Bread and Liberty (MPL) and the Trotskyist Socialist Workers Party (PST), part of which later withdrew and the Revolutionary Socialist Party (PSR). The movement grew rapidly, mainly because many people on the left distrusted the peace plan and feared that false expectations would break up the popular movement.

A Luchar sought to build a broad mass-based movement on the grounds that, although the country had strong social and guerrilla organisations, there was no political movement through which the people's protest could be turned into political challenges to the state. As a result, their activities were often ineffectual or isolated. *A Luchar's* combative politics (the name means 'to struggle') attracted people who

Military police stand next to A *Luchar* graffitti calling for another civic strike, Barrancabermeja.

rejected the UP's cautious electoralism and it won influence within the peasant (and to a lesser extent the workers') movement. Many of *A Luchar*'s members had strong ELN sympathies, but both organisations insisted on retaining their complete independence.

The three organisations had very different ideas about how to work with popular movements. In joining forces to support the third national civic strike of 1985, the FP and UP saw their role as calling for greater democracy and the fulfillment of the peace agreements, whereas *A Luchar* saw its as a protest against the government's demagogic behaviour over the peace issue. While their differences persisted, the organisations none the less cooperated over minimal common demands — the right to life, the dismantling of the paramilitary groups, the defence of national sovereignty.

In September 1988 the three groups announced their intention to join forces in a political front (*Frente Político de Convergencia*), but it had great difficulty getting off the ground. The UP saw it as broadly based and encompassing both the left and other progressive forces; similarly, the FP saw it as generally anti-imperialist and anti-fascist; but *A Luchar* saw it solely as a front of the left.

The three movements had varying degrees of support by the late 1980s, but were leading the people in different directions. The UP had lost hundreds of lives and endured considerable repression for a tiny opening into the political system. The traditional elite was unlikely to allow more than the minimal participation of opposition forces.

The guerrilla movements

Though the storming of the Palace of Justice in 1985 had severely weakened M-19, there was none the less a resurgence of guerrilla activity as a whole. The ELN in particular, which had not backed the 'national dialogue', grew considerably. In 1985 it took the first step towards coordinating its activities and, by October 1987, had formed the Coordinadora Guerrillera Simón Bolívar (CGSB). Shortly before, in July 1987, the FARC had ambushed an army unit in Caquetá, killing 17 soldiers and breaking its truce with the government.

No reliable information exists on exactly how many guerrillas there are, though some suggest a figure of around 12,000. Reyes Posada and Bejarano (1988) show that between 1985 and 1987 the guerrillas had been active in 339 of the country's 1,009 municipalities, which represented a considerable geographical area. They had infiltrated all the departments except Guajira, Chocó, Nariño and the *comisarias* of Amazonas and Vaupés. Though once confined to isolated marginal regions, they were now strong in some economically strategic ones. They were weakest, however, in the urban areas, particularly the large cities.

Each movement had a base in certain regions. The FARC, with nearly 50 fronts, covered the largest geographical area, but was strongest in places of peasant colonisation, the eastern plains, the Magdalena Medio, the Alto Magdalena and in some parts of the south and east. The ELN was strongest in the north-east, particularly Arauca, along the frontier with Venezuela and in the east of Antioquia. The EPL was strongest in Urabá, Córdoba and Antioquia, and had a small operational base in Norte Santander and Putumayo. M-19's operational base was in the south-east, in Valle, Cauca and Tolima. The map on page 282 shows where the guerrilla movements operated. Their relationship to these conflicts varied from place to place, but in many areas the peasants came to regard them as a serious political option and this support alone can account for their growth.

Strategic differences divided the guerrilla movement, but remarkably the CGSB survived. The FARC (still under the Communist Party's political direction) and the ELN were at opposite ends of the tactical and strategic spectrum. In an interview with Martha Harnecker in 1988 (*Foro Nacional* 1989) Gilberto Vieira, the Communist Party's

Regions affected by guerrilla actions 1985-7

Bogotá

KEY

- EPL
- M-19
- FARC
- ELN

1   ANTIOQUIA
2   BOYACÁ
3   CALDAS
4   CAQUETÁ
5   CASANARE
6   CAUCA
7   CÓRDOBA
8   META
9   NORTE DE SANTANDER
10 TOLIMA
11 VALLE

general secretary, supported the idea of combining all forms of struggle — a view confirmed at the party's fifteenth congress at the end of 1988.

For the Communist Party, the FARC and the UP were both important vehicles for political change. The FARC provided the bargaining power necessary to force an opening into the political system, and a defence against the armed forces, landowners and drug traffickers. The UP provided it with the opportunity to broaden its support and to test the electoral battleground. As Vieira put it at the close of the congress, the tactical and strategic objective for combining various forms of struggle is 'not war, but the democratic peace which the Colombian people desire'. However, during 1989 the UP took steps towards complete independence from the Communist Party in a bid to attract a wider following and to reduce the level of repression against its activists.

The ELN, on the other hand, was clear that what it sought was the seizure of power. Its growth between 1986 and the end of 1988 (which it itself estimated at 500 per cent) was rapid (Harnecker 1988:87). In June 1987 it had merged with the MIR-*Patria Libre* (a split from the PC-ML) and was subsequently known as the *Unión Camilista-ELN* (UCELN). In 1987 it held its first national assembly which elected the national leadership.

The organisation now had a social base and needed to put forward political as well as military proposals. It had to ensure that those who did not form part of the guerrilla army could participate politically and, in areas where it held influence, the idea of popular power, though also part of a national programme to build an alternative popular, democratic and revolutionary government, grew out of this concern.

The ELN's decision to blow up oil pipelines engendered intense debate on the left (a large sector disapproved of such tactics), but the campaign was none the less launched at the end of 1986 under the slogan 'Awake Colombia . . . they are stealing the oil'. It cost the government millions in lost oil revenues and (between early 1988 and mid-1989 alone) nearly US$400 million in damage to pipelines. The ELN made large sums of money out of kidnapping oil executives and forcing their companies to invest in health, education, water and sewerage in the areas in which they operated. Among the guerrillas' demands have been the resignation of the minister responsible for oil and of the president of ECOPETROL, the nationalisation of the Caño Limón oil field, an end to association contracts with foreign companies and a nationwide forum to discuss oil policy. Their objective is to draw attention to the issues of self-determination and national sovereignty. In November 1989 the government did agree to an energy forum in which the ELN could put its case. The Minister of Mines was forced to resign, and the ELN stopped blowing up the pipeline. For the first time, the national press began to debate the energy issue, the role of the multinationals and the nature of the contracts signed with them.

As Colombia's guerrilla movements began to build popular support, they found their spaces for political work starting to close. Defending the civilian population was difficult, but recruiting large numbers of civilians under threat into the guerrilla movements was logistically and politically impossible. They were too weak in the urban areas to claim that a revolution was imminent in the short or medium term.

The guerrillas had to respond to the political impasse, but the government had yet to recognise that it could not defeat them militarily. A massive army campaign during 1989 had failed to weaken the ELN and, within this context, the guerrillas had to decide how to use their armed strength. Should they, as the ELN wished, deepen the revolutionary process through a prolonged popular war? Or, as the EPL insisted, find political openings by uniting all forces against 'fascism'? Or, as the FARC and M-19 argued from their different perspectives, win reforms and the right to participate electorally? In 1989 arguments for peace or war, reform or revolution were once again being debated. William Ramírez Tobón (*Analísis Política,* no.5, 1988) feels that the 'enemy in the peace negotiations is more than a military opponent or an opposition force. The guerrilla represents, whether we like it or not, a dream of a new society, a project different from the established order in existence today in Colombia. Behind the guns are voices that cry out for employment, education, health and the right to life'.

Peace or war?

In the first years of his administration President Barco had little interest in talking to the guerrilla movements. But when M-19 kidnapped and subsequently released the veteran right winger, Alvaro Gómez Hurtado, a new peace process was triggered off; this began (without the government) in July 1988 as one of the conditions for the hostage's release.

Taking part were business leaders, the representatives of political parties and popular organisations, and (significantly and after some initial reluctance) members of the church hierarchy. The church was under pressure from international human rights organisations to investigate abuses — 18 priests had been murdered between January 1980 and June 1988. In some regions local bishops, such as Bishop Serna in Florencia and Bishop Samuel Silverio Buitrago in Popayán, had already begun to encourage local dialogue.

Finally, on 1 September, the government produced its own peace proposal, but imposed a series of pre-conditions on the talks which were unacceptable to the guerrillas. Eventually only M-19 agreed to a dialogue which was held on a farm in the Cauca. In April three of its members, including one the movement's leaders, Afranio Parra, were murdered, apparently by drunken policemen. Parra had joined a long list of guerrilla leaders murdered during a truce; it included some Liberal guerrillas and Guadalupe Salcedo in the 1950s, and Carlos Toledo Plata and Oscar William Calvo in the mid-1980s.

M-19 continued to talk. Most of its demands were conditions for electoral participation, including electoral reforms, control over party and campaign funding, and a second-round voting system which would break the dominance of the two parties. Such guarantees went to the heart of the bipartisan state. As the leader of M-19, Carlos Pizarro, explained, 'we are not going into politics on the basis of our historic suicide' (*Colombia Hoy* April 1989:10). But in October, the guerrillas voted by a margin of 227 to 3 in favour of laying down their arms and forming a political party.

M-19 made their disarmament dependent on congressional approval of a referendum, a proposal which had been presented along with the constitutional reform and which was due to be passed by 16 December 1989, the last day of Congress. Also essential was the passing of measures to facilitate political minorities' access to congressional seats. These conditions were fulfilled, M-19 announced its intention of becoming a legal political group, the M-19 Party, with Carlos Pizarro as its presidential candidate for the 1990 elections.

The FARC called a unilateral ceasefire in March 1989 and, because the government refused to talk until it was convinced the ceasefire was genuine, began talks with a 'commission of notables'. The EPL and Quintín Lame followed suit. The ELN agreed to stop blowing up oil pipelines in exchange for the energy forum, the resignations of the manager of ECOPETROL and the Minister of Mines, and talks on reducing the scale of violence in relation to civilian victims. Many more civilians were killed during the paramilitary's 'dirty war' than were guerrillas or soldiers during the armed confrontations. Over 3,000 civilians were killed in 1988 compared to 393 policemen and soldiers and 549 guerrillas. Application of the Geneva convention would reduce the war's impact on the civilians.

The guerrillas disagreed over the contents of the peace plan, as did the forces of the state. As always, political and military realities and class interests intervened. The traditional elite, with a 100,000-strong army to defend its interests, had not even accepted the right of the UP to participate in elections and, in the midst of the peace initiatives, the 'dirty war' continued:

There are zones in the country where the word dialogue does not figure in the dictionaries, such as in Urabá, where the population organised a civic strike on 10 and 11 April [1989] to protest against the arrest, torture and murder of banana workers during 31 March and 3-4 April, of which they directly accuse the military *jefatura* commanded by Brigadier General Hernán José Guzmán Rodríguez. The stoppage also demanded the right to form unions, which the army wishes to prevent at the moment when the unification of all the banana unions in one organisation, SINTRAINAGRO, affiliated to the CUT, was under preparation. (*Solidaridad* April 1989:6)

Colombia's political time-bomb

Colombia has been described as a country of different 'political time zones'. In 1989 Puerto Boyacá was in the hands of the organised right, while Arauca, except for its municipal towns, was in the hands of the ELN. Urabá was in a state of virtual civil war, but in the big cities the left had minimal political weight. The cities' middle classes were attracted to charismatic politicians like Andrés Pastrana (elected mayor of Bogotá in 1988), while the poor were engaged in a daily struggle for survival and few bothered to vote. Popular movements everywhere were divided on how to respond to the political options on offer.

These options varied. Many progressive urban intellectuals rejected armed struggle and traditional left-wing politics and wanted to build a third force based on civic movements and broad social alliances. They formed a movement in early September 1989, called *Colombia Unida*. The UP hankered for a still elusive 'bourgeois democracy'. In some regions the guerrillas had simply replaced the state. In others they were emphasising grassroots politicisation and popular power, from which they could build a revolutionary alternative in Colombia.

No political project (right, left or centre) had national legitimacy and, though with insufficient bipolar conflict to generate civil war, this contributed to a sense of social and political decomposition. There were wars in regions such as Urabá and the Magdalena Medio, where class conflict was particularly acute, but in the cities, where there were no clear political options other than cocaine and crime, violence bred violence.

Meanwhile the traditional elite was still searching for a political formula that would restore its hegemony more permanently with a minimum loss of power. The modernisers wanted to strengthen the state further, reform institutions and pursue a peace plan on their own terms. The majority of the elite were concerned at the loss of political legitimacy, but their main interest was the preservation of their own privileges. In that sense, a weak state served them best.

The right still supported a military solution directed against the popular movement. At the end of 1988 the Minister of Defence, General Rafael Samudio, spoke at the burial of some soldiers killed in a guerrilla ambush of the need to 'destroy the enemy and break its will to struggle. Subversion', he said, 'requires a military response and we are going to provide it'. Samudio subsequently lost his job, but there were plenty in the army who supported his position. Meanwhile, the rise of a new elite, enriched by cocaine dollars, seriously threatened the search for reform on the part of the modernisers, as well as the quest for representation and economic justice undertaken by the popular movements. In this respect, the outcome of the 'cocaine wars' will be more important than any electoral contest.

The Colombian journalist Antonio Caballero once called Colombia a 'political time-bomb'. Can an economy that has created only 500,000 jobs in manufacturing, which a leaked World Bank report (July 1989) describes as closed and meeting the needs of only a minority, provide the majority of its population with a humane existence and the means to a livelihood? The archaic political order that has kept that minority in power has proved incapable of taking on this responsibility. The bomb will carry on ticking until it does, or until the left proves itself able to unite the people around an alternative social and political project.

Appendix: Colombians abroad

Much of the interview material used in this appendix is drawn from Nony Ardill and Nigel Cross, *Undocumented Lives: Britain's Unauthorised Migrant Workers,* (Runnymede Trust, 1988). Other interviews were conducted by Catherine Hill.

Colombia has a considerable tradition of emigration. Since the 1930s Colombians have gone to Venezuela, and since the 1950s to the US. The 1960s and 1970s were the decades of highest emigration, with a sharp increase during the late 1970s. People left for neighbouring Venezuela, Ecuador and Panama, as well as for the US, Canada and Western Europe.

Studies show that people left Colombia not just because they were unemployed, but because of low salaries for those in work. The salary differential between Colombia and neighbouring countries narrowed a great deal during the recession of the early 1980s, making Ecuador and Venezuela less attractive and the US and Europe more so. The search for social mobility has been a factor amongst the lower and middle classes, particularly in emigration to the US, as Colombia has not been able to provide jobs for newly educated sectors of the population. Considerable numbers of women and young people between 15 and 25 have emigrated to find skilled and professional work.

In 1980 there were just under one million Colombians abroad, according to calculations by a study for the Chenery report on the Colombian labour market, though others have suggested that some three to five million Colombians have emigrated at one time or another since the early 1970s (Ocampo and Ramírez, 1987). The Colombian government has encouraged emigration, because the migrants send back foreign exchange. There is significant social status attached to having a family member abroad, especially in the US or Europe, and there are frequent programmes on television which depict the affluent life-style enjoyed by emigrants. A number of agencies help people move abroad and find jobs, although they are mostly unregulated and there is little protection against exploitation.

In Britain today, there are an estimated 25,000 Colombians, living mostly in London. Most came to this country during the 1970s and have taken up low-paid jobs in the service sector. Many have come from the south-west of Colombia, from Cali and Valle del Cauca, a region where agricultural modernisation from the 1950s onwards disrupted the peasant economy of the region and forced many into the city of Cali. The city has one of Latin America's largest shanty towns, Aguablanca, housing some 300,000 people in squalid shacks.

The majority of Colombians living in Britain have come in search of a better life. Many are women, who came initially to work as au pairs and stayed on in the country. Their stories are very varied. Agencies in Colombia arrange the trip, but migrants often have to incur debts guaranteed by their remaining friends or relatives to pay their passage which they repay in installments from future earnings:

> There are agencies in Colombia that cheat workers, giving them false documentation... a woman here was was left stranded in Piccadilly Circus with no passport, no money and so on. That man was operating an office in Cali, south-west Colombia, where most of us come from....We found quite a lot of people from small villages who had never been in the capital, not even in the capital of their own districts let alone the capital of Colombia. They only passed through there when they were coming here. We have found cases where we just don't know how they managed to get here at all. ('José')
>
> The more reputable agencies book you into a hotel, explain where to get a job and how to find a room. The crooks wait until you are through immigration, take their fee and then disappear. At first people are fascinated by Britain. Here there are lots of commodities we don't have at home. Until the visa expires, it's like a long working holiday. Then reality hits them, and they get scared because if they get caught they will be thrown out. (LeBor 1989)

A significant sector of Colombians living in Britain came to escape political harassment, particularly in the late 1970s. The political problems they face were brought home dramatically and tragically, when Herbert Marín ('José' in the interviews cited by Ardill and Cross), a Colombian who had lived in London since 1979 and worked with the Colombian community, particularly the human rights committee, returned to Colombia for a visit. He was kidnapped, tortured and murdered on 9 October 1986 one day before he was due to return home to London. No-one was found responsible for the murder, but members of the army's Third Brigade are thought to have been involved.

The political situation in the country has led more Colombians to seek asylum in Britain in the 1980s, although the vast majority fleeing the death squads have gone into internal exile or to neighbouring countries, so that they can return to their homes as soon as possible. In 1988 there were about sixty applicants for asylum in Britain, including a lawyer of the banana workers' union of Urabá, victim of a death squad attack in Medellín, who was sent out of the country on a stretcher in February 1988. Another was a leader of the civic movement of Itagüí, who was living in constant fear with his wife and new-born baby after narrowly escaping the death squads.

Most Colombians living in Britain are illegal immigrants who have overstayed the tourist visa they were given when they entered the country and who live in fear of the immigration authorities. Many have been tacitly allowed to stay and fill low-paid jobs in the services which British people do not want:

> Several immigration organisations believe that the government has a policy of allowing overstayers to fill poorly paid jobs that do not attract British citizens who can claim welfare benefits. At the same time, they say, guerrilla raids by immigration officials keep overstayers fearful and unorganised. 'If the Home Office wanted to get rid of everybody in one go, they could' says Rosa Gómez, coordinator of the Latin American Advisory Committee. 'They know where the Colombians are, They know we are working in cleaning and catering, in jobs where you don't need a P45 or a work permit. It's easy to get a job and if you're desperate you take £60 a week to wash dishes. But who else would work such long hours for such low pay?' (Le Bor *op cit*)

Overstayers live in a state of insecurity and prefer not to use the state social services and the national health service, for fear of being reported to the Home Office. Housing, for instance, is a major problem as most are restricted to the private sector where landlords ask no questions. But this often means being at the mercy of racketeers, living in poor and cramped conditions and paying high rents:

Any relationship with the authorities is a risk. 'Lara' tells how late one night she called the police because her boyfriend had beaten her up. The police were not interested in the domestic violence but immediately questioned her about her status. At that time she was in the process of applying for refugee status and had no official papers. After thoroughly questioning her on what she was doing in Britain, the police searched the rooms of everyone who lived in the house, saying they were looking for drugs.

The Colombians' illegal status also puts them at the mercy of unscrupulous employers. Most work in restaurants, hotels and as domestic cleaners, often casual work in which workers go from job to job, working long hours:

> I work five days a week, seventy-five hours a week. I have three jobs: cleaning in the morning, working in a restaurant, then cleaning in the evening. For the three jobs I get £120.

> Of course I feel exploited...the employers are asking every day for more, but they always pay the same ('Luis')

Many Colombians who do this type of work, particularly those escaping political threats, are very over-qualified. 'Luis', for instance, was once an area manager for a furniture factory in Colombia. 'José' described his experience:

> After coming here I was doing a full-time job as a cleaner. There are other people who are professionals, doing the same thing — they do the washing up or the cleaning. Their education might help them to improve their prospects. For instance, you start by washing the pots — in three months you might be outside washing the tables! So obviously, someone like that, if they manage to learn English very quickly, they are more likely to end up serving behind the counter.

Anxiety is endemic among Colombians in Britain. In addition to the threat of deportation and the problem of housing, work and health, there is the stress of trying to understand a new society and a new language:

> People usually envisage staying two years and then they think they will go home. It is very stressful being away from your family. Couples adjust more easily, they are more stable. However, the stress does cause couples to split. Family violence is common, as male and female roles change when families come here. Many women have found work, they are more independent and less subservient.
>
> People miss their families in Colombia. Family ties are very strong and sometimes when people have a drink they start talking about maybe their mother or brother and sisters, also those who have left boyfriends or girl friends behind. People always talk about the letters they have received or tapes of music. People phone home a lot. A Colombian psychologist did some research into the effects of anxiety on the Colombians living here. She found symptoms such as trembling and feeling you are going to have a heart attack. According to her, the Colombian community in London is very ill. ('Jorge')

The cocaine issue has added to the problems of ordinary Colombians, as many are automatically suspected of having connections with the drug trade. This means they are searched at airports and seaports just for being Colombian. Press articles have also hinted at connections between the Colombian community in London and drugs. There is one group of

Colombians here as a direct result of the drug trade. These are the *mulas* or carriers of the drug into Europe. Many of them are women who agreed to do this to escape poverty, pay off a debt or some other reason. When they are caught, they are given extremely high sentences, although they represent the lowest rung of the drugs hierarchy, the top of which escapes unpunished. The women suffer badly in prison; they know little English, and have often left their children behind in Colombia.

Exiled in Britain: a Colombian testimony

'The Thatcher government has tried to criminalise immigration offences. People are fined, detained and then sent back to their country. They detect illegal immigrants through landlords and employers. If the migrant workers create any difficulties, either at work or at home, then it is very easy for an employer or landlord to say he will inform the Home Office. This threat is also used if the landlord wishes to increase rents and wants the tenant out. An illegal immigrant is powerless once he has been reported. If an employer does not want to pay holiday money, then it is a very effective way of dismissing an employee. There are also people inside the Colombian community who might inform the police on somebody's illegality, but this usually arises if there is a dispute between two families.

The fear of deportation creates fantasies in peoples' minds and they think anybody might arrest them. Some people never go out because of that and feel under permanent threat. They start to think that the Home Office is much bigger than it is and much more powerful, with information on everybody, and that the police are the same Big Brothers who know everything. The same happens with rumours in the community, it all gets out of proportion.

There used to be only one detention centre, but today there are six serving London. The government is trying to maintain only the number of migrant workers it needs, while politically it sees it as unacceptable to legitimise them. Racism lies behind these policies. To focus on the problems of immigrants is an easy way to detract from the real causes of economic problems, and so migrant workers become scapegoats. The government says there are too many foreigners here and that it must crack down on the illegal immigrants who are taking jobs from other people. The migrants are in fact usually doing the jobs which no English person would do as they are so badly paid. At least once a month there is an article on the problem of illegal immigrants in the *Sun, Star* or *Daily Mail*. For instance, when there was a dispute with workers at Wimpeys, the papers immediately highlighted the fact that there were illegal immigrants working there, rather than talking about the strike and the fact that the workers were paid terribly low wages. They accused the workers of being trouble-makers.

In the past, the police did not have the instructions they have today. Now they are well briefed by the Home Office, and communications are also much better. For example, in the case of a driving offence, any foreigner is immediately asked about his or her status — this is called internal immigration controls. Local authorities have to co-operate with the Home Office on finding illegal immigrants, as well as the DHSS. They also have direct links with the Home Office. For instance, if you go to the DHSS, the first question if you are not British, is to see your passport. If you haven't got, it they will immediately contact the Home Office to establish if you are here legally. If you go to your local health centre, you will be asked the same questions. The Colombians know that they cannot go to the DHSS or look for housing through the services. They cannot use the normal services that someone working and paying taxes in this country is able to use. These are internal immigration controls.

The police enforce them. They cannot arrest anyone without instructions from an immigration officer, so they have direct links with the Home Office. They may hold someone who has not committed an offence until the Home Office has proved that they are allowed to stay. It can sometimes take the Home Office a week to clarify this, and a week to move the person from the police station to the Home Office detention centres. These are better than the police stations, where conditions are terrible. They are crowded, people cannot change, they cannot wash. There are cases of people being kept a month at the police station. And then they may remain in a detention centre for several months or a year before someone outside can get hold of a ticket to send them home. The Home Office cannot deport anyone until the airline has a free seat.

The Home Office regularly raids the Colombian community. This is not just because they think there may be illegal immigrants, but because they want to be seen to be doing something about the immigration problem. Nobody is interested in the Latin American community and it is not well organised. It is an easy target. The Asian and Black communities are much better organised politically. It is the Latin American and Turkish communities which are now taking the butt of Thatchers' policy of controlling immigration. The Latin American communities are unable to express what happens to them as they have no forum in which to make their voice heard.'

Bibliography

Abel, Christopher, *Política, iglesia y partidos en Colombia.* Universidad Nacional de Colombia, 1987

Acosta, Daniel and López, Gilma, 'Violencia capitalista en el Magdalena Medio', in *La Realidad del 'si se puede': demagogia y violencia.* Comité de Solidaridad con los Presos Políticos, Bogotá, 1984

ALAI, *El Movimiento popular en Colombia.* Documentación Política, vol 3, no 3, Bogotá, June 1985

Alape, Arturo, *El Bogotazo: memorias del olvido.* Pluma, Bogotá, 1983

Alape, Arturo (ed), *La Paz, la violencia: testigos de excepción.* Planeta Colombiana, Bogotá, 1985

Amnesty International, *Colombia Briefing.* London, 1988

Amnesty International, *Colombia: Human Rights Developments - 'Death Squads' on the Defensive?* London, 1989

Andean Commission of Jurists, Colombian section, *Dirty War and State of Siege.* mimeo, Bogotá, 1989

ANUC, *El Avance de la guerra sucia en Colombia: el caso del Magdalena Medio.* mimeo, Bogotá, 1988

ANUC, *Conclusiones: tercer encuentro nacional.* Bogotá, July 1985

ANUC, *¡De Pie! Ponencias y conclusiones del congreso de unidad y reconstrucción de ANUC.* Bogotá, 26-28 August 1987

Arango, Carlos Z., *FARC Veinte Anos, de Marquetalia a la Uribe.* Aurora, fourth edition, Bogotá, 1986

Arango, Mariano, 'La Reforma agraria y alcances de la nueva ley', *Revista Foro*, no 7, Bogotá, October 1988

Arango, Mario and Child, Jorge, *Coca-Coca: historia, manejo político y mafia de la cocaína.* Dos Mundos, Bogotá, 1986

Arango, Mario and Child, Jorge, *Narcotráfico: imperio de la cocaína.* Percepción, Medellín, 1984

Archila, M., *Aquí nadie es forastero: testimonios sobre la formación de una cultura radical, Barrancabermeja 1920-1950.* CINEP, Bogotá, 1986

Ardill, Nony and Cross, Nigel, *Undocumented Lives: Britain's Unauthorised Migrant Workers.* Runnymede Trust, London, 1988

Arrubla, Mario *et al, Colombia hoy*, Siglo XXI, Bogotá, 1978

Article 19, *Commentary*, Colombia. London, 1988

Atehortua, Adolfo, *Café: bonanza y realidades.* Escuela Nacional Sindical-SINTRAFEC, 1986

Avila Bernal, Alvaro, *Corrupción y expoliación en América Latina*. Grijalbo, Bogotá, 1987

Barco, Virgilio, *Plan de ecónomica social*. Departamento Nacional de Planeación, Bogotá, 1987

Behar, Olga, *Las Guerras de la paz*. Planeta Colombiana, Bogotá, 1985

Bejarano, Jesús A., *Economia y poder: la SAC y el desarrollo agropecuario colombiano, 1871-1984*. CEREC-SAC, Bogotá, 1985

Berquist, Charles W., *Labor in Latin America: Comparative Essays on Chile, Argentina, Venezuela and Colombia*. Stanford University Press, Stanford, 1986

Bermúdez Rossi, Major Gonzalo, *El Poder militar en Colombia: de la colonia al Frente Nacional*. Expresión, Bogotá, 1982

Bourguignon, François, 'L'Emploi et le marché du travail', *Problèmes d'Amérique Latine*, no 84, Paris, 1987

Broderick, Walter J., *Camilo, el cura guerrillero*. El Labrador, fifth edition, Bogotá, 1987

Buendia, Aureliano, 'La Zona esmeraldífera: una cultura de violencia', *Revista Foro*, no 6, Bogotá, June 1988

Rod Burgess, 'The Political Integration of Urban Demands in Colombia', *Boletín de Estudios Latinoamericanos y del Caribe*, no 41, Amsterdam, December 1986

David Bushnell, 'Política y partidos en el siglo XIX: algunos antecedentes históricos' *in* Sánchez, Gonzalo and Peñaranda, Ricardo

Cabrera, Alvera *et al*, *Los Movimientos cívicos*. CINEP, Bogotá, 1986

Castillo, Fabio, *Los Jinetes de la cocaína*. Documentos Periodísticos, Bogotá, 1988

Castro, Jaime, *Elección popular de alcaldes*. Oveja Negra, Bogotá, 1986

Castro, Jaime, *Respuesta democrática al desafío guerrillero*. Oveja Negra, Bogotá, 1987

Conclusiones del Segundo Congreso Nacional de Movimientos Civicos y Organizaciones Populares, Consejo Nacional de Organizaciones Populares, Bogotá, July 1986

Consejo Regional Indígena del Cauca-CRIC, *Diez años de lucha: historia y documentos*. CINEP, Bogotá, 1981

Consideraciones generales para el tratamiento del fenómeno de violencia en el Magdalena Medio Boyacense, caso Puerto Boyacá. mimeo, Bogotá, 1989

Corporación Colectivo de Abogados, *Informe analítico de la situación de derechos humanos en Colombia.* Bogotá, January-May-September 1989

Craig, Richard B.,'Illicit Drug Traffic: Implications for South American Source Countries', *Journal of Interamerican Studies and World Affairs,* vol 29, no 2, Miami, Summer 1987

CRIC, 'El CRIC, una experiencia regional de participación y organización', *in* de Botero, Margarita J. and Uribe Echeverria, F., *Pobreza, participación y desarollo.* CIDER, Universidad de los Andes, Bogotá, 1986

CRIC, Equipo de capacitación del, *El Movimiento indígena.* mimeo, 1986

Cuervo, Luis Mauricio, *Conflicto social y servicios publícos en Colombia.* CINEP, Bogotá, 1987

Deas, Malcolm, 'Algunos interrogantes sobre la relación guerras civiles y violencia' *in* Sánchez, Gonzalo and Peñaranda, Ricardo

Delgado, Alvaro, *Luchas sociales en Caquetá.* Ceis, Bogotá, 1987

Departamento Administrativo Nacional de Estadística (DANE), Bogotá, 'Resultados de la investigacion 'Población afectada por la delincuencia: una aproximación a la criminalidad real', 1986
- , *Colombia Estadística 1986*
- , *Colombia Estadística, Vol 1, 1987*
- , *Boletín de estadística especial: pobreza y desnutrición en el area rural colombiana.* March 1988
    - , *Boletín de estadística especial: la pobreza en 13 ciudades colombianas.* December 1988

de Rementería, Ibán, 'Hipótesis sobre la violencia reciente en Magdalena Medio' *in* Sánchez, Gonzalo and Peñaranda, Ricardo

Díaz Uribe, Eduardo, *El Clientelismo en Colombia.* El Ancora, Bogotá, 1986.

Dix, Robert H., *Colombia: The Political Dimensions of Change.* Yale University Press, Newhaven USA, 1967

FAO, *The World Banana Economy, 1970-84.* Economic and Social Development Paper 57, Rome, 1986

FARC, *Las FARC: semilla fecunda.* Bogotá, May 1989

Fernando Ocampo, José, *Dominio de clase en la ciudad colombiana.* Oveja Negra, Bogotá, 1972

Galeano, Eduardo, *Open Veins of Latin America: Five Centuries of the Pillage of a Continent.* Monthly Review Press, New York, 1973

Gallón Giraldo, Gustavo, *La Arbitrariedad mesurada.* mimeo, Bogotá, January 1989

García Martínez, Mery, *Diagnóstico de la zona de Urabá.* IPC, Medellín, 1987

Gilhodes, Pierre, 'Les Elections de 1986', *Problèmes d'Amérique Latine*, no 84, Paris, 1987

Gilhodes, Pierre, *La Question agraire en Colombie, 1958-71*. Armand Colin, Paris, 1974

Giraldo, J., 'Los Modelos de la represión', *Revista Solidaridad*, Bogotá, no 101, December 1988

Giraldo, J. and Camargo, S., 'Paros y movimientos cívicos en Colombia' *in* Giraldo, J. *et al, Movimientos sociales ante la crisis en Sudamérica.* CINEP, Bogotá, 1986

González, Fernán, *Iglesia católica y sociedad colombiana (1886-1986)*. mimeo, Bogotá, 1987

González Posso, Camilo, 'Movimientos sociales y políticos en los años 80: en busca de una alternativa' in Moncayo, V.M. *et al, Entre la guerra y la paz: puntos de vista sobre la crisis colombiana de los años 80*. CINEP, Bogotá, 1987

Guzmán Campos, Germán, Fals Borda, Orlando, Umana Luña, Eduardo, *La Violencia en Colombia.* 2 volumes, 9th edition, Carlos Valencia, Bogotá, 1986

Harnecker, Marta, *Reportajes sobre Colombia: entrevista a dirigentes de la UCELN.* Quimera, Quito, 1988

Hartlyn, Jonathan, *The Politics of Coalition Rule in Colombia.* Cambridge University Press, Cambridge, 1988

Heinz, Wolfgang, 'Impunity in Colombia', paper presented to Pax Christi conference, Geneva, February 1989

Helmsing, A.H.J., *Firms, Farms and the State in Colombia.* Allen & Unwin, London, 1986

Informe de la Comisión Internacional de Observación Judicial en Colombia (24 de febrero al 5 de marzo de 1988), Fondation France Libertés, Paris, 1988

International Bank for Reconstruction and Development (IBRD), *The World Bank Group in Colombia.* Washington, August 1967

Jaramillo Uribe, Jaime, 'Etapas y sentido de la historia de Colombia' *in* Arrubla, Mario *et al*

Justicia y Paz, *Boletín Informativo.* Vol 1, Nos 1-4, Bogotá, 1988

Kalmanovitz, Salomón, *El Desarrollo de la agricultura en Colombia.* Carlos Valencia, Bogotá, 1982

Kalmanovitz, Salomón, *Economía y nación: una breve historia de Colombia.* Siglo XXI, Bogotá, 1985

Kalmanovitz, Salomón, 'El Pequeño milagro: economía subterránea y reestructuración industrial', *Revista Solidaridad*, no 100, Bogotá, November 1988

Kline, Harvey F., *The Coal of El Cerrejón: Dependent Bargaining and Colombian Policy-Making*. Pennsylvania State University Press, 1987

Landazábal Reyes, General Fernando, *Páginas de controversia*. Bedout, Medellín, 1983

Lara, Patricia, *Siembra vientos y recogerás tempestades*. Planeta Colombiana, Bogotá, 1986

Leal Buitrago, Francico, *Un Bipartidismo en crisis*. mimeo, 1986

Leal Buitrago, Francisco, 'La Crisis política en Colombia: alternativas y frustraciones', *Análisis Político*, no 1, Bogotá, May-August 1987

Leal Buitrago, Francisco, *Estado y política en Colombia*. Siglo XXI, Bogotá, 1984

Le Bor, Adam, 'Out of Colombia, in Search of a Life,' *The Independent*, 2 February 1989

LeGrand, Catherine, *Frontier Expansion and Peasant Protest in Colombia, 1850-1936*. University of New Mexico Press, Albuquerque, 1986

LeGrand, Catherine, 'Labor Acquisition and Social Conflict on the Colombian Frontier, 1850-1936', *Journal of Latin American Studies*, vol 16, part 1, Cambridge, May 1984

Lievano Aguirre, Indalecio, *Bolívar*. Oveja Negra, Bogotá, 1979

Londoño, Rocio, Grisales, Orlando and Delgado, Alvaro, 'Sindicalismo y empleo en Colombia' *in* Ocampo and Ramírez (eds)

Manual de historia de Colombia. 3 vols, Procultura-Instituto Colombiano de Cultura, Bogotá, 1984

Mauleón, José Ramón, *Assassination of Banana Workers in Colombia*. Colombia Committee for Human Rights-Colombia Solidarity Committee, London, July 1988

Ken Medhurst, *The Church and Labour in Colombia*. Manchester University Press, Manchester, 1984

Merino, E., *Sobreexplotación y desprotección del proletariado bracero de la zona bananera de Urabá*. Cenasel, Medellín, 1987

Molano, Alfredo, *Selva adentro: una historia oral de la colonización del Guaviare*, El Ancora, Bogotá, 1987

Molano, Alfredo, 'Violencia y colonización', *Revista Foro*, no 6, Bogotá, June 1988

Molano, Alfredo, 'Colonos, estado y violencia', *Revista Foro,* no 9, Bogotá, May 1989

Nieto Arteta, Luis Eduardo, *El Café en la sociedad colombiana.* La Soga al Cuello, Bogotá, 1971

Ocampo, José Antonio and Ramírez, Manuel (eds), *El Problema laboral colombiano: informes de la Misión Chenery.* Contraloría General de la República, 2 vols, Bogotá, 1987.

Ocampo, José Antonio (ed), *Historia económica de Colombia.* Siglo XXI, Bogotá, 1987

Oquist, Paul, *Violence, Conflict and Politics in Colombia.* New York, Academic Press, 1980

Ortiz Sarmiento, Carlos Miguel, *Estado y subversión en Colombia: La Violencia en Quindío años 50.* CEREC, Bogota, 1985

Osorio, Ivan D., *Historia del sindicalismo antioqueño, 1900-1986,* IPC, Medellín, n.d.

Palacios, Marco, *El Café en Colombia (1850-1970): una historia, económica, social y política.* El Ancora, Bogotá, 1983

Pax Christi Netherlands and Dutch Commission Justitia et Pax, *Impunity in Colombia,* The Hague, 1989

Pécaut, Daniel, 'Crise, guerre et paix en Colombie', in *Problèmes d'Amérique Latine,* no 84, Paris, 1987a

Pécaut, Daniel, *L'Ordre et la violence.* Editions de l'Ecole des Hautes Etudes en Sciences Sociales, Paris, 1987b

Pécaut, Daniel, *Política y sindicalismo en Colombia.* La Carreta, Bogotá, 1973

Pinzón, Patricia, *La Oposición política en Colombia: aproximación al itinerario de la fórmulas.* FESCOL, Bogotá, 1986

Pizarro Leongómez, Eduardo, *La Guerrilla en Colombia.* CINEP, Bogotá, 1987

Pizarro Leongómez, Eduardo, 'La Profesionalización militar en Colombia, 1907-1944', *Análisis Político,* no 1, Bogotá, May-August 1987

Prieto, Jaime, 'El Lamento de la Mojana', *Colombia Hoy,* no 50, Bogotá, July 1987

Quintero Latorre, Julio César, *Qué pasó con la Tierra Prometida?* CINEP, Bogotá, 1988

Restrepo, Laura, *Colombia: historia de una traición.* IEPALA, Madrid, 1986

Restrepo, Luis Alberto, 'El Protagonismo de los movimientos sociales', *Revista Foro,* no 2, Bogotá, February 1987

Reyes Posada, Alejandro and Bejarano, Ana María, 'Conflictos agrarios y luchas armadas en la Colombia contemporánea: una visión geografica', *Análisis Político,* no 5, Bogotá, September-December 1988

Rodríguez, Ana Lucía P.(ed), *Debates sobre la paz.* CINEP, Bogotá, 1988

Rodríguez Solano, Ana and García, William, 'La Lucha cívica del Bagre: no todo lo que brilla es oro', *Revista Foro,* no 6, Bogotá, June 1988

Romero Vidal, M., *De la Factoría a la microempresa: el desmonte del sindicalismo* in Giraldo, J. et al

Sánchez, Gonzalo, 'Los Bolcheviques del Líbano' *in Ensayos de historia social y política del siglo XX.* El Ancora, Bogotá, 1984

Sánchez, Gonzalo and Meertens, Donny, *Bandoleros, gamonales y campesinos: el caso de la Violencia en Colombia.* El Ancora, Bogotá, 1983

Sánchez, Gonzalo and Peñaranda, Ricardo (eds), *Pasado y presente de la violencia en Colombia.* CEREC, Bogotá, 1986

Santamaría, Ricardo and Silva Luján, Gabriel, *Proceso político en Colombia: del Frente Nacional a la apertura democrática.* CEREC, Bogotá, 1984

Santana, Pedro, *Desarrollo regional y paros civícos en Colombia,* CINEP, Bogotá, 1983

Santana, Pedro, *Colombia: el difícil camino de la unidad popular.* mimeo, Bogotá, September 1986

Santana, Pedro, 'Crisis municipal, movimimientos sociales y reforma política en Colombia', *Revista Foro,* no 1, Bogotá, September 1986

Santana, Pedro, 'Los Movimientos cívicos: el nuevo fenómeno electoral', *Revista Foro,* no 6, Bogotá, June 1988

Santana, Pedro, *Movimientos sociales, gobiernos locales y democracia,* mimeo, Bogotá, 1988

Santana, Pedro, 'Violencia política y diálogo nacional', ALAI, no 113, Quito, March 1989

Silva Colmenares, Julio, *Los Verdaderos dueños del país: oligarquía y monopolios en Colombia.* Editorial Suramérica, Bogotá, 1977

Thoumi, Francisco, 'Some Implications of the Growth of the Underground Economy in Colombia', *Journal of Interamerican Studies and World Affairs,* Vol.29, no2, Miami, Summer 1987

United Nations Consejo Económico y Social, *Informe del grupo de trabajo sobre desapariciones forzadas o involuntarias: informe de la visita realizada a Colombia por dos miembros del Grupo de Trabajo sobre desapariciones forzadas o Involuntarias, (24 de Octubre a 2 de Noviembre 1988),* UN, New York, 6 February 1989

Urrutia, Miguel, *Gremios, política económica y democracia*. Fondo Cultural Cafetero-FEDESARROLLO, Bogotá, 1983

Urrutia, Miguel, *Los de arriba y los de abajo: la distribución del ingreso en Colombia en las últimas décadas*. FEDESARROLLO-CEREC, Bogotá, 1984

Varón, Miguel, 'Colombians bootleg everything from cigars to computers, chickens and Spanish bulls', *Latinamerica Press*, Lima, 27 October 1988

Vázquez Carrizosa, Alfredo, *Betancur y la crisis nacional*. Aurora, Bogotá, 1986

Villegas, Jorge, *Petróleo colombiano, ganancia gringa*. El Ancora, Bogotá, 1985

Vivas Reyna, Jorge, *Descentralización administrativa, política fiscal y de la planificación regional: una visión general*. Federación Nacional de Cafeteros de Colombia, Bogotá, 1987a

Vivas Reyna, Jorge, *Recesión, ajuste económico y política de salud*. FEDESAROLLO-Unicef-DNP, Bogotá, 1987b

Washington Office on Latin America (WOLA), *Colombia Besieged: Political Violence and State Responsibility*. WOLA, Washington, 1989

Wilde, Alexander W., 'Conversations among Gentlemen: Oligarchical Democracy in Colombia' in Linz, Juan and Stepan, A. (eds), *The Breakdown of Democratic Regimes*. Johns Hopkins University Press, Baltimore, USA, 1978

Wilde, Alexander W., 'The Contemporary Church: the Poiitical and the Pastoral' in Berry, Albert, Hellman, Ronald and Solaun, Mauricio (eds), *Politics of Compromise: Coalition Government in Colombia*. New Brunswick, Transaction Books, 1980

World Bank, *World Development Report 1989*. World Bank-Oxford University Press, New York, 1989

Zamosc, Leon, *The Agrarian Question and the Peasant Movement in Colombia: Struggles of the National Peasant Association, 1967-1981*. Cambridge University Press, Cambridge, 1986

Journals and Newspapers:

Cien Días (CINEP, distributed every three months in El Espectador)
Colombia Hoy, Bogotá
Solidaridad, Bogotá
ALAI, Quito, Ecuador
Revista Foro, Bogotá,
Opción, Bogotá
A Luchar, Bogotá

Polémica, Bogotá
Voz, Bogotá
Semana, Bogotá
Economía Colombiana, Bogotá
Coyuntura Económica, FEDESAROLLO, Bogotá
Petroleum Economist, London
Latin America Newsletter Reports, London
Latin America Press, Lima
El Espectador
El Tiempo
La Prensa
El Mundo

Acronyms

ACDEGAM	Asociación de Campesinos y Ganaderos del Magdalena Medio
	Peasants and Ranchers of the Magdalena Medio
ADO	Autodefensa Obrera
	Workers' Self-Defence
ANAPO	Alianza Nacional Popular
	Popular National Alliance
ANDI	Asociación Nacional de Industriales
	National Association of Industrialists
ANTA	Asociación Nacional de Trabajadores Agrarios
	National Association of Agricultural Workers
ANUC	Asociación Nacional de Usuarios Campesinos
	National Association of Peasant Users
APRA	Alianza Popular Revolucionaria Americana
	American Popular Revolutionary Alliance
AUCURA	Asociación de Bananeros de Urabá
	Banana Growers of Urabá
CCC	Comunidades Cristianas Campesinas
	Peasant Christian Communities
CEB	Comunidades Eclesiales de Base
	Christian Base Communities
CGSB	Coordinadora Guerrillera Simón Bolívar
	Simon Bolivar Guerrilla Coordination
CGT	Confederación General del Trabajo
	General Confederation of Labour
CIA	Central Intelligence Agency
CIMARRON	Movimiento Nacional por los Derechos Humanos de las Comunidades Negras de Colombia
	National Movement for the Human Rights of the Black Communities of Colombia
CINEP	Centro de Investigación y Educación Popular
	Centre for Popular Research and Education
CRIC	Consejo Regional Indigena del Cauca
	Regional Indigenous Council of the Cauca
CRIT	Consejo Regional Indigena del Tolima
	Regional Council of the Indigenous of the South of Tolima
CSTC	Confederación Sindical de Trabajadores de Colombia

	Union Confederation of Colombian Workers
CTC	Confederación de Trabajadores de Colombia
	Confederation of Colombian Workers
CUAN	Comité de Unidad Agraria Nacional
	National Agrarian Unity Committee
CUS	Comité de Unidad Sindical
	Committee of Trade Union Unity
CUT	Central Unitaria de Trabajadores
	United Confederation of Workers
DANE	Departamento Administrativo Nacional de Estadística
	Department of National Statistics
DAS	Departamento Administrativo de Seguridad
	Administrative Security Department
DRI	Desarrollo Rural Integrado
	Integrated Rural Development
ECOPETROL	Empresa Colombiana de Petróleos
	Colombian Petrol Company
ELN	Ejército de Liberación Nacional
	National Liberation Army
EPL	Ejército Popular de Liberación
	Popular Liberation Army
FANAL	Federación Nacional Agraria
	National Agrarian Federation
FARC	Fuerzas Armadas Revolucionarias de Colombia
	Revolutionary Armed Forces of Colombia
FECODE	Federación Colombiana de Educadores
	Colombian Federation of Teachers
FEDERACAFE	Federación Nacional de Cafeteros de Colombia
	National Federation of Colombian Coffee Growers
FEDEGAN	Federación Nacional de Ganaderos
	National Federation of Cattle Breeders
FENALCO	Federación Nacional de Comerciantes
	National Federation of Traders
FENSUAGRO	Federación Nacional Sindical Unitaria Agropecuaria
	National United Agricultural Federation
FN	Frente Nacional
	National Front
FP	Frente Popular
	Popular Front
INCORA	Instituto Colombiano de Reforma Agraria
	Colombian Institute of Agrarian Reform
JAL	Junta Administradora Local
	Local Administrative Council

LIGA M-L	Marxist-Leninist League
M-19	Movimiento 19 de Abril
	April 19 Movement
MAN	Movimiento de Acción Nacional
	Movement of National Action
MAS	Muerte a Secuestradores
	Death to Kidnappers
MIR-Patria Libre	Movimiento de Izquierda Revolucionaria-Patria Libre
	Revolutionary Left Movement
MOEC	Movimiento Obrero-Estudiantil Campesino
	Workers', Students' and Peasants' Movement
MOIR	Movimiento Obrero Independente Revolucionario
	Independent Revolutionary Workers' Movement
MPL	Movimiento Pan y Libertad
	Movement for Bread and Liberty
MRL	Movimiento Revolucionario Liberal
	Revolutionary Liberal Movement
ONIC	Organisación Nacional Indigena de Colombia
	National Organisation of the Indigenous People of Colombia
ORIT	Organisación Regional Inter-Americana del Trabajo
	Inter-American Organisation of Labor
PC-ML	Partido Comunista-Marxista Leninista
	Communist Party — Marxist-Leninist
PRI	Partido Revolucionario Institucional
	Institutional Revolutionary Party
PRN	Plan de Rehabilitación Nacional
	National Rehabilitation Plan
PRT	Partido Revolucionario de los Trabajadores
	Workers' Revolutionary Party
PSR	Partido Socialista Revolucionario
	Revolutionary Socialist Party
PST	Partido Socialista de los Trabajadores
	Socialist Workers Party
SAC	Sociedad de Agricultores de Colombia
	Society of Colombian Farmers
UNIBAN	Unión de Bananeros
	Union of Banana Producers of Urabá
UNIR	Comités de Unidad Intersindical Regional
	Committees for Regional Inter-Union Unity
UP	Unión Patriótica
	Patriotic Union
USO	Unión Sindical Obrera

Oil Workers' Union
UTC   Unión de Trabajadores de Colombia
          Union of Colombian Workers

Index

Latin America Bureau

LAB

The Latin America Bureau is a small, independent, non-profit making research organisation established in 1977. LAB is concerned with human rights and related social, political and economic issues in Central and South America and the Caribbean. We carry out research, publish books and lobby on these issues, and establish support links with Latin American groups. We also brief the media, organise seminars and have a growing programme of schools publications.

Recent LAB books include:

Fight For the Forest: Chico Mendes in his own words
Chico Mendes and Tony Gross

". . . a short but vivid study . . . This is a book to show your friends, to influence people with, and to campaign with."

The Ecologist

96 pages £4.70/US$7.50 ISBN 0 906156 51 3

Ecuador: Fragile Democracy
David Corkill and David Cubitt

"This survey of Ecuadorean politics continues the Latin America Bureau's tradition of providing rigorous and readable overviews."

NACLA, Report on the Americas

114 pages £5.75/US$9.00 ISBN 0 906156 39 4

The Dance of the Millions: Latin America and the Debt Crisis
Jackie Roddick et al.

"A crisp and informative introduction to the Latin American debt crisis . . . Price, clarity of presentation, and a robust grasp of the structural characteristics of the world economy will ensure the success of this carefully reasoned polemic."

Times Higher Education Supplement

258 pages £8.00/US$12.50 ISBN 0 906156 30 0

Prices are for paperback editions and include post and packing. For a complete list of books write to Latin America Bureau, 1 Amwell Street, London ECIR IUL. LAB books are distributed in North America by Monthly Review Press, 122 West 27th Street, New York, NY 10001